The Door of Liberation

The DOOR of LIBERATION

ESSENTIAL TEACHINGS OF THE TIBETAN BUDDHIST TRADITION

Translated by
GESHE WANGYAL

WISDOM PUBLICATIONS • BOSTON

WISDOM PUBLICATIONS
361 Newbury Street
Boston, Massachusetts 02115
United States of America

First published in 1973 by Maurice Girodias Associates Inc.
Republished in 1978 by Lotsawa.
This revised edition, 1995

©Joshua and Diana Cutler, 1995
All rights reserved.

No part of this book may be reproduced in any form or by any means, electronic or mechanical, including photocopying, recording, or by any information storage and retrieval system or technologies now known or later developed, without permission in writing from the publisher.

ISBN 0 86171 032 0

Library of Congress Cataloging-in-Publication Data

The door of liberation / translated under the supervision of Geshe Wangyal.
p. cm.
Originally published : New York : Lotsawa, c1978.
Includes index.
ISBN 0-86171-032-0
1. Buddhism—China—Tibet—Doctrines—Early works to 1800.
I. Thupten Wangyal.
[BQ7630.D66 1994]
294.3'42--dc20 94–29623

99 98 97 96

6 5 4 3 2

Cover Art: Tsong Khapa, Chahar, Inner Mongolia, c.1700. Gilt brass, with pigments. Folkens Museum Etnografiska, Stockholm. Photography by John Bigelow Taylor, NYC.
A Tibetan Door, illustration derivative from original photograph, *Detail of Door,* by Magnus Bartlett.

Typeset in Adobe and Diacritical Garamond and Truesdell at Wisdom Publications

Designed by: L.J.SAWLIT

Wisdom Publications' books are printed on acid-free paper and meet the guidelines for permanence and durability of the Committee on Production Guidelines for Book Longevity of the Council on Library Resources.

Printed at Northeast Impressions, Fairfield, NJ USA.

Contents

Foreword to the First Edition
by His Holiness the Fourteenth Dalai Lama *vii*
Response *ix*
Preface to the New Edition *xi*
A Note on the Translations *xxix*
Acknowledgments *xxxi*

I INTRODUCTION *3*

II THE LINEAGE OF THE TEACHING *19*

III DISCOURSES FROM THE SUTRAS *45*
A Prayer by the First Panchen Lama *46*
The Miraculous Deeds of Śākyamuni Buddha *50*
The Story of Prince Gendun *65*
The Nun Utpaladok *77*

IV KADAMPA PRECEPTS *83*
Precepts Collected from Here and There *83*

V THE ESSENCE OF GOOD EXPLANATION: PRAISE OF MUNĪNDRA *123*
Poem by Tsongkhapa *124*

VI THE THREE PRINCIPLES OF THE PATH *135*
Root Text by Tsongkhapa *135*
Instructions for Meditation by the Fourth Panchen Lama *138*

VII THE CONCISE MEANING OF THE STAGES OF THE PATH *173*
Root Text by Tsongkhapa *173*

VIII THE FOUNDATION OF ALL EXCELLENCE *183*
Root Text by Tsongkhapa *183*
Commentary by Kushri Kabchu Sudhi *185*

CLOSING DEDICATION *213*

Notes 215
Glossary 223
Index 251

Foreword to the First Edition

LONG AGO, THE TEACHER, the victorious Buddha, prophesied, "Two thousand five hundred years after my *parinirvāṇa*, the holy Dharma will spread to the land of the red-faced people." According to different ways of reckoning time, some say that the country referred to is Tibet, while others feel that the land of the red-faced people is Europe and the other regions of the West. However it may be, a small number of people in the West have recently become interested in the teachings of Buddha. At this time of rising enthusiasm, Geshe Wangyal, who is a Mongol, has translated into English this selection of Tibetan texts. I am certain that these will be invaluable to those who are interested in the Dharma, and I extend my best wishes to the translator and my thanks to those who assisted him.

Although there are many concepts expressed in the various selections, the essence of them all is contained within the three principles of the path: renunciation, bodhi-mind, and right view. Seeing that the nature of all saṁsāra is suffering, and seeing that only in liberation is there final happiness, one can produce the thought of renunciation: the desire for liberation. Contemplating that suffering, which is unbearable to us and unbearable to others as well, one can produce bodhi-mind, which arises from the compassion that wishes to free all living beings from suffering. Finally, one can produce right view, the understanding that all phenomena are not established by self-nature.

Without renunciation, interest in liberation will not arise. Without the mind of enlightenment, Mahāyāna will be merely a name. Without the view of voidness, it is not possible to attain even liberation. Therefore, if one is intent on one's own liberation, it is necessary to develop renunciation and the view of voidness. If one aspires to the Mahāyāna, it is necessary to develop the mind of enlightenment and the view of voidness, preceded by renunciation. When the Tantrayāna is added to this, it is indeed very profound.

The Dalai Lama
2517 years after the Sugata
April 1973

Response

AFTER RECEIVING THIS FOREWORD from His Holiness the Dalai Lama, I had a dream that I was on a long and difficult journey to a distant harbor, trying to reach a ship that was waiting to cross the great ocean. I was following His Holiness, who was already on board. How happy I was when I finally reached my destination!

In Tibet, it was rare for people such as myself even to see His Holiness's face from a distance, but in India I have had the great fortune to meet with him personally on several occasions. The great blessing of hearing his teachings, as when I recently heard him read Nāgārjuna's *Mūlamadhyamakakārikā* in Mundgod, has increased my deep loyalty to and faith in him and his great knowledge. In his foreword to these translations, he has shown the true substance of all the teachings of Buddha. His omniscient wisdom is unsurpassed. His bodhi-mind turns iron into gold, and his great mercy is deeper than the ocean. I pray from the depth of my heart that his life be long. May his great wisdom and compassion lead all living beings to the door of liberation.

Geshe Wangyal
May 1973

Preface to the New Edition

IT IS VERY IMPORTANT that Wisdom Publications is republishing this book. This collection of teachings first was published in 1973, a time when there was very little available in English about Tibetan Buddhism. Nowadays there is a great abundance of such books, thanks to the good efforts of many competent authors, but this special selection of teachings has not lost its significance in any way. This is mainly due to the continual ability of such authentic teachings to inspire the reader.

This book's lasting significance, however, also stems from the unique perspective and character of the late venerable Geshe Wangyal, the teacher who chose and translated the variety of works herein. Geshe-la (*la* is a term of respect), a Kalmyk Mongolian, although born a Tibetan Buddhist, was born outside of Tibet and its culture. Thus, he had a Tibetan's natural devotion to the religion, but the outsider's perspective of a non-Tibetan. The latter made it possible for him to be especially sympathetic to the intended readers of this book, persons new to Tibetan Buddhism. This perspective was enhanced by Geshe-la's training as a translator from around the age of twelve, for the Tibetan scriptures had yet to be translated in their entirety into Mongolian. At an early age he was challenged to interpret the Tibetan scriptures and their teachings for others. As a natural consequence of this training, he learned English in Beijing in the early 1930s (after training to become a geshe, or doctor of Buddhist philosophy, for nine years at Drepung Monastery in Lhasa), and became a teacher and translator in English in China, Tibet, England, India, and then finally the United States, where he died in January of 1983 after twenty-eight years of residency.

I had the great privilege of apprenticing under Geshe-la for the last thirteen years of his life and directly observing his dedication to the teachings presented here. The selection of teachings in this book is special, because they were chosen by a remarkable person. He was a very wise and compassionate man who lived a very full and purposeful life. Geshe-la's deep devotion to the teachings herein was clear to all who knew him and saw his great efforts to promote Buddha's teachings. This devotion was certainly assisted by the circumstances of his upbringing, for Buddhism permeated his Mongolian culture, much the same as it does for a Tibetan. I used to hear many stories of his youth. I would like to share some of those stories with the reader in order to show who the author was and, especially, to illustrate how unique his devotion to Tibetan Buddhism was, for he was born into one of the few non-Himalayan cultures to adopt Tibetan Buddhism to such a great degree. The stories show how Geshe-la's Buddhist upbringing and subsequent training as a monk were much the same as would be expected for a Tibetan, but with one exception—a high reverence for Tibet. As Geshe-la said, even the name 'Tibet' is from the Mongolian term *tüvot*, which means central—for to the Mongolians, Tibet is the center of their religion, their holy land. Tibetans in their literature show a similar attitude towards the land from which they had received their religion, referring to India as the "land of the Noble Ones" (*'phags pa'i yul*). Geshe-la cherished Tibet and its teachings, and the teachings in this book are the treasures that he chose with that attitude.

Geshe-la was born in 1901 amongst the Kalmyk Mongolian people of what is now called Kalmykia, a region of Russia that is west of the Volga River and just to the north of the Caspian Sea. Though Kalmykia was part of Russia, the Kalmyks were mostly left alone by the Russians, especially those Kalmyks who were settled in the center of their region, as Geshe-la was. They were primarily semi-nomadic, living in tents made of animal hides, and tending sheep, cows, camels, and horses. Originally, they had been part of the Western

Mongolian clans, and starting in around 1632, they emigrated from Dzungaria (now western Mongolia and Xinjiang) in Central Asia to the lower Volga region. They brought with them their devotion to Tibetan Buddhism, particularly their devotion to the Tibetan teachings of the Gelug (*dge lugs*) tradition of Tsongkhapa, whose writings are amply represented in this book. Geshe-la used to take pride in the fact that the Kalmyks were part of the same Mongolian clans that allied themselves with the Fifth Dalai Lama, and were then responsible for consolidating Tibet under the leadership of the Dalai Lamas. "Dalai" is a Mongolian word for ocean, indicating that the Dalai Lama possesses an ocean of wisdom. The present Fourteenth Dalai Lama often mentions this traditional relationship as one reason for the close friendship that Geshe-la and he enjoyed after Geshe-la came to America.

As measured by the amount of livestock they kept, Geshe-la's parents were moderately wealthy. His father, Leiji, died when he was less than one year old, so young that the only remembrance Geshe-la could call up was "that man [in our home] must have been my father." His father did not even have an opportunity to give his young son a name. Thus, his mother, Bolgan, called him *shikker* (sugar), or *bota* (cherub), two terms of endearment that Kalmyk mothers commonly used. Being the last child, Geshe-la could get anything that he asked for. Honey was a very rare commodity in Kalmykia, but Geshe-la could ask for it at any time and receive a piece of bread dripping with butter and honey. As Geshe-la so aptly put it, "I ordered my mother around, and she did her best to spoil me."

But it was also his mother whom Geshe-la credited with inspiring him to undertake a religious way of life. In fact, Geshe-la was always amazed to recall how much she knew about religion. He used to tell the story of how his mother took him to the temple when he was around three years old. He remembered asking his mother where they were going and why. When they had entered the temple, he asked how to bow down. Instructing him, his mother said, "Buddha is a special being to whom we bow and pray. He will bless you. When you bow down and pray, you must do so for the sake of all living beings." Showing an innate sharp intelligence, Geshe-la asked, "If I pray for others, how will I get what I want?" She then replied, "By helping others your own aims will be achieved incidentally." About a year later Geshe-la went to the monastery to ask permission to become a monk, but was refused because he was too young.

Finally, at age six Geshe-la was allowed to enter the local monastery. Becoming a monk in Kalmykia was a very precious thing. When a young monk first returned to his home, his family placed him in a high seat and bowed down to him. Although the Kalmyks practiced Tibetan Buddhism, they had some religious customs that were not observed in Tibet, such as this unusual respect for young monks. Geshe-lahad an explanation for this, a legend that illustrates the high regard that the Kalmyks have for their religion. It is said that such customs were left over from a period in their history when they had originally received Buddha's teachings directly from India during a time when their ancestors, mountain Mongols, lived in northern Afghanistan. They were asked at that time whether they wanted a pure transmission that would last for one hundred years or an impure one that would last for one thousand years. Of course, they chose the former, and traces of that one hundred year period still remained.

Geshe-la had three siblings. His eldest brother, Morsang, was sixteen years his senior; then came a sister, Jugda, who was twelve years older, and another brother, Gunsang, who was eight years older. Gunsang had become a monk before Geshe-la was born and had entered a monastery that was far from his home. Therefore, Geshe-la did not know him well when he was young. However, he did admire Gunsang greatly, because Gunsang was praised and honored in the family. In fact, it was partly this admiration for his distant brother that caused Geshe-la to enter the monastery. He wanted to be just like him.

At the time Geshe-la entered the local monastery, his brother also was in residence, along with about forty other monks. Gunsang now became responsible for his development, and he was a very stern instructor. Geshe-la later surmised that his brother must have thought, "My mother has spoiled this boy so much, I will have to frighten him." Geshe-la always remembered his brother with great gratitude. Without Gunsang's stern tutelage, the spoiled young Geshe-la would never have made progress in his spiritual development. Thus, Geshe-la remembered his brother's love for him as actually being equal to that of his mother.

Gunsang molded Geshe-la into an excellent student and scholar. All young monks were put quickly to the task of learning the Tibetan language and then memorizing many pages of Tibetan prayers and important Tibetan texts. The young Geshe-la was very adept at memorizing many pages of text in one sitting. He had a great competitive spirit and excelled in his class, though he had a classmate who was always slightly ahead of him (which undoubtedly worked to his advantage).

When Geshe-la was sixteen years old, he decided to enter a medical school that had been recently established by a famous doctor from what was then known as Outer Mongolia. There he demonstrated a voracious appetite for knowledge, studying in one year the books that were normally covered in two years. His teacher was very proud of him and said, "You can recognize a wish-fulfilling horse when it is a colt," meaning that he saw that Geshe-la would be very successful in his life.

However, at the year's end his teacher suddenly died. Geshe-la lost his interest in medical studies, but was swept up quickly by the great lama, Agvan Dorzhiev.[1] Although Lama Dorzhiev was a Buryat Mongolian from the Siberian region of Russia called Buryatia, he was very devoted to the Kalmyks. From time to time throughout his life he would visit Kalmykia to teach and promote the religion. Lama Dorzhiev had established there two monastic colleges for the study of

Buddhist philosophy, known by the Kalmyks as the *chö-ra* (*chos grva*), a Tibetan term meaning "religious institution." Hearing of Geshe-la's great abilities, he conscripted him into one of these chö-ra. Lama Dorzhiev was a man of such immense presence and reputation that there was no question of Geshe-la's considering whether he would go or not. In awe, he went.

Thus started a teacher-student relationship that shaped the rest of Geshe-la's life. Lama Dorzhiev became his root lama, giving him all the principal vows and initiations. He was such a strong role model that when Geshe-la came to America in 1955, he too worked to establish a center for learning amongst the Kalmyks, a group of whom had emigrated from the European refugee camps after the Second World War and settled in central New Jersey. One of his elderly Kalmyk disciples who had emigrated to the United States once remarked to me that Geshe-la was just like his teacher Lama Dorzhiev in that he was very successful at everything he undertook.

At the chö-ra Geshe-la was a very confident and effective student and debater. He became very proud of the fact that no one could surpass him. Geshe-la caught the attention of the leader of the Kalmyk religion, the Shachin Lama, at that time a young man who had studied for a while in Tibet and had recently been appointed to his position with the help of Lama Dorzhiev. The Shachin Lama gave Geshe-la the rank of head scholar, and rewarded him with many privileges that the other students did not have.

But unfortunately Geshe-la's studies gradually became sporadic because of the great changes going on around him. At first the only evidence of the Bolshevik revolution was the sound of distant explosions. But the Kalmyks eventually became the victims of theft by marauding bands of soldiers from the various warring groups. Therefore, by 1921 Geshe-la was spending more time at his home monastery than at the chö-ra. Then one day he was summoned to appear before the chö-ra's executive secretary, who told him that he had been selected by Lama Dorzhiev to go to Tibet to further his studies.

It is hard to imagine the excitement that Geshe-la must have felt. He had been selected to go to center of the religion to which he had devoted his life! His brother Gunsang's reaction gives us a small indication of how Geshe-la felt. Gunsang wept tears of joy—not for just a short time, for ten days! He would get up in the morning, wash his hands and face, begin to have his tea, and immediately start to cry. Geshe-la would plead with him, "O brother, do not cry so much. You will get sick!" His brother would reply, "I am not crying with sorrow. I am crying because I am so happy."

Two other Kalmyk monks had also been selected, and Geshe-la quickly prepared to leave with them to meet Lama Dorzhiev in Volgograd, the largest city in the region. Geshe-la did not know it then, but the trip to Tibet would take fourteen months. From Volgograd he would go with Lama Dorzhiev to Moscow in order to catch the Trans-Siberian Railway to Ulan Ude, the largest city in Lama Dorzhiev's region of Buryatia. Parting there from Lama Dorzhiev, he would then head south by boat and ox cart to Urga (now known as Ulan Baatar), the holy city of the Kalka Mongolians of Outer Mongolia. Then came the most difficult part of the journey: a caravan across the Gobi Desert to the Tsaidam (Tshva 'dam) region in northernmost Tibet, then south across Tibet's great northern plain, Changtang (Byang thang), to Nakchuka (Nag chu kha) at the frontier to central Tibet, and finally to Lhasa.

When it came time for Geshe-la to leave, his brothers, sister, sister-in-law, and two young nieces were there to say good-bye (his mother had died a few years earlier). One of his young nieces grabbed his leg and pleaded with him not to leave. Everyone wept. As he mounted his horse, Gunsang asked him to circumambulate their monastery's entire complex of three temples and twenty small residence buildings on his way out.

Geshe-la's oldest brother, Morsang, accompanied him as far as Volgograd in order to sell some of the family's cows and horses to finance the trip to Tibet. They easily sold their livestock for a good price in gold. Here Geshe-la and Morsang parted, never to see one another again. But Geshe-la wrote to him from Urga and asked him to sell off all his livestock, because he was accumulating too much non-virtuous karma by keeping animals. He asked him to use the money to plant fruit trees instead. It is a measure of the great respect Kalmyks had for monks that Morsang—a nomad and Geshe-la's elder by sixteen years—followed his little brother's advice.

In Volgograd Lama Dorzhiev took charge of the three young monks. Geshe-la did not think that Lama Dorzhiev himself had chosen him to go to Tibet. They did not have such a close relationship. He imagined that he must have been recommended by the Shachin Lama. But by the time that they reached Moscow, it was clear that a special relationship was developing between Geshe-la and his root lama. Of the three young monks, Lama Dorzhiev especially liked Geshe-la, for he gave only him the task of procuring his drinking water and favorite cheese, which he would then share with Geshe-la. Moreover, one day, before leaving the room in which he was staying with his three young charges, Lama Dorzhiev gave Geshe-la the responsibility of watching the room, entrusting him with the keys and ordering him not to leave under any circumstances. But Geshe-la could not contain himself. Locking the door, he set out to see the city. Just as he started down the street, much to his astonishment Lama Dorzhiev was standing before him, laughing.

"Did you lock the door?" he asked.

"Yes," Geshe-la replied, meekly.

"Well then, give me the keys, and have a good walk!"

Geshe-la's faith in his lama greatly deepened. He was sure that he was traveling with a buddha. If Lama Dorzhiev was not a buddha, how did he get there before him? How did he know what he was planning? Geshe-la's experience reminded him of the story of Buddha Śākyamuni appearing before his younger half-brother, Saundarananda, who was very attached to his wife, even though she had given her consent for him to become a monk. Just as Geshe-la had tried to sneak out to see the city, so had Saundarananda tried to sneak out to see his wife when the Buddha and the other monks were not there. And just as Lama Dorzhiev suddenly appeared before Geshe-la, so did the Buddha suddenly appear before Saundarananda—there was no way to outwit an omniscient being. Buddha understood his half-brother's great potential, for Saundarananda later attained the high state of an *arhat.*

Indeed, Lama Dorzhiev was a man of no small spiritual accomplishments. He was at that time about sixty-seven years old. When he was twenty-six, he entered Gomang Monastic College in Lhasa, and, after a short eight years, achieved his geshe degree with great honors. That same year he became an assistant tutor to the teenage Thirteenth Dalai Lama of Tibet, and taught him for ten years, establishing a very close relationship. Throughout most of Lama Dorzhiev's life this relationship proved to be the basis for many endeavors to forge an alliance between Russia and Tibet. Theoretically, such an alliance should have ensured the security of Tibetan Buddhism in the Tibetan and Mongolian regions, for Lama Dorzhiev also had great influence with the Tsar's government and the subsequent Bolshevik regimes. It was only due to this influence that Geshe-la was able to get through Russia to Urga.

From Moscow, Lama Dorzhiev sent Geshe-la and the other two monks on the Trans-Siberian Railway as far as Ulan Ude. He joined them there ten days later, bringing with him another Kalmyk monk. As it turned out, in Moscow Lama Dorzhiev had been organizing a secret delegation with which Geshe-la would travel from Urga to Tibet. The leader was Sergey Stepanovich Borisov, a member of the Peoples' Commissariat of Internal Affairs. He was on a mission to open diplomatic relations with Tibet, and was to bring many guns and much ammunition as an offering to the Tibetan government. Borisov was carefully chosen because he was of Turkic descent and his dark skin made him look Mongolian, which made it more likely that he would not be expelled as a foreigner at Nakchuka, the main checkpoint in northern Tibet on the way to Lhasa. Another monk—

this time a Buryat Mongolian—was added to the party, which would total around twelve people (all Mongolians except for Borisov) when it left Urga. The presence of the five monks made the caravan look more like a party of pilgrims. But Lama Dorzhiev seems to have been advancing his two intertwined objectives, religious and political, for he carefully advised Geshe-la to separate himself from Borisov in Nakchuka so as not to be detained.

Lama Dorzhiev said good-bye to his five young monks in Ulan Ude, sending them to meet the readying caravan in Urga, known to the Mongolians as Da Küree, 'the Great Monastery.' With its thirteen thousand monks, thirty monastic colleges, huge assembly halls, and numerous temples, Urga must have been an overwhelming sight to the faithful young Geshe-la when he first arrived. There, he frequently visited Ganden Monastery, where the philosophical studies were located, and watched the monks debate. It was at Ganden that His Holiness the Thirteenth Dalai Lama stayed in 1904 at the beginning of his five-year self-imposed exile. At the time, Lama Dorzhiev was accompanying him. The Dalai Lama was greatly impressed by the abilities of the Mongolian geshes and asked Lama Dorzhiev if there were many such geshes in Tibet. Lama Dorzhiev replied enigmatically, "Yes, there are. They are located in the basement of Drepung," meaning that they were kept in very low positions. When the Dalai Lama returned to Tibet, he dismissed many of the monks in authority, and set up a system based on scholarly merit in order to give the best geshes the greatest responsibility for teaching the other monks.

But the great religious purpose in this city did not shelter it from the upheaval in Russia. At Ganden, Geshe-la heard the monks chant prayers to eliminate such obstacles to the teachings as the Kalmyks, for the Bolshevik government had sent five hundred young Kalmyk soldiers to take possession of Urga. They had been terrorizing the local populace, imprisoning and killing many wealthy residents, and stealing their money. Even Geshe-la and his four companions were threatened by this group, even though they were mostly Kalmyk and Lama Dorzhiev had provided the necessary papers and permits from the Moscow government. One evening they were stopped by some young guards who wanted to check the contents of the cart in which they were riding. One of Geshe-la's companions recognized the leader of the group, but the young guard pretended not to hear him calling out his name. When they showed him their papers from Moscow, he paid no attention. Geshe-la's companions were ready to resist, but Geshe-la cooled down the tensions by pointing out that they should allow the search because they had nothing to hide. Indeed, finding nothing, the guard let them go on.

Like a true pilgrim, Geshe-la found his way through many such difficulties and obstacles on his way to Tibet because of his strong faith. But his sharp intelligence, strong will, and sense of purpose were also great assets. Further, Lama Dorzhiev's favoritism had bolstered his great self-confidence. He was very proud of his abilities, but he never let that pride blind him. This allowed him to be open to some help from a great Kalmyk teacher in Urga, Tourgüt Jentsen, who had thousands of students. Geshe-la visited him with Chö-nyen, the Kalmyk monk who had joined the group in Ulan Ude and with whom he had already become an inseparable friend. Chö-nyen was from the same region of Kalmykia as Tourgüt Jentsen and, therefore, was granted an audience. The great teacher seemed to know very well the problem of increased pride that the honor of a trip to Tibet was giving Geshe-la when he said, "Don't think proudly, 'I am going to Tibet,' but remember, even camels go to Tibet!"

After the young monks met Borisov, it did not take them long to learn that they were under a capable leader. One time, Chö-nyen went out by himself to one of the monasteries and got in trouble with the authorities. Borisov decided that he would be a problem for the caravan as well and therefore should return to Kalmykia. This caused Geshe-la to assert brashly that if Chö-nyen was forced to go, he would join him. Oddly enough, this caused Borisov to relent. It seemed that Lama Dorzhiev was looking after Geshe-la still, for he must have informed Borisov to favor Geshe-la because he was a reliable person.

Borisov organized the caravan like a military expedition. An all night watch was kept with each member of the party standing guard for two hours. Most of the members were able marksmen. Geshe-la was the only one who refused to carry a gun. When he was asked, Geshe-la replied, "No, I don't want a gun. I am going to Tibet, a holy place. I don't want to kill anyone. I would rather die myself." Since Geshe-la did not have his hands occupied with holding a rifle, Borisov ordered him instead to take hold of the camels' lead and keep them in tow from the early morning start until the end of the day. Geshe-la must have been often reminded of Tourgüt Jentsen's words during the journey, for there were more than one hundred camels for carrying the supplies and gifts.

They started in the winter of 1922 and planned to reach Nakchuka in twenty-two days. But it took them almost fifty, because, in spite of their two Mongolian guides from Tsaidam, they still got lost. The thick snow on the ground and frequent snow storms made proper navigation too difficult. After losing their way, they also started to run out of food. The horses could hardly walk for want of nourishment and due to snow blindness. The camels fared a little better, though the narrow mountain paths were difficult for their large feet. Usually the party would have had plenty to eat from just the wild animals that they could hunt, but no animals appeared. When resentment started to rise against the two guides, Borisov quickly ordered everyone not to say a thing to them. He very cleverly did not want to lose what slight hope they had of finding their way.

Finally, they reached the snowless banks of a large river, and the men started to net small minnows; but these provided hardly any nourishment. As they rested at the river's edge for three days, Borisov announced that they would share equally what food they had (some dried vegetables), for, he said, if they must die, they would die together. Suddenly, a large herd of wild yaks appeared. The marksmen quickly shot about thirty of the yaks, and the young monks were ordered to extract the meat. Although the meat was tasteless and very tough because they could not boil it enough on their small dung fires, it was enough to give them energy.

Having reached the river, Borisov was able to assist the guides by locating where they were on a map that he had brought. After more than a week, they reached Nakchuka, but not before they lost one man, the Buryat monk, in a blinding blizzard. They were able to find him, but he was terminally ill from exposure and died in Nakchuka.

Exhausted, hungry, and saddened by their friend's misfortune, the party was nevertheless glad to be able to buy some real food. As monks, the young Kalmyks were treated very well by the local people and ate until they were sick. Luckily, Borisov was able to get by the government authorities (who were later punished). Because the camels could not make the journey to Lhasa, Borisov made arrangements for them to be taken care of until he returned, and rented some horses.

The trip to Lhasa took about twelve days, and was fortunately uneventful. When they were within sight of the golden roofs of the Potala, they made camp for the night. Geshe-la was overwhelmed with excitement and could not sleep. Late at night Geshe-la and Chö-nyen stole quietly out of camp, and rode off to reach the city before sunrise. Geshe-la had rationalized that, following Lama Dorzhiev's advice, it would be best not to be seen arriving with Borisov's party.

To travel virtually unarmed through the outskirts of Lhasa at night was very foolish. The area was full of robbers, and Chö-nyen's small handgun would not have afforded much protection, especially in the hands of a monk. When Borisov realized that they had gone, he was furious that they had put their lives in jeopardy. But he placed all the blame on Chö-nyen, who he was sure had misled Geshe-la, for by this time he liked Geshe-la very much. Geshe-la met up with him again in Lhasa after the main party arrived around mid-day, but Borisov did not scold him. Indeed, when they finally parted, Borisov gave him his address and asked him to write.

As most Mongolians did when they came to study in Lhasa, Geshe-la entered the Gomang College of Drepung Monastic University. But there was no fear of his wasting his opportunity and being like the camels Tourgüt Jentsen had referred to. Instead, he again demonstrated his great capacity to absorb knowledge. In Kalmykia he had started a rigorous scholastic training that was organized along the same lines as the program of geshe studies at Gomang. In that program, there are five primary areas of study (*po ti lnga*), covered in the following order:

(1) Topics of Valid Cognition (*rnam 'grel*)—logic, reasoning, and debate;
(2) Perfection of Wisdom (*phar phyin*)—the factors of the path;
(3) Madhyamaka (*dbu ma*)—the philosophy of emptiness;
(4) Discipline (*'dul ba*)—vows and ethical discipline;
(5) Higher Knowledge (*dzod*)—presentation of the Vaibhāṣika school of Buddhist tenets.

The Kalmyk monks who went to Tibet to attain a geshe degree entered this program of studies at the level of the Perfection of Wisdom, which they had started already in Kalmykia (it took about five years to complete this area of studies). Thus, they had a great advantage over their Tibetan classmates, and Geshe-la did not squander this advantage. In order to quickly finish his full course of studies, he made good use of the spare time that resulted from his already having started the Perfection of Wisdom. While his classmates were training in the first year's topics, Geshe-la studied the next year's topics as well. He continued this pattern until he finished all five areas of study in nine years, less than one-half the twenty years that it would normally take.

At the end of the nine years Geshe-la decided to return to Kalmykia in order to find funding to continue his studies. He went by way of Beijing, but ended up going no further than that after some Buryat monks at the monastery in which he was staying warned him of the great persecution of monks in Russia. Indeed, Geshe-la had no way of knowing then, but at about this time his brother Gunsang was arrested because he was an abbot of the monastery, and imprisoned three times, finally dying in jail. Geshe-la never returned to Kalmykia, nor did he ever contact his family, fearing that he would bring some form of persecution upon them.

Instead, Geshe-la became a citizen of the world. He stayed in Beijing and northern China for a few years. During this time he earned money for his studies by working on a translation project that had been organized by Russian scholars, wherein he was responsible for comparing various editions of the Tibetan Buddhist canon. He also raised money by teaching in Inner Mongolia for a year amongst the Ijlin Tourgüt, a settlement of Western Mongolians, who were similar to the Kalmyks. He eventually learned English in Beijing, and in 1935 became an interpreter for the great English representative to Tibet, Sir Charles Bell, during Bell's travels in China and Manchuria. Geshe-la then returned to Tibet to get his geshe degree, and in 1937 traveled to England for about four months at the invitation of Marco Pallis, a mountaineer and author on Buddhism whom he had met in India on his return from China. During the war years, Geshe-la spent the winters in India and the summers in Tibet. He earned enough money through trading to support himself and a number of Mongolian monks who were studying to attain their geshe degrees. He had wanted to return to Beijing to live and practice his religion, but the revolution there made his plans impossible. In 1951 Geshe-la was about to buy a retreat house and settle in Tibet when he heard that the Chinese army was moving towards Lhasa. He immediately fled to India.

It was from India that he finally had an opportunity to rejoin his Kalmyk people, but this time in New Jersey. From the time he left Gomang in 1931 until that time he had not wavered in his religious conviction. When he arrived in the United States in 1955, he was intent on helping the new immigrants keep their religion. To this end he worked at two teaching jobs and founded the Lamaist Buddhist Monastery of America in 1958, using his own money to build a temple and residence. Although he intended to teach the young Kalmyks, Geshe-la was open to anyone who wanted to learn about the teachings that he so cherished. Soon he was teaching many more new Buddhists from America than new immigrants from Kalmykia. He made America his home, becoming a citizen after five years. He devoted the rest of his life to his students out of a conviction that Tibetan Buddhism offered something that would be helpful to the American way of life. By the time of his death, he had spent more time in America than anywhere else in the world. As one of his Kalmyk-American students, David Urubshurow, points out, he had become the first American lama.

The teachings in this book are what Geshe-la read to his students in the manner described in the following "Note on the Translations" written by the final editors. These teachings were delivered with great devotion, some understanding of which is conveyed in the stories I have told. That devotion and Geshe-la's strong character inspired his students to transform their lives through the practice of the teachings and also to do what they could to assist Tibet and its teachings. Many of these students are now teaching in universities and colleges throughout the country. I have the responsibility of continuing Geshe-la's work of teaching and translating in accordance with his advice at the center of learning that he founded, now known as the Tibetan Buddhist Learning Center, in Washington, New Jersey, where he spent the last fifteen years of his life. I am assisted by my wife, Diana, who apprenticed under Geshe-la for eleven years. We reside at the center with four Tibetan monk-scholars.

The recent fall of the Soviet Union and the subsequent opening up of Kalmykia has provided an interesting postscript to Geshe-la's life story. David Urubshurow visited Kalmykia in 1990 and met descendants of Geshe-la's siblings—his sister Jugda's two sons and a grand-niece. They informed him that the last time the family had heard from Geshe-la was the letter to Morsang that he had sent from Outer Mongolia. They assumed that Geshe-la had died in Outer Mongolia on his way to Tibet! In Kalmykia almost all traces of the monasteries, temples, and memorials to Buddha's enlightenment had been removed. Geshe-la's grand-niece showed David a small fenced-in area that marked where Geshe-la's monastery had been, and she also pointed out the fruit trees that Morsang had planted.

His Holiness the Fourteenth Dalai Lama visited Kalmykia in 1991 to assist in the revival of Buddhism there. In front of a large gathering of the Kalmyk people, he paid Geshe-la the greatest tribute by holding him up as a good model for the Kalmyks in their religious endeavors, saying, "[This] single Kalmyk human being eventually did a lot not only to preserve Buddhism but, I think, to propagate it as well. I have always admired his activities and his determination. Therefore, I am extremely happy to be here with you today, and if Geshe Wangyal were here, I would be even happier."

Joshua W. C. Cutler
Tibetan Buddhist Learning Center

A Note on the Translations

"The precept of the lama is more important than the scriptures and commentaries." —Atīśa

The term *precept* refers to the personal advice or instruction given by a spiritual teacher for the immediate, practical needs of a disciple. The *scriptures* of Buddhism consist of the recorded precepts given by the Buddha to his various disciples on different occasions. The *commentaries* on the scriptures consist of the clarifications and systematizations composed by later teachers for use as precepts by their own disciples.

In utilizing these written records it is difficult to know which of the many precepts given by the Buddha and the great teachers is applicable and most beneficial at any particular stage of development. Even if the appropriate teaching is known, it will not be effective unless it is well applied—just as the appropriate medicine will not produce the desired cure unless it is taken properly. This is the special importance of the precept of the lama—the spiritual friend—who, with superior vision of the realities of our condition, knows exactly what is needed at any particular time to further our growth, and can select and apply the most beneficial teaching.

These recorded precepts were translated by a lama in the lineage of the original authors, Geshe Wangyal. Through the period of his residence in the United States, well over a decade, Geshe-la has used the process of translating these and other works as a vehicle of instruction for his disciples as well as for the eventual reader.

The selections in this book were taught to various disciples on different occasions, and over the years English versions of most were written down a number of times; this work was the foundation from which the present volume was prepared. All the selections were translated to the disciples by Geshe-la a final time and a few new ones were added. All available material was reviewed and a tentative manuscript was made. This was then read and criticized by others—both with and without a usable knowledge of the Tibetan language—and their suggestions were used in numerous revisions. We feel that this method of translation, involving the cooperation of many people, has refined the work and increased its comprehensibility for those readers who are approaching this material for the first time. We hope that our collaboration has been auspicious.

Deborah Black
Joshua W. C. Cutler
Elizabeth Napper
Retreat House, 1973

Acknowledgments to the First Edition

I WOULD LIKE TO EXPRESS my sincere appreciation to all those who helped make this book possible. To begin, I would like to thank Mr. Marco Pallis, whose advice and prophetic statements in my youth have now been proven so accurate; Dr. J. J. Robinson, who first urged me to publish these translations; the Reverend Dr. Marion L. Matics, who, through his interest in translating the Buddhist teachings, has given me much helpful encouragement and spiritual support; my friends Ted Jacobs and Elsy Becherer, whom I have known since I first arrived in this country; Mr. Johann J. Blomeyer, whose goodwill towards my work I hold in high regard; and Dr. Josef Kolenski, Dr. Peter Beskyd, and Dr. and Mrs. A. U. Bertland, who, through their sympathetic interest in Tibetan Buddhism, have unselfishly provided medical assistance to the monks of the Lamaist Buddhist Monastery of America.

I would particularly like to express my deep gratitude to the late Mr. Chester Carlson, whose goodwill and deep inspiration are felt even now, and to Mrs. Carlson, whose extremely kind encouragement and support has made so much of my work possible.

The great help and friendship of my students Mr. and Mrs. Robert Fulton also deserve particular mention here. For many years they have put forth great effort to portray on film the religious practices of Tibetan Buddhism, even accompanying me on my recent visit to India.

I am also thankful to Mr. C. T. Shen, who, through his devotion to the Dharma, has extended his generous support to further the work of translation being undertaken by our newly formed Buddhist Studies Institute.

In connection with the Buddhist Studies Institute, I must acknowledge the efforts of two of my students, Dr. Christopher George and Dr. Robert Thurman, who are now coordinating the activities of the Institute. Many years ago, they were among my earliest students and helped work on the versions of the translations in this book.

Also, I appreciate very much Dr. Jeffrey Hopkins' many years of dedicated service to the Lamaist Buddhist Monastery of America.

Finally, I would like to thank Maurice Girodias for his patience and enthusiasm throughout the preparation of this manuscript, and his editors Grant Fisher and Diane di Prima. And last but certainly not least, I extend my thanks to my students: to Brian Cutillo, for his devotion and effort in our work of translation; to Debby, Betsy, and Josh, who worked closely with me in preparing this manuscript; and to all my other students and friends, too many to name, who assisted me in so many ways.

Geshe Wangyal
May 1973

The Door of Liberation

I

Introduction

I BOW DOWN TO Buddha Śākyamuni, the teacher without equal, who attained the highest state and possession of the four aspects of fearlessness through his perfect accomplishment of the six *pāramitās* and the four ways of assembling. He is the great Compassionate One, the originator of the teaching, who, in order to deliver all living beings, has shown the path that he himself traveled to liberation.

Buddha taught two great paths: to the *bodhisattva* Mañjuśrī, he taught the path of profound view, and to the bodhisattva Maitreya, the path of extensive deeds. After several hundred years, as Buddha had prophesied, these two paths were extended by Nāgārjuna and Asaṅga. From them, these undefiled teachings descended in an unbroken succession through many great Indian and Tibetan scholars, such as Atīśa and Tsongkhapa. Remembering their kindness in extending the teaching, I bow to these great beings.

I bow down to His Holiness, Tenzin Gyatso, the Fourteenth Dalai Lama. By the radiant illumination of his great compassion, his wonderful methods and skillful deeds emanate in all directions, causing the lotus within all beings to blossom forth. May his blessings grant peace and happiness to all living beings.

I bow down especially to my own teachers, the lamas from whom I directly received these precious teachings. Even that knowledge I have of English came from them, and from my heart I honor them as would a son, though I can never repay their great kindness. I have tried to translate their teachings into English with the sincere prayer that their profound meaning might be extended to others.

This teaching appeared in the world through the miraculous manifestation of Buddha Śākyamuni, who, descending from the buddha-field of Akaniṣṭha ('Og min), took rebirth as the bodhisattva-prince Tampa Dokar in the Tuṣita heaven. In order to benefit all living beings, he then descended to Jambudvīpa, taking rebirth as Siddhārtha, prince of the Śākyas. The events of his illustrious life are widely known. Manifesting full enlightenment, he revealed his perfect teaching to the world. To guide all living beings to the door of liberation, he presented his teaching by many wonderful methods. A few descriptions of Buddha's miraculous activities have been translated here. These activities demonstrate the authority of his teaching, for in the Tibetan tradition, the reliability of a teaching is established by the qualifications of the teacher.

Buddha showed his omniscience in many ways. One day while he was teaching a gathering of his disciples, a crow flew over and defecated on his robe. The bodhisattva Avalokiteśvara stood up from among the assembly and asked Buddha to explain the significance of this occurrence. Buddha replied with a prophecy. He said that in the future that crow would be reborn as a powerful non-Buddhist pandit, Aśvaghoṣa, or Mātṛceta, who would severely criticize the Dharma. After being defeated in debate, he would see the truth and would write many famous praises of the Buddha. Avalokiteśvara then asked Buddha, "May I be the one to subdue this great opponent of the teaching?"

Centuries later Buddha's prophecy was realized. Many Buddhist teachers in India were being defeated in debate by a non-Buddhist pandit named Mātṛceta. After he had conquered all the Buddhists in his region, Mātṛceta's mother, a devout Buddhist, persuaded him to challenge the monks of the renowned Buddhist center of Nālandā. At that time, Ārya Avalokiteśvara, incarnated as the great Buddhist scholar Āryadeva, met Mātṛceta in debate and defeated him. Mātṛceta then began to study the Buddha's teachings and was compelled to acknowledge their truth. He sincerely repented his previous harmful deeds. Completely abandoning his wrong views, he said, "I have given up my other teachers, and I take refuge in Buddha, for Buddha has no faults and possesses perfect omniscience."

The goddess Tārā appeared before Mātṛceta in a dream and advised him to purify himself by writing praises to the Buddha and commentaries on the *Jātakas.* Following her advice, Mātṛceta wrote many volumes extolling the *Tathāgata* and his teaching. His praises of Buddha demonstrate the truth of the Dharma with particular effectiveness, as they were written by a former opponent of Buddha's teaching. An account of the debate between Mātṛceta and Āryadeva has been included in chapter 2 of this book.

Buddha Śākyamuni also prophesied that, after he had passed into *parinirvāṇa,* there would appear in the world many great scholars who would disseminate his teaching. Therefore, the first chapter also includes short histories of some of these great Indian teachers, such as Nāgārjuna and Asaṅga, as well as those who spread the teaching in Tibet, such as Atīśa and Tsongkhapa. These great teachers are respected as is the Buddha himself. Their teachings are as clear and unerring as those of the Buddha and are directly or indirectly those which have been translated in this book.

In the Tibetan tradition, which follows a system set forth centuries ago by the Indian poet Daṇḍin, books begin with an expression of salutation, to show respect to the Buddha and the bodhisattvas and scholars through whom his teachings have descended to the present. This is followed by the subject matter of the book, which is written according to two purposes, temporary and final. The temporary purpose is to produce in people an understanding of the Buddha's teaching, which will inspire them to enter into the Dharma and make effort in its practice. Realization of this purpose can be seen in the history of the non-Buddhist pandit Mātṛceta. Having himself begun to follow the Dharma through the study of scriptures, he wrote commentaries on the *Jātakas* and praises of the Buddha, so that others might understand Buddha's perfect knowledge and develop faith in the teaching. Through practice of the Buddha's teaching, one can attain, temporarily, rebirth in happy states of existence and, finally, the ultimate goal of liberation. This is the final purpose of the book: to show the way to reach the final attainment of buddhahood. Although presented from a variety of viewpoints, all the translations in this book share in these two purposes. All show the way to reach the door of liberation.

According to the *Mahāyāna* tradition, the ultimate door of liberation is the realization of voidness. However, to actually open this door, one must produce the bodhi-mind of love and compassion. The generation of bodhi-mind is the basis for method, and the realization of voidness is the basis for wisdom. To reach the door of liberation, according to the Mahāyāna tradition, the practice of method and wisdom must be inseparably joined. The following verse from the sutras is the origin of the teaching of the door of liberation:

> As those who do not understand voidness, peace,
> and birthlessness
> Wander in the world,
> The Compassionate One
> Taught method and many different reasonings.

To elaborate on this: seeing that living beings suffer in the world through their lack of understanding of voidness, peace, and birthlessness, the threefold door of liberation, Buddha was moved to great compassion. In order to show living beings the way to free themselves from *saṃsāra*, Buddha taught many different teachings, expressed in a variety of ways according to the capacity of his listeners to understand them.

His teachings are of two kinds: those of direct meaning and those of derived meaning. Buddha's sole purpose is to guide living beings to liberation, and all his teachings are correct and non-contradictory. However, due to different understandings of Buddha's words, according to whether they are interpreted to be of direct or of derived meaning, there developed different systems of Buddhist tenets and the differentiation into *Hīnayāna* and Mahāyāna.

There are four main schools of Buddhist tenets: the *Vaibhāṣika*; the *Sautrāntika*; the *Cittamātra*, or *Vijñānavāda*; and the *Madhyamaka*, which is divided into the *Svātantrika-Madhyamaka* and the *Prāsaṅgika-Madhyamaka*. The former two schools belong to the Hīnayāna tradition, and the latter two to the Mahāyāna tradition. The translations in this book are primarily from the viewpoint of the Prāsaṅgika-Madhyamaka.

All the schools of tenets base their viewpoints on statements of the Buddha; the differences between them arise through their varying interpretations of those statements. This is seen in their different understandings of Buddha's teaching that all compounded phenomena are like a magician's illusions.

The Vaibhāṣikas feel that this example indicates impermanence, in the sense that all things must be given up at the time of death. Though the illusory elephant and horse of the magician exist during his magical show, they cease to exist once the show is over; in the same way, the body and the enjoyments of this life must be abandoned at the time of death. This is the ordinary level of understanding of impermanence, as found among people like ourselves.

The Sautrāntikas feel that what is being indicated is impermanence in the sense of the momentary nature of phenomena. Just as the illusory emanations of the magician change from moment to moment, so all phenomena are disintegrating in each moment, not depending on any later cause, but depending merely on having been produced.

The Cittamātrins, or Vijñānavādins, feel that this example indicates that phenomena are not established depending on the nature of external objects, but are merely the nature of the inner mind, just as the horse and elephant that the magician manifests from pieces of stone and wood are not actually horses and elephants, but are merely the perceptions of a consciousness deluded by the power of the magician's *mantras* or power objects.

The Mādhyamikas feel that Buddha's example indicates that phenomena do not exist truly, but are merely put forth by the power of their appearing to the mind. However, the Svātantrika-Mādhyamikas further say that it is not enough that an object be put forward by the power of its appearing to the mind; the object must also be established from the nature of its own basis of imputation. That is, the illusory horse and elephant of the magician are put forth not only by the power of their appearing to the mistaken mind, but also from the nature of the pieces of stone and wood that are their bases of emanation. They say that if this were not the case, one would be able to see the horse and elephant just from the delusive power of the magician's mantras or power objects, without need for the pieces of stone and wood which serve as their bases of emanation.

The Prāsaṅgika-Madhyamaka school refutes this position of the Svātantrika-Mādhyamikas. They say that one does not see the illusory emanations of the magician by the power of their being established from the nature of the pieces of wood and stone that are their bases of emanation. If the sight of "horse" were to depend on the nature of a particular piece of wood or stone, then that particular piece of wood or stone could be seen only as "horse," and not as "elephant." Further, if the sight of "horse" were produced from the nature of its basis of emanation, even those not under the magician's power would have to see the horse. The Prāsaṅgika-Mādhyamikas say that one sees the illusory horse and elephant of the magician by the power of whether or not one's mind imputes "horse" or "elephant" to those bases of emanation, for they say that phenomena are established by the mere imputation of concepts and terms. According to the Tibetan scholarly tradition, the Prāsaṅgika system of interpretation expresses the actual meaning of Buddha's teaching.

This short description of the tenets of the different schools is included here because they are not specifically described in any of the translations. An understanding of them helps to clarify the concept of the illusoriness of phenomena, as that concept appears throughout the various translations from the viewpoint of the Prāsaṅgikas. Ultimately, thorough study of the tenets is necessary in order to develop the understanding needed to achieve the realization of voidness.

In all the teachings of Buddha, mind is essential. It is first of all necessary to have mind-practice, whether following the Hīnayāna or the Mahāyāna path, for it is only from mind-practice that one can abandon wrongdoing and purify oneself from all defilements. Therefore, throughout all of Buddhism, there is nothing that is not based upon mind. In the systems of practice that follow the Hīnayāna tradition, one develops the mind-practice of controlling selfish feelings and extending the concept of renunciation of saṃsāra. The final goal of this practice is the attainment of *arhatship*. According to the Mahāyāna tradition, it is most important to develop mind-practice from the viewpoint of the deeds of the bodhisattvas. These deeds are the six pāramitās, or transcendences: giving, moral practice, patience, effort, meditation, and wisdom. From this viewpoint one develops the bodhi-mind of love and compassion and the realization of voidness. Through the joint practice of these two, a bodhisattva can ultimately attain buddhahood, the final goal of the Mahāyāna.

The beginning of all mind-practice in the Buddha's teaching is the taking of refuge. In order to free oneself from the pain and suffering of existence, one must seek protection from the best possible source. Just as one must have a reliable guide when undertaking a long and difficult journey to an unknown place, so one must follow a guide who has the proper qualifications when seeking to travel the path to liberation.

Śākyamuni Buddha attained the final goal of the path, buddhahood, by first generating the mind of compassion and then perfecting himself during many lifetimes through the stages of the bodhisattvas. He practiced the difficult bodhisattva deeds of compassion and purified himself of all the defilements of the three mental poisons. Having attained perfect omniscience, even now he works exclusively for the benefit of other living beings, and, by the power of this great compassion, is able to guide living beings to liberation. Buddha's compassion is such that he feels toward all living beings as a mother feels toward her children. He makes no discrimination between those who are good or bad, high or low, friend or enemy—he works for all living beings equally without expecting that his kindness will be repaid.

Therefore, Buddha can be relied upon as a guide. Knowing that his motivation is pure and his knowledge complete, one can understand that the *Dharma,* his teaching, is the right teaching to follow, and that the *Saṅgha,* those who practice and teach the Dharma, can be depended on for help. Thus the *Three Jewels,* the Buddha, the Dharma, and the Saṅgha, are the most suitable objects of refuge.

All three objects of refuge are indispensable. For example, if one is sick, a doctor is needed to diagnose the illness, medicine is needed to cure the sickness, and attendants are needed to give medicine and care until one is cured. The Buddha is the doctor, the Dharma is the medicine, and the Saṅgha are the attendants. All three are needed to eliminate the suffering of saṃsāric existence.

The Three Jewels can be understood in both their relative and their actual sense. The *trikāya* of the Buddha—*nirmāṇakāya, saṃbhogakāya,* and *dharmakāya*—comprise the actual Buddha, while images, paintings, and statues are the relative Buddha. Because the relative is an aspect of the actual, images of the Buddha are placed in the temples and respected in the same way as is the actual Buddha. By honoring these relative images, one can receive the actual blessings of the Buddha.

The Buddha's teaching is the actual Dharma; the books in which this teaching is written down are the relative Dharma. In these books one can find all the ways of practicing the teachings for the attainment of buddhahood. Therefore, in temples one finds books placed even higher than images of the Buddha. One should respect the books, not place them on the ground or mistreat them.

The actual Saṅgha are those who have attained the position of an *ārya,* but we respect as Saṅgha all those who have taken the vows of a monk or nun, because they are the representatives of the actual Saṅgha.

Taking refuge in Buddha, Dharma, and Saṅgha produces great

benefits. One enters the path of the Buddha and is able to take the vows of that path. One is able to purify oneself of defilements and accumulate immeasurable merit; by this one will not fall into lower states of being and will never be harmed by natural or supernatural obstacles. One can achieve one's right desires and will be able to attain buddhahood quickly.

There are different levels of taking refuge in the Three Jewels. At the lowest level, one sees only one's own misery and, seeking happiness, takes refuge in the Buddha from faith in his qualifications rather than from great understanding of his teaching. Here, one follows the precepts of the teaching and learns that the practice of virtue brings happiness.

At the middle level, one sees that the nature of all saṃsāra is suffering, and being afraid of this pervasive suffering, one takes refuge in the Buddha and seeks the happiness of *nirvāṇa.* This person begins the practice of the *three precepts*—exceptional moral practice, exceptional meditation, and exceptional wisdom. At this stage one can either immediately enter the highest level or one can become a *śrāvaka* or a *pratyekabuddha.* However, even śrāvakas and pratyekabuddhas will eventually admire the compassionate deeds of the bodhisattvas and will enter the highest level.

At the highest level, one sees the misery of all sentient beings and seeks to attain the perfect enlightenment of buddhahood for the sake of all beings. Motivated by this, beings of the highest level take refuge in the Three Jewels. They generate bodhi-mind and, practicing the six transcendences and the four ways of assembling, attain the qualities of a buddha.

Those who have reached the highest level and selflessly seek only to help others are called bodhisattvas, the offspring of the buddhas. Though they could seek to escape the misery of existence, they wish instead to be reborn in saṃsāra in order to help living beings. They accept the conditions of life wherever they are born, whether good or bad, and suffer along with other living beings. Yet they are never corrupted by worldly attachments; each one is like the lotus, which is itself pure and undefiled though it grows from the mud. One can recognize bodhisattvas from their deeds, just as when one sees a sea-gull, one knows that water is near, and when one sees smoke, one knows there is fire.

An example of such a being is the bodhisattva Ārya Avalokiteśvara, known in Tibet, the Land of Snow, as Chenrezig. While listening to the Mahāyāna teaching as a disciple of Buddha Śākyamuni, Ārya Avalokiteśvara vowed to help all living beings. Even long before this, he had made his renowned vow before the thousand buddhas to liberate every single sentient being and spread the Buddha's teachings "in the barbaric Land of Snow," making that "gloomy, barbaric country... bright, like an island of precious jewels" (see p. 32 in chapter 2). Throughout Tibetan history Ārya Avalokiteśvara has manifested himself in Tibet in many different forms: sometimes as a *dharmarāja*, sometimes as a lama, sometimes even in the form of an animal, such as the bodhisattva-monkey, as described in chapter 2. From the time of Tsongkhapa's disciple Gendun Drup until the present, he has manifested himself as the Dalai Lama of Tibet. The present Dalai Lama, His Holiness Tenzin Gyatso, is the Fourteenth Dalai Lama. It is our good fortune that Ārya Avalokiteśvara has manifested in the world even now, seeking to help all living beings.

One reaches the level of such a high bodhisattva through many lifetimes of unselfish deeds. However, if one makes exceptional effort in this life, one can enter the path of the *Mantrayāna*, through which it is possible to attain buddhahood in one lifetime. Even on entering this path, one takes refuge in the Three Jewels.

In short, taking refuge is intrinsic to all the Buddha's teaching. Though bodhi-mind is the gateway to the Mahāyāna and initiation is the gateway to the Mantrayāna, the foundation of both is refuge. Refuge is taken not only on entering the path to liberation but repeatedly throughout the path. The refuge prayer is repeated before every meditative session as part of the preliminary practice. One says:

Lama la kyap su chio.	I take refuge in the lama.
Sangye la kyap su chio.	I take refuge in the Buddha.
Chö la kyap su chio.	I take refuge in the Dharma.
Gendun la kyap su chio.	I take refuge in the Saṅgha.

The lama is not considered a fourth object of refuge but, in the Tibetan tradition, embodies all Three Jewels—Buddha, Dharma, and Saṅgha. When Buddha Śākyamuni was about to enter parinirvāṇa, he told his disciples, "In the future I will appear in the form of the lama. Feel that your lama is the Buddha and have the same faith in the lama that you have in me." The lama is the one who transmits the teaching to us, and he is the spiritual friend who assists us on the way. From him we derive the benefit of the Buddha's actual presence as a teacher.

Reliance on the lama is the foundation of all excellence. It is not enough merely to learn from books and accumulate knowledge; one must learn from a teacher who has internal realizations and then follow his precepts. In following the lama, one must develop faith in him through the purification of one's own perceptions. One must always hold in mind the thought that one's lama is the manifestation of all good qualities. If one perceives a fault in the lama, it should be accepted as one's own fault arising through the influence of desire, hatred, and ignorance. Buddha's cousin Devadatta could not even see the wonderful qualities of the Buddha because of the great force of his own obscuring passions.

Therefore, one should always listen to the words of the lama and learn from him the precepts of the teaching and the way to practice. Because this is so essential, Atīśa, when asked which was more important, the precept of the lama or the scriptures and commentaries, always answered, "The precept of the lama." Chapter 4 is a translation of a collection of many precepts, given by different lamas of the Kadampa lineage to their disciples. This lineage, begun by Atīśa, has always placed strong emphasis on the precept of the lama. A true lama is in a direct lineage descended from Buddha Śākyamuni himself. The lama's teaching, therefore, never contradicts the intention of the Buddha, the teachings of the bodhisattva path, or the precepts of the great lamas.

The bodhi-path is the path traveled by all the buddhas of the three times: past, present, and future. It is the system of the two great charioteers: Nāgārjuna, who extended the lineage of the profound view of voidness, and Asaṅga, who extended the lineage of the extensive deeds of compassion. It is the teaching followed by the highest level of beings who travel to enlightenment, the perfect omniscience of buddhahood. Atīśa, or Dīpaṃkara Śrījñāna, gathered these two lineages of the teachings, descended from Nāgārjuna and Asaṅga, into the teaching of the stages of the path of the three levels of beings, which are set forth in his book, the *Bodhipathapradīpa* (*Lamp of the Bodhi-Path*). Though this book is very short, it includes the essence of all the Buddha's teachings. Because of its conciseness and clarity, it is easy to practice. As it is ornamented by the two great lineages, it is pre-eminent among all other systems of explanation.

In praise of Atīśa's teaching of the stages of the path of the three levels of beings and of the lamas through whom it has descended, Tsongkhapa wrote:

> I bow down to my spiritual teachers,
> Who, moved by mercy and by skillful means, illumine
> This best gate for the fortunate traveling to liberation,
> This eye through which all the glorious scriptures are seen.

Though an eye is very small, through it one can see a vast area. In the same way, though the teaching of the stages of the path is very concise, through it one can see all the teachings of the sutras and *tantras.* It is the great entrance to the Mahāyāna teaching, the entrance of fortunate beings who seek to attain buddhahood for the sake of all living beings. By entering and following this path, one can reach the door of liberation.

The great Tsongkhapa, king of Dharma, then developed and explained this teaching from Atīśa. In the later chapters of this book, several short works by Tsongkhapa have been translated, that express this teaching from slightly different viewpoints. Tsongkhapa wrote his books through the direct inspiration of Mañjuśrī, the bodhisattva of wisdom, and therefore, his teachings are accorded highest reverence.

Another verse work of Tsongkhapa, *The Essence of Good Explanation: Praise of Munīndra*, in which Tsongkhapa praises Buddha Śākyamuni from the viewpoint of *dependent origination*, has been translated in chapter 5. The usual understanding of Buddha's teaching of dependent origination is by means of the twelvefold interdependent chain of cause and effect, by the power of which all living beings wander in saṃsāra. This corresponds closely to Buddha's first teachings of the *Four Noble Truths*. However, Buddha taught dependent origination from a different viewpoint in the following three lines:

> By existence of this, that comes forth;
> By production of this, that is produced;
> Conditioned by ignorance come conditioned activities.

The concept indicated by this statement—that by the existence of a previous cause, an effect comes forth—has been widely commented upon by Buddhist scholars, for its profound meaning indicates the highest teachings of Buddha and clearly shows his skillful means. Tsongkhapa praised Buddha from this viewpoint in order to honor him in the highest manner.

Such renowned members of the Saṅgha as Tsongkhapa and other great commentators did not create any new teachings but, rather, clarified the original word of Buddha as it is preserved in the *Tripiṭaka*—the sutras, the *vinaya*, and the *abhidharma*.[2] Through their great kindness they have shown us the way in which to apply the teachings contained in these Three Baskets.

The teachings contained in the *Tripiṭaka* are divided into three precepts for practice: the vinaya is the basis for the precept of exceptional moral practice, the abhidharma is the basis for the precept of exceptional meditation, and the *prajñāpāramitā* sutras are the basis for the precept of exceptional wisdom. These three precepts comprise the instruction aspect of the Dharma: all that one studies, memorizes, and practices. The corollary to the instruction aspect of the Dharma is the understanding aspect: the inner realizations attained as a result of the practice of the three precepts.

Once one has decided to follow the teaching, one should listen to, contemplate, and meditate on the precepts with great care. Through this one can develop the understanding leading to the realization of voidness, the ultimate door of liberation.

Having obtained the leisure and opportunity necessary to practice the Dharma, one should strive to use one's life purposefully rather than wasting it. If we devote ourselves to senseless worldly activities, we are like the man who spent his whole life rubbing a stone. When his friends asked him to go with them to gather precious gems and not waste his time rubbing the stone, he told them, "I am too busy. I have to rub my stone." After spending his whole life rubbing the stone, he finally found that it was useless and threw it away.

Therefore, do not just accumulate senseless bits of knowledge when studying the teaching, but try to increase your understanding. The story is told of a man who was listening to a lecture on the stages of the path. At the end of the lecture, a friend asked him what he had learned. He answered, "Something very important. I learned that Mrayicakra is another name of the old Lhundrup Dzong fort to the north of Lhasa."

❧

For the proper transmission of the teachings, three conditions must exist. Not only must the teacher and the teaching be pure, it is also necessary that the listener be a suitable vessel. Such a listener is honest, intelligent, and intent on the teaching. If one is inattentive, one is like a vessel turned upside down into which nothing can be poured. Therefore, one must listen closely. One must also attempt to retain what one hears, for otherwise one is like a vessel that has no bottom. Although something may be poured into it, nothing will remain, and one gains no understanding or benefit from listening. One should not listen to the teaching when filled with passion, hatred, or ignorance, or out of desire for name, fame, or wealth, because then one is like a vessel tainted with poison. When the pure nectar of the teaching is poured into it, the teaching will be contaminated and will not take effect.

All happiness in the world comes from virtuous activities, and all miseries from wrongdoing. From the teaching of Buddha one can learn to discern what activities are to be taken up and what activities are to be abandoned in order to achieve happiness and avoid suffering. Therefore, you should attend to the teachings without distraction and with awareness. Listen correctly and concentrate on the meaning, remembering it and making every effort to put it into practice. Buddha Śākyamuni himself said: "I have shown the method of liberation. Remember, to actually achieve it, you must rely upon yourself."

2

The Lineage of the Teaching

THIS CHAPTER CONTAINS histories of some of the great teachers in the lineage that has descended to us in an unbroken succession from Śākyamuni Buddha. These histories are not mere myths; they are incidents drawn from those teachers' lives and passed on as examples of the activities of those who were masters of Buddhist practice.

The import of these narratives lies in their actual relevance to us. The practices and realizations of the beings described are real and can be developed by individuals capable of applying themselves with similar effort.

Though the histories are often humorously expressed, their subject matter is as serious as religion itself. They serve as inspiration for self-development and as assurance that such attainment is possible.

Śākyamuni, the teacher without equal, first generated bodhi-mind. Then he accumulated merit and wisdom for three *kalpas*, and finally, while seated on the *vajra throne* at Bodhgayā, he became the perfect Buddha. After his enlightenment he turned the first *wheel of the Dharma*, that of the Four Noble Truths, for the five ascetics at Vārāṇasī. Then he turned the second wheel of the Dharma while teaching at Vultures' Peak. Finally, at Vaiśalī, he turned the third wheel of the Dharma. In his glory, he outshone all erroneous teachers, such as the six Indian pandits, and made known his precious teaching, the origin of happiness and blessings.[3] When Buddha passed into parinirvāṇa at the age of eighty, thousands of his followers, who had attained arhatship and thus had the power of voluntary death, chose to enter parinirvāṇa with him. Mahākāśyapa, Buddha's appointed successor, was forced to decree that those who had this power and wished to join the Buddha should refrain from dying so that the teachings of Buddha might remain in the world. At that time, many of those who had met Buddha, as well as many who had not had that good fortune, deeply regretted that they had not followed his teaching more diligently while he was alive. By the force of their regret, they were inspired to make a one-pointed effort and a vast number of them attained one of the *four stages of perfection*: stream-winning, once-returning, non-returning, and arhatship.[4]

The arhats had memorized the teachings as Buddha taught them, and many were able to recite the entire *Tripiṭaka* by heart. To provide for the future, Mahākāśyapa called a great convocation of all *bhikṣus* in order to write these teachings down. When they had gathered in a cave near Rājagṛha, Mahākāśyapa realized that there were only four hundred and ninety-nine arhats—one less than the necessary five hundred, the number that had been decided upon by a council of monks at the time of Buddha's parinirvāṇa. Ānanda—Buddha's cousin and disciple and for twenty years his closest attendant—was also there, but he had not yet attained arhatship. To help Ānanda attain arhatship quickly, Mahākāśyapa ordered him to bring water for the assembly, though Mahākāśyapa knew there was no good water in the area. When Ānanda returned with dirty water from a muddy pond, Mahākāśyapa scolded him severely: "Ānanda, you have too many faults to be allowed to stay among the arhats. You did not ask Buddha to remain in the world, you answered incorrectly when Buddha questioned you, you used to step on Buddha's robe, and you did not ask any questions about metaphysics. Now you bring dirty water into this assembly: you can no longer be allowed to stay with the arhats."

Ānanda sorrowfully left the assembly but went only a short distance away. There he meditated unceasingly for an entire day and night and attained arhatship, as Mahākāśyapa had intended. Ānanda returned to the gathering at once. The completed assembly of five hundred arhats proceeded to collect the discourses of Buddha, gathering them all into the *Tripiṭaka*: *sūtrapiṭaka*, *vinayapiṭaka*, and *abhidharma-piṭaka*. Mahākāśyapa supervised the collection of the abhidharma, Ānanda, that of the sutras, and Upāli, that of the vinaya.

After training Ānanda for some ten years to be his successor, Mahākāśyapa entered parinirvāṇa. At that time, Ajātaśatru was king of Magadha. He was the son of King Bimbisāra, one of Buddha's most loyal followers. During Buddha's lifetime, Ajātaśatru had followed Devadatta, who was envious of Buddha and of the support King Bimbisāra gave him. Devadatta had persuaded Ajātaśatru to seize the throne and imprison his father. After many years, however, Ajātaśatru realized how very kind his father had been to him, and he repented and sent men to release him. But when King Bimbisāra saw the men coming, he thought they had been sent to kill him, and he died before they could reach him. When Ajātaśatru heard of his father's death, he truly regretted his evil deeds and became a disciple and patron of Ānanda.

During Ānanda's years as successor, there was great happiness and peace in the land, and the people were devoted in their practice of religion. After Ānanda had led the Saṅgha for fifteen years, a young boy named Suvarṇavarṇa became his disciple and quickly attained arhatship. The people were impressed that such a young boy could attain arhatship without difficulty, and the fame of Ānanda spread far and wide.

Hearing of his fame, a brahmin named Bharadvājā, who was a great sorcerer, came from Kimmilimālā in south India to challenge the bhikṣus to a contest of magical powers. King Ajātaśatru, with all his ministers, and Ānanda, with all his arhats, assembled to witness the spectacle. With great pomp, Bharadvājā magically created four mountains: one of gold, one of silver, one of ruby, and one of blue *indranīla*. In the midst of the mountains were four pleasure gardens full of blossoming fruit trees and exotic birds. Each garden had a pond covered with lotuses of many colors. Regarding his work with pride, Bharadvājā challenged Ānanda to outdo him.

With his miraculous powers, Ānanda in his turn created a herd of fierce elephants who ate the lotuses and trampled the ponds. Then he raised a great wind that felled the fruit trees, and a terrible thunderstorm whose lightning bolts shattered the four precious mountains. Then Ānanda multiplied his body into five hundred emanations, of which some rained like giant thunderclouds, some rose in the sky, and some radiated fire. Then they all vanished at once, leaving Ānanda sitting quietly as usual. Bharadvājā was completely overcome, and he and his attendants became disciples of Ānanda. For seven days and nights Ānanda taught them the holy Dharma. They achieved understanding of the Four Noble Truths and attained various stages of realization.

Ānanda taught for forty years, ordaining tens of thousands of bhikṣus and leading thousands to arhatship; finally he perceived that it was time to die. In order to divide his relics equally between the people of Vaiśalī and the people of Magadha—for he knew the two would dispute over them—he created an island in the middle of the Ganges, the border between the two lands, and went there with five hundred bhikṣus. Five hundred *rishis* joined him on the island and asked to be admitted to the Saṅgha. Ānanda ordained them and, in one hour, magically established them in arhatship. Then, before the thousand assembled arhats, he passed into parinirvāṇa. His body spontaneously consumed itself in fire and the waves of the river divided his relics into two parts. One part was carried to the north bank of the river, where the Licchavis of Vaiśalī took them and built a great *stūpa* in which to enshrine them. The other part was carried to the south bank, where King Ajātaśatru of Magadha also built a stūpa to house the relics.

Śāṇavāsika was the third successor. He had been a wealthy householder and had maintained Ānanda and five thousand bhikṣus for five years, at which point Ānanda had told him to take the bhikṣu vow himself. As soon as he did so, Śāṇavāsika attained arhatship, and Ānanda then appointed him successor.

King Ajātaśatru died shortly after Ānanda. Because he had caused his father's death, he was born in hell for an instant of time, but he was then reborn in a godly realm as a disciple of Śāṇavāsika. He attained the state of stream-winner.

While Śāṇavāsika remained in Magadha teaching the doctrine, another arhat, Mahāmadhyāntikā, the foremost of those rishis who had obtained arhatship in the middle of the Ganges, went to Kashmir with five hundred bhikṣus. There he subdued the demons and *nāgas* and spread the practice of Buddhism. He obtained saffron from the nāgas and gave it to the people of Kashmir. From that time it grew abundantly there, its golden hue reflecting the light of the bhikṣus' robes.

The fourth successor was Ārya Upagupta. He traveled far and wide disseminating the teaching and in his travels happened to come to the city of Mathurā. After he had taught there for a time, many people were ordained as bhikṣus and obtained great realizations. The demon-king Māra became jealous and, with his followers, assumed the forms of heavenly dancers in order to distract people from attending to the teaching of the Dharma. Seeing this, Ārya Upagupta went to their show place and said to the dancers, "I am delighted to see you dance and sing. I would like to offer you these flowers." He then presented them with exquisite garlands of many-colored lotuses.

The dancers were delighted and placed the garlands around their necks. As soon as they did so, they turned back into demons. They were old and ugly, clothed in rags; the lotus garlands became the rotting corpses of dogs. All the spectators were filled with fear and disgust, and the stench was so foul that many could not help vomiting.

Then Ārya Upagupta approached the demons and addressed them gently: "This is the effect of your resentful minds. It is the retribution you receive for distracting my disciples, who were peacefully listening to the teaching."

The demons replied, "We regret our actions; please get us out of this predicament."

"I will help you," Ārya Upagupta said, "but first you must promise not to disturb my disciples any more."

"We promise, we promise," they said. "We will die before we ever harm them again."

Immediately, the demons became beautiful as before. "O reverend sir," they said, "you should not be so harsh. We were merely having a little fun, and you caused us great trouble. We also tried to harm Buddha when he was sitting under the bodhi tree, but he did not retaliate. He remained seated in the meditation of love and compassion."

Ārya Upagupta said to the demons, "I was never privileged to see the rūpakāya of Buddha; I have only seen his dharmakāya. Please, O magical actors, show me his physical form as you saw him under the bodhi tree." At once the demons created the form of Gautama Buddha. When Ārya Upagupta saw their creation, he wept tears of pleasure and bowed down before the image of the Buddha. Unable to bear his devotion, Māra and his demons disappeared.

After Ārya Upagupta, Ārya Dhītika was appointed successor. The sixth successor was Ārya Kṛṣṇa, and the seventh was Ārya Sudarśana.[5]

❧

During the centuries that followed, there were many schisms among the followers of Buddha's teachings. There arose variations in the understanding of the path to enlightenment, and Śākyamuni's teachings became clouded by the misinterpretations of false teachers, all of which disturbed the flow of his doctrine.

About four hundred years after Buddha, Ārya Nāgārjuna was born. The coming of Ārya Nāgārjuna fulfilled a prophecy made by Buddha in several sutras. This prophecy stated that in the time when the teaching had deteriorated, there would come one who would clarify the teaching and thus revive it. Though he would state the teachings in a new form, their intent would be the same.

Nāgārjuna was born in south India, in the country of Vidarbha. His brahmin parents were childless and had begged the rishis to give them a son. When he was born, the rishis gave him only seven days to live, but by worshipping and begging the rishis, his parents were able to extend his life to seven months and then to seven years. Hoping that Nāgārjuna could find a way to keep himself alive beyond that span, his parents sent him to study Buddhism at the great Buddhist university of Nālandā. There, after taking the vows of a novice, he received training in the way of extending his life.

Nāgārjuna lived for six hundred years, and his life is divided into three stages. For almost a century he was prefect of Nālandā, during which time he sustained and taught the many monks of that university. The second stage of Nāgārjuna's life began when he was nearly one hundred years old. He went to the land of the nāgas, where he taught the doctrine of Buddha. He received from the nāgas the *One Hundred Thousand Verse Prajñāpāramitā Sūtra* and returned with it to India. Nāgārjuna then composed many commentaries on this sutra, the highest of Buddha's philosophical teachings. In these writings he explained the sutra's meaning, and in so doing, developed the viewpoint that avoids all extremes—the viewpoint of the Madhyamaka system he founded.

When he reached the age of three hundred, Nāgārjuna visited the northern continent; this was the beginning of the third stage of his life. He stayed in that continent for two hundred years and then returned to south India, where he retreated into the mountains to meditate in seclusion.

Nāgārjuna's death is attributed to the son of his life-long friend, King Antīvāhana.[6] One day Antīvāhana's queen made a marvelous robe for her son, Prince Śāktiman. The prince said, "I will save it to wear when I am king."

His mother replied, "I am afraid you will never be king, for your father and Nāgārjuna are of 'one life.' They both will live the same length of time, and it is said that Nāgārjuna will never die."

Her son began to weep bitterly, asking, "Then what is the use of being a prince?"

Greatly distressed, and desiring only the happiness of her son, she told him, "Neither Nāgārjuna nor your father are subject to natural death. But Nāgārjuna is a bodhisattva. If you ask for his head, he will surely give it to you. Then, after Nāgārjuna dies, your father will soon follow, and you will become king."

The prince went to the cave where Nāgārjuna was meditating and made his request. Without a moment's hesitation, Nāgārjuna bared his neck to the prince's sword, but as Nāgārjuna could not be pierced by any weapon, his neck was not even scratched by the prince's blow. Nāgārjuna then said to the prince, "Get a blade of kuśa grass. When I was still a common person, I killed an insect in a clump of kuśa grass, and now, by the return of karma, I can be killed by a blade of this grass and in no other way." The prince got a blade of *kuśa* grass and began cutting off the bodhisattva's head. While Śāktiman was hacking away at his neck, Nāgārjuna's voice proclaimed, "I am going from a happy life to bliss, but I will use this same body again." The words filled the prince with fear. In order to keep Nāgārjuna's head and body from reuniting, he placed them far apart. Even today they are said to be moving toward each other. When they meet, Nāgārjuna will once more live in the world in order to help living beings.

❧

Nāgārjuna's spiritual heir was Āryadeva. Āryadeva was miraculously born from a lotus on the island of Sri Lanka and was adopted by the king of that country. Later, Āryadeva went to study with Nāgārjuna and was highly successful in all his studies.

At that time there was a great non-Buddhist teacher named Mātṛceta (Aśvaghoṣa) living in western India. He was a renowned physician and had saved thousands of lives during an epidemic. He was also called the Black Conqueror, because no man born from a human womb could defeat him in combat or in debate. In just seven days of meditation, he had received the full realization of Maheśvāra.

Empowered by Maheśvāra, he was able to shoot fire from his forehead and destroy anyone or anything he wished. When Mātṛceta debated, Maheśvāra would enter his body to help him, a pandit in the form of a parrot would whisper advice in his ear, Śīva would write invisible advice in the sky, and Sarasvatī would come to his aid with beautiful and wise phrases.

After he had debated and defeated all the pandits in western India, Mātṛceta traveled around looking for other scholars to challenge. Eventually, at the urging of his mother, a devout Buddhist, he arrived at Nālandā, a renowned Buddhist learning center. The monks of Nālandā recognized him and decided not to confront him as they knew that no one born from a human womb could defeat him. Mātṛceta's followers surrounded the university and completely blockaded it. They set up a drum and began to beat it, declaring themselves victorious. Sometimes they would enter the grounds and beat the monks on the head and mock them, asking, "Shavepates, where did your bald heads come from?"

One night an abbot of Nālandā had a dream in which Mahākāla, one of the fierce defenders of the Dharma, spoke to him: "These non-Buddhists drove a stake into my head and put dirt on my body. Clean and repair my image in the temple. Perform prayers to me and invite Nāgārjuna, who is meditating on Bell Mountain in the south, to come and challenge these non-Buddhists." As they were repairing the image of Mahākāla the next morning, a crow emerged from it and allowed the abbot to tie a message to its leg. It then flew to the cave where Nāgārjuna was staying.

Nāgārjuna wanted to go at once, but Āryadeva objected, saying that Nāgārjuna was too old. Āryadeva volunteered to go in Nāgārjuna's place, and Nāgārjuna agreed on the condition that he first allow Nāgārjuna to train him in the art of debate. To do so, Nāgārjuna took the non-Buddhist viewpoint in debate and had Āryadeva argue the Buddhist side. Then they switched positions, and Nāgārjuna argued the Buddhist position while Āryadeva took the non-Buddhist view on various subjects. In both cases, Āryadeva won, and so he received permission to depart. As he was leaving, Nāgārjuna advised him, "If you are to subdue Mātṛceta, do not be attached to your eye." The purpose of this advice was soon realized for, as he was traveling to Nālandā, Āryadeva met a god in the form of a blind beggar, who asked him for one of his eyes. Being a bodhisattva, Āryadeva willingly gave it.

When Āryadeva arrived at Nālandā, he disguised himself as a water carrier in order to pass by Mātṛceta's followers and enter the university. But once he was inside, his disguise aroused the monks' suspicions. "How old are you?" they asked. "Five hundred years," he replied. "Are you Nāgārjuna?" they asked. "No, I am his disciple Āryadeva." They were glad to hear that and welcomed him with music, incense, and prayers, for they knew Āryadeva was not born from a human womb and thus could perhaps defeat Mātṛceta. Āryadeva had them beat the drum to assemble the bhikṣus and then addressed them, saying: "We are beating our sandalwood drum, which is worshipped by gods, nāgas, and ḍākinīs; in this way we will demoralize those non-Buddhists."

He then approached some of Mātṛceta's followers, who were performing a religious ceremony with water, and asked them, "What are you doing with that water?"

One of them replied, "I am offering it to my dead grandparents." He then asked Āryadeva, "What are you going to do with that water you are carrying?"

Āryadeva replied, "I am going to water that completely dried up garden over there."

The man laughed and asked, "What is the use of watering dead plants?"

"Well," Āryadeva returned, "what is the use of giving water to dead people?" This made the non-Buddhists angry, but they continued their religious ablutions.

Āryadeva came before Mātṛceta's followers again, this time carrying a pot filled with excrement. He sat down and began to wash the outside of the pot.

"How can you clean that chamber pot by washing the outside?" one of them asked.

"How can you purify the dirty mind by washing the body?" Āryadeva returned, and the non-Buddhists were unable to answer.

It was not long before Mātṛceta arranged to meet Āryadeva in a formal debate. Nine scholars were chosen to be judges, and the king and his ministers attended, promising to cut out the tongue of the loser. It was also agreed that the loser would follow the religious doctrine of the victor.

To counter the divine aid that Mātṛceta usually received while debating, Āryadeva first placed a dirty boot near his opponent. He then released a cat, spread vanishing ointment in the sky to erase the skywriting, and finally, led a naked man to the debate area.

Mātṛceta spoke first. "One-eyed man, how dare you debate me?"

"Indradeva with his thousand eyes cannot see reality. Maheśvāra with his three eyes cannot see the nature of all existents. But Āryadeva with his one eye has seen it." At that the cat jumped up and killed Mātṛceta's parrot.

"I thought you Buddhists disliked harming living beings," said Mātṛceta accusingly.

"That is true," Āryadeva replied, "but such is the nature of cats."

Then Mātṛceta discovered that he could not read the skywriting, that the dirty boot had caused Maheśvāra to leave in disgust so that Mātṛceta could no longer shoot flame from his forehead, and that Sarasvatī had had to turn away from the naked man. In desperation, Mātṛceta tried to escape by flying up into space, but Āryadeva followed close behind. As they approached the limit of existence, beyond which everything disappears, Āryadeva warned Mātṛceta, "Do not pass beyond this point, for that which does never returns. If you do not believe me, toss your hair beyond it." Mātṛceta did not believe him but, just to be sure, shook his long hair beyond the point.

It all disappeared. He was impressed by his opponent's compassion and agreed to return to Nālandā with him.

Upon their return, all Mātṛceta's numerous followers accepted the teachings of Buddha, but Mātṛceta himself remained recalcitrant. Nonetheless, he was made to study Buddhist scriptures. One day, as he was studying, pages of mantras fluttered down to where he sat. The mantras were excellent and beautiful, and Mātṛceta was impressed by them but doubted that they were Buddhist. At this, a deity appeared and beat him senseless. When he came to, he looked more closely at the pages and discovered that they contained a prophecy of his own life, saying that he would become a great Buddhist teacher. He immediately realized his error and said, "I have been wrong. I will cut out my tongue according to the conditions of the debate, and if I am correct in following Buddha's teachings, it will grow back again." Indeed it did, and Mātṛceta quickly obtained realizations. In later years he composed many famous praises of the effectiveness of Buddha's teachings.

Though the Mahāyāna arose simultaneously with the Hīnayāna and is said to have spread widely in the lands of gods and nāgas, it disappeared from the earth forty years after Buddha's parinirvāṇa. Nāgārjuna founded the Madhyamaka system to restore the Mahāyāna teaching in this world.

Nāgārjuna and his disciples spread this system far and wide, but some later philosophers, both Buddhist and non-Buddhist, misinterpreted his terse and subtle writings. They began to feel that Nāgārjuna, though he claimed to avoid either extreme, had fallen into the extreme of nihilism in his explanations of reality and voidness. Bhāvaviveka, who had studied with Nāgārjuna toward the end of the great teacher's life, put forth another Madhyamaka system, the Svātantrika-Madhyamaka, which claimed to avoid the extreme of nihilism by accepting the self-nature of existence.

No one was able to refute him except Candrakīrti. A great bodhisattva who was said to have been a pandit for five hundred incarnations, Candrakīrti had studied with Nāgārjuna and was also under the protection of Mañjuśrī, the bodhisattva of wisdom. Candrakīrti wrote a clear, powerful refutation of Bhāvaviveka's assertion of self-nature. He then gave his own, correct interpretation of Nāgārjuna's philosophy and thus was able to establish the Prāsaṅgika-Madhyamaka system of the Mahāyāna.

One day, while circumambulating the main temple at Nālandā, Candrakīrti hit his head on a pillar. A scholar who was with him asked, "You are the believer in the self-naturelessness of both persons and phenomena. Why, then, does anything happen when your head hits this column?"

The bodhisattva replied, "Column? What column?" and put his hand through the column as though it were not there.

Another time there was an extremely heavy rainy season, and all the cows sought shelter deep in the jungle. The monks wanted milk and said to Candrakīrti, "If everything is really without an intrinsic nature of its own, why don't you get us some milk from that picture of a cow?" Candrakīrti milked the cow in the picture and presented the milk to the Saṅgha. In such ways he led many followers of the other Mahāyāna schools to the system of the Prāsaṅgika-Madhyamaka.

❧

Nine hundred years after the parinirvāṇa of Gautama Buddha, Ārya Asaṅga was born. In his youth he completed intensive studies in a monastery and in middle life withdrew to a cave to meditate. He determined not to give up his meditation until Maitreya, the bodhisattva of love and compassion and the buddha-to-come, manifested himself openly before him.

When, after three years, he had no results, Asaṅga became discouraged and left his cave. Nearby, he met a man who was making a needle from an iron spike by rubbing it with a piece of cotton. Seeing this, Asaṅga's patience returned, and he went back to his cave and meditated unceasingly for six more years. Still Maitreya did not manifest himself. Disheartened that he had meditated for nine years without even a sign of success, Asaṅga again left his cave. Outside he saw how a rock had been completely worn down by single drops of water and the beating wings of passing birds. Again his patience returned, and he resumed his meditation; this time for another three years. But finally, Asaṅga despaired completely of realizing his aim and set out on the journey to return to his monastery.

On the outskirts of Acinta he saw an old she-dog whose hindquarters were raw and crawling with maggots. He felt great pity for her and wanted to relieve her suffering, but he could not bear to harm the maggots. Instead, he cut a piece of flesh from his own thigh and placed it near the dog. He then put out his tongue and prepared to transfer the larvae one by one, but the sight of the wound was so disgusting that he had to close his eyes. Suddenly, there was a great ringing in his ears, and he opened his eyes. Standing before him, in a magnificent, radiant light, was Maitreya. Despite his joy, Ārya Asaṅga exclaimed without thinking, "Why did you never come to me during the twelve years I earnestly meditated?"

Maitreya answered, "I was with you all the time, but you could not see me, because you did not yet have great compassion. If you do not believe me, carry me through the town on your shoulders and try to show me to the people."

Then Ārya Asaṅga raised Maitreya on his shoulder and carried him through the town, hoping to let everyone see the wonderful buddha. But no one in the town saw Maitreya, and only one old woman saw a dog on his shoulder.

After this, Maitreya magically transported Ārya Asaṅga to Tuṣita heaven, where he stayed for fifty earth-years studying the Dharma. When he returned to India, he brought with him the five treatises of Maitreya,[7] the central teachings of the lineage of compassion, used in the Tibetan tradition as root texts for the study of abhidharma and the prajñāpāramitā.[8]

In a prophecy made in the *White Lotus Sutra,* Śākyamuni Buddha himself predicted the spread of his teaching to Tibet. Once, while the great teacher was staying in the Bamboo Grove with his disciples, a rainbow-colored ray of light emanated from his forehead toward the north, and he smiled. His disciples were surprised and begged him to explain. He said, "Fortunate youths, the snowy country of Tibet, long the abode of demons and devils, has never been subdued by any of the buddhas of the past, present, or future, but it will be subdued in the future by the bodhisattva Ārya Avalokiteśvara. He will lead its inhabitants to the path of enlightenment, and the holy Dharma will blaze there like a rising sun. Long ago Ārya Avalokiteśvara made this vow before the thousand buddhas:

> May I be able to establish in emancipation all living beings in the barbaric Land of Snow, where beings are so hard to discipline and none of the buddhas of the three times have stepped. May these beings be disciplined by me. May I be like father and mother to those who are now helpless. May I be their guide, leading them to freedom. May I burn the lamp to chase away the gloom of barbarism. In that country, may I extend, for as long as possible, the teachings of the tathāgatas of the three times. In hearing the name of the Three Jewels, may the many beings of the Land of Snow go for refuge and obtain rebirth as men or gods. May they have the opportunity to enjoy the holy Dharma. May I be able to mature and emancipate them, each according to his own way. May that gloomy, barbaric country become bright, like an island of precious jewels.

After his speech, another ray of light in the form of a white lotus emanated from Buddha's heart. It illuminated all the world and radiated to Amitābha in *Sukhāvatī* Pure Land, the western paradise—an ineffable land of light sustained by the power of the buddhas, in which there is no material creation. That ray of light then emanated from the heart of Amitābha and dissolved into the Lotus Lake. Thereupon, Amitābha prophesied that an incarnation of Buddha would subdue the beings in the barbaric Land of Snow.

At that time there lived in Sukhāvatī the dharmarāja Sangbochok. One day he sent a group of his attendants to Lotus Lake to gather offerings of flowers for Buddha. In the middle of the lake they saw a lotus from whose great stem extended a canopy of leaves; showing through the petals of the lotus was a cushion from which radiated rays of light. The attendants immediately ran to tell the king, who, amazed, filled his royal barge with offerings and went with his attendants to see this miraculous lotus. In front of the lotus he and his attendants made offerings and prayers.

The center of the lotus opened in four parts, revealing, miraculously born from the lotus, the incarnation who would subdue the barbaric Land of Snow. He was seated in the cross-legged position. His face was smiling and beautiful; his hair fell in five locks and was ornamented with precious jewels. He had four arms. Two of his hands were folded at his heart; his lower right hand held a white crystal rosary, and his lower left hand held the stem of a white lotus that blossomed at his ear. His body was the color of sunlight reflected on ranges of snowy mountains and was ornamented by the special signs and marks. He was adorned with jeweled ornaments and wore garments of beautiful silks. Across his left shoulder was draped the skin of a black antelope. From his body, rays of light emanated to the ten directions.

The king and his attendants welcomed him with many kinds of

music and invited him to the palace. The king then went to Amitābha and asked, "Who is this incarnation magically born from the center of a lotus, who has five flowing locks, who is ornamented with precious jewels, who is the color of snowy mountains, whose beautiful appearance captivates the mind, and who has the extraordinary signs and marks? Is he a prince of my lineage, or is he one who will help living beings?"

Amitābha replied, "This incarnation is a bodhisattva, the great compassionate Ārya Avalokiteśvara. He is not of your kingly lineage."

Then Amitābha, putting his hand on the head of Ārya Avalokiteśvara, spoke these words: "Noble son, those beings who abide in the barbaric Land of Snow have not been subdued by the buddhas of the three times. Because of the power of your previous supplication, you, excellent one, will subdue them. Wondrously well done! By merely seeing your ārya body and hearing the sound of the six syllables, may the beings in the Land of Snow be delivered from the three lower states of being and obtain rebirth as humans or gods.

"When all the demons and devils living in the Land of Snow see your body and hear the six syllables, may their harmful minds be calmed, and may they develop helpfulness, compassion, and the bodhi-mind.

"When all the carnivorous animals in that country, whose very voices are frightful, see your body and hear the six syllables, may their harmful thoughts be calmed, and may they live together peacefully.

"When beings in the Land of Snow who are hungry, thirsty, and miserable see your ārya body and hear the six syllables, may they receive a rain of ambrosia. Drinking this, may they be satisfied according to their wishes.

"When those who live in the Land of Snow who are unfortunate, blind, and sick, who have no protection and no refuge, see your ārya body and hear the six syllables, may they be completely freed from all sickness and disabilities.

"When all these beings see your ārya body and hear the six

syllables, may their lives be prolonged and free from illness.

"May you be the protector of those without protection, the refuge of those without refuge.

"As the beings in the Land of Snow depend on the six syllables, may all the teachings of the Buddha spread throughout the land, and may all delight in the holy Dharma. *Oṁ maṇi padme hūṃ.* In these six syllables are found the intent of all the buddhas and the root of the eighty-four thousand aggregates of Dharma."

❧

It came to be that there was a monkey king who was an emanation of Ārya Avalokiteśvara. This monkey king took the *upāsaka*, or layman's, vows and went to the mountains of the Land of Snow to meditate. In the Robo cave, he tirelessly meditated on the extensive compassion of bodhi-mind and the profound view of voidness. One day, a demoness of the mountain noticed the bodhisattva-monkey and immediately fell in love with him. She courted him, showing many signs of affection, while he sat undistracted in meditation. Finally, she appeared before him in the shape of a beautiful woman and begged him to marry her. He refused, telling her that he was an upāsaka and that for him to marry her would corrupt his vow. Bursting into tears, she told him that she would die if he did not marry her. She pleaded with him in this way for a week and finally threatened that her desire would compel her to marry a demon and conceive innumerable demon children who would devour all the living beings in the Land of Snow.

The bodhisattva-monkey did not know what to do. To marry her would break his vow, and not to marry her would bring great misery to the living beings of that country. In dire distress, he called for the assistance of Ārya Avalokiteśvara.

The wise bodhisattva and two manifestations of the goddess Tārā appeared and told him to marry the demoness. Ārya Avalokiteśvara performed the wedding ceremony, during which he made this prophecy: "In the future, the doctrine of Buddha will flourish in the Land of Snow. Spiritual teachers will come forth ceaselessly, and there will blossom many treasures of hidden teaching."

The demoness and the bodhisattva-monkey had six children, each born from one of saṃsāra's six realms. The child born from hell had a dark face and was very patient and uncomplaining; the child born from the realm of hungry ghosts was very greedy for food and drink; the child born from the animal world was stupid and brutish; the child born from the world of humans was intelligent and humble; the child born from the realm of the demigods was strong and prone to quarreling and jealousy; and the child born from the world of the gods was forbearing and virtuous.

At first the family ate wild fruit that grew in the forest, but as their numbers increased they exhausted the supply of fruit. All the children cried incessantly for food, and the bodhisattva-monkey fell into deep despair, knowing of no way to satisfy their hunger. Again, he prayed to Ārya Avalokiteśvara and in response to his devout plea, the earth was miraculously covered with an abundance of food crops. Eating these, the monkey-demon children gradually lost their fur. Eventually their tails fell off, and they stood erect like human beings.

These were the first Tibetans. Their temperament is said to stem from their ancestors, bodhisattva and demon. Thus, from their father they are hard-working, kind, and attracted to religious activity; from their mother they are quick-tempered, passionate, prone to jealousy, and fond of play and meat.

❧

Before his teacher Amitābha, Ārya Avalokiteśvara also vowed:

> May I have the opportunity to establish all living beings in happiness, beginning with those in the Land of Snow. Until I relieve all living beings, may I never, even for a moment, feel like giving up the purpose of others for my own peace

> and happiness. If I should ever think of my own happiness, may my head be cracked into ten pieces like the ardzaka plant, and may my body be split into a thousand pieces, like the petals of a lotus.

Having made this promise, Ārya Avalokiteśvara traveled throughout the six realms of saṃsāra, teaching all living beings the eighty-four thousand teachings of Dharma by means of the six-syllable mantra, *Oṁ maṇi padme hūṃ*. In each realm he freed beings from their particular miseries and taught the Dharma to those who wished to hear it.

Finally he went to Tibet, the Land of Snow. Gazing over the Tibetan nation from the peak of Red Mountain, he had a vision of countless beings burning alive in an ocean of fire. Witnessing the misery of these beings, he wept heartfelt tears. The goddesses Tārā and Bhṛkuti[9] miraculously appeared from his teardrops and encouraged the bodhisattva, promising to help him with the great task of teaching the Tibetans.

Avalokiteśvara went among the Tibetans and taught them the mantra *Oṁ maṇi padme hūṃ,* pronouncing the words of the Dharma with infinite compassion. Then he entered the meditation of the bodhi-mind, making long and intense effort to dispel the misery of beings and bring them to happiness. Exhausted by his efforts, he entered the meditation of restoration. For a second time, he gazed out over the land and saw that he had not helped even a hundredth of the beings of the Land of Snow to enter the bliss of liberation. He was seized by bitter sorrow, and for an instant the thought arose, "What is the use? I can do nothing for them. It is better for me to be happy and peaceful myself."

At that moment, his head cracked into ten pieces, and his body split into a thousand parts. In agony, he cried out to Amitābha Buddha, who appeared before him in the sky. Placing his hand on Avalokiteśvara's shattered head, he said:

All circumstances come from cooperative causes
Conditioned at the moment of intent.
Every fortune that arises to anyone
Results from his own former wish.
Your powerful expression of supplication
Was praised by all the buddhas.
In a moment of time,
The truth will certainly appear.

Then Amitābha blessed him and transfigured the ten pieces of his head into ten faces, one for each of the ten transcendences.[10] He also blessed the broken body, transfiguring the torn flesh into a thousand hands, each with its own wisdom-eye. Thus, the bodhisattva had a thousand eyes, and his vision became as that of the thousand buddhas of the golden eon. On the crown of the ten-faced head, Amitābha placed himself, and he radiated boundless, inconceivable light.[11]

Since that time, Ārya Avalokiteśvara has often manifested himself in Tibet. His various forms have included laymen and lamas. The first of the three great Tibetan dharmarājas, King Songtsen Gampo, who ruled in the seventh century, was considered an incarnation of Avalokiteśvara, and his two Buddhist queens, one a Nepali princess and the other a Chinese princess, were believed to be the two manifestations of Tārā born from Avalokiteśvara's tears. Historically, this king is credited with bringing Buddhism to Tibet, for he sent his counselor Thomi Sambhota to India to study the teaching and to learn the art of writing from the great Sanskrit scholars. Returning to Tibet, Thomi Sambhota developed the written form of Tibetan and began the great task of translating the sutras and commentaries from Sanskrit to Tibetan.

The second great dharmarāja, King Trisong Detsen, reigned in the eighth century. He was considered an incarnation of the bodhisattva Mañjuśrī. King Trisong Detsen invited the teacher Padmasambhava to come to Tibet and subdue the many local demons and deities, who were jealous of the spread of Buddhism. Padmasambhava's teachings flourished, and he had many followers, who later came to be known as the Nyingma sect. Also, during King Trisong Detsen's reign, the great Indian scholar Kamalaśīla was invited to Tibet to challenge the Chinese Ch'an teacher, Huashang Mahāyāna. After much debate, Huashang Mahāyāna was declared the loser and was asked to leave Tibet. Since that time the Buddhism of Tibet has been based primarily on Indian rather than Chinese sources.

The third great dharmarāja was King Ralpachen, who reigned in the ninth century. He was considered an incarnation of Vajrapāṇi. King Ralpachen organized large-scale, systematized translation of the Sanskrit texts, but this work was cut short by his assassination. This marked the end of the early spread of Dharma in Tibet, for his successor, the evil King Langdarma, was able in only five years almost completely to destroy the teaching there. King Langdarma was also assassinated, but it was many years before Buddhism became strong again in Tibet.

For almost a century there were few teachers with any real insight into the teaching and few reliable translations of the Buddhist texts. A deep schism developed between the followers of the sutras and followers of the tantras. Of the many who professed to follow the Dharma, some were merely scholars who went about arguing obscure theoretical points, and some were yogis who understood the practice of magic but not that of religion. There were few who continued to put into practice the pure aims and actions of Buddha.

In the early eleventh century, a great king of western Tibet, Yeshe Öd, and his son, Jangchub Öd, were able to bring Atiśa, then the most renowned teacher in India, to Tibet to restore the purity of the teaching. At this same time, Marpa, the great translator, made several journeys to India, where he studied with the famous siddha, Nāropa. Marpa brought from India many important yoga treatises as well as the lineage of Nāropa, which he passed on to his greatest disciple, the unsurpassed yogi Milarepa.

❧

Atīśa, or Dīpaṃkara Śrījñāna, was born in the late tenth century in eastern India. He was the second son of Kalyāna Śrī, a rich and powerful king. At a very young age Atīśa entered Nālandā university. He studied there for many years and, by the time he was thirty-one, had mastered the entire *Tripiṭaka*—sutra, vinaya, and abhidharma—as well as the teachings of the Mantrayāna. Atīśa then traveled to Suvarṇadvīpa—present-day Sumatra—to study with Ācārya Dharmakīrti (Lama Serlingpa), from whom he received the teaching of bodhi-mind. Because of the greatness of this teaching, Atīśa considered Ācārya Dharmakīrti the kindest of his many teachers.

While studying in Sumatra, Atīśa became skilled in the two great lineages: that of Maitreya, which is the lineage of compassion descended through Asaṅga; and the lineage of Mañjuśrī, which is the lineage of wisdom descended through Nāgārjuna. He then returned to India and, as he was the foremost teacher of his time, became head of the one hundred and eight temples of the university of Vikramaśīla.

Some years later, a delegation, the first of three, arrived at the university to invite Atīśa to Tibet. Atīśa refused the request of the first delegation. The second delegation, headed by King Yeshe Öd, was captured en route by a barbarian king who held Yeshe Öd for ransom. The Buddhist king's son, Prince Jangchub Öd, collected the necessary gold, but the king refused to be ransomed, saying that he was old and would soon die anyway and would rather that the money be used to bring Atīśa to Tibet. The good king was then executed by his captor. The third delegation reached Vikramaśīla and told Atīśa all of this. Atīśa felt great respect for the determination of the king and his subjects and agreed to go to Tibet.

Atīśa arrived in Tibet in A.D. 1042. He first stayed in the land of his benefactor, King Jangchub Öd, where, at the king's request, he wrote the famous *Lamp of the Bodhi-Path.*[12] In this treatise is the first formulation of the three levels of beings—lower, middle, and higher—in the three stages of renunciation, bodhi-mind, and the view of reality. This text contains the lineages of profound view and extensive deeds, descended through Nāgārjuna and Asaṅga, respectively. In it are brought together the teachings of the Hīnayāna, Mahāyāna, and Mantrayāna, in stages of practice leading to highest enlightenment. Tsongkhapa praised Atīśa's teaching in a work called *The Concise Meaning of the Stages of the Path,* saying:

> Through it one can realize that the teachings are without contradiction
> And understand all of the doctrines as precepts;
> One can easily find the intention of Buddha,
> And avoid the abyss of wrongdoing.
>
> Thus, this precept is relied on by many of good fortune,
> The wise of India and Tibet.
> What sensible mind would not be captivated
> By the path of stages of the three types of beings?

Atīśa later traveled to Lhasa and other parts of Tibet, strengthening and purifying the practice of Buddhism there. During this time he gathered many disciples, the foremost among them being the teacher Dromtönpa, the founder of the Kadampa sect, which carries the lineage of Atīśa's teaching.

⁂

Tsongkhapa (1357–1419) was born in Amdo, a province of eastern Tibet, in Tsongkha, "the region of onions." Thus he is known as the "man of the onion region." His religious name is Losang Drakpa.

When he was very young, he entered a monastery of the Kadampa sect. There, he was taught the lineage of compassion and quickly mastered the five treatises of Maitreya, the books Asaṅga brought back from Tuṣita heaven. Tsongkhapa then learned all of the vinaya and abhidharma.

When he began to study Madhyamaka, Tsongkhapa found that the available collection of texts was very confused, for many scholars had attempted to interpret them in their own way. Through his teacher, Lama Umapa, Mañjuśrī told him that the writings of Candrakīrti were in all ways reliable. From then on, Tsongkhapa studied the commentaries of Candrakīrti and soon attained highest realization. By this realization, he was able to converse directly with Mañjuśrī, who gave him many precepts as well as instructions to write *The Great Stages of the Path* (*Lam-rim Chenmo*) and *The Stages of Mantra* (*Ngag-rim Chenmo*).

Tsongkhapa founded Ganden monastery in Lhasa, where he established the Gelug order. It became one of the four main schools of Tibetan Buddhism, the other three being the Nyingma, the Kargyu, and the Sakya. Tsongkhapa's third successor, Gendun Drup, was recognized as an incarnation of Avalokiteśvara and became the First Dalai Lama.

The present Dalai Lama, His Holiness Tenzin Gyatso, fourteenth incarnation of that unbroken succession, currently lives and teaches in India. His Holiness continues the compassionate deeds of Avalokiteśvara, guiding the Tibetan people in exile, and extending the teachings of Buddha to many, both Eastern and Western.

3

Discourses from the Sutras

The following stories were translated from the Damamūrkhanāmasūtra, *in the Tibetan* Kangyur, *Volume 40, Peking edition as published by the Suzuki Research Foundation. The first, "The Miraculous Deeds of Śākyamuni Buddha," tells of Buddha's victory over the six Indian pandits. As great teachers of that time, these six pandits were resentful of Buddha's large following and attempted to discredit him by a show of magical powers. Buddha's purpose in accepting their challenge was not simply to overcome the six pandits and their teaching but, by performing great miracles and expounding the doctrine, to lead many beings toward enlightenment. Thus, he was motivated by compassion. The fifteen days of miraculous deeds took place during the first lunar phase of the new year at the beginning of spring, and they are still remembered in the Tibetan New Year celebrations. We have prefaced the story with a poem on the same subject written by the First Panchen Lama, Losang Chökyi Gyaltsen (1569–1662).*

"The Story of Prince Gendun" concerns one of the former lives of Śākyamuni Buddha. Known as Prince Gendun in that life, he underwent great hardships to obtain the wish-fulfilling jewel and thus benefit all living beings.

The last story, "The Story of the Nun Utpaladok," illustrates the karmic law of cause and effect and also shows the high position that women were able to attain within the Saṅgha.

This chapter illustrates the inconceivability of a buddha, who is able to accomplish extraordinary feats through his great compassion for living beings. These stories indicate the radical metamorphosis that takes place with the attainment of buddhahood—that buddhahood is not simply the mental realization of some inner buddha-nature that we already have but is a physical change of our whole being in all its relationships and interactions. They give us the first hint of a behavior actuated by bodhi-mind: what a buddha is and what he can do. We can realize the great distance between our present state of being and the state of a buddha. We become aware that the events of birth and death are but instants in a larger continuum, that what we are now is a product of what we have done, and that what we will be is produced by what we do now. In this immensity of time, we can see the difficulty of attaining buddhahood but also the possibility of effecting in ourselves the changes necessary in order to attain buddhahood.

A PRAYER BY THE FIRST PANCHEN LAMA, LOSANG CHÖKYI GYALTSEN

Namo Munīndrāya

I bow down to Prince Śākyamuni, the all-knowing one,
God of gods, who drew the great ones to follow him,
Subdued the four inner and outer demons,
And completely accumulated merit and wisdom.

I bow down to the protector who, dwelling in the Bamboo Grove,
At the request of many great kings
Subdued the six jealous pandits with miraculous deeds
And welcomed their disciples to follow his teaching.

I bow down to him who left the print of the auspicious wheel
On the fields of many countries,
Drawing countless humans and gods
To increase their virtue by his miracles.

I bow down to the one who, having purified by the fire of wisdom
And soothed by truthful words

The differences of the king and his brother,
Performed in Śrāvastī many miraculous actions.

I bow down to him who planted in the earth a toothpick,
Which, growing into a wish-fulfilling tree,
Satisfied all desires of humans and gods
When King Prasenajit made offerings on the first day of spring.

I bow down to him who, to the right and left of his throne,
Created great jewel mountains
Covered with excellent food and sweet grasses,
When worshipped by Udrāyaṇa on the second day.

I bow down to him who, on the third day,
Having been offered food by King Shun Tsin,
Rinsed his mouth and created a lake of eight wondrous attributes
On which bloomed lotuses of laughing, radiant light.

I bow down to him who, when offered midday food by Indravarma,
Manifested a pond from which eight streams
Rippled in a circular path, showing by their sound
The teachings of the three vehicles of the holy Dharma.

I bow down to him who, on the fifth day, when Brahmadatta made offerings,
Radiated from his smiling face a golden light that filled the three thousand worlds.
It purified those in the lower states
And filled all beings with the joy of samādhi.

I bow down to him who, when offered food by the Licchavi on the sixth day,
Generated faith and belief in those assembled

By enabling them to read one another's minds
And see the white and black thoughts of themselves and others.

I bow down to him who transformed
Each of those assembled in the field of virtue
Into a world sovereign having seven magical jewels
When the Śākyas made offerings at the end of the first week.

I bow down to him who performed limitless miraculous deeds:
From his lion throne issued five demons and Vajrapāṇi,
Vanquishing the six pandits and freeing their ninety thousand
followers,
On the eighth day when Indra paid respectful homage.

I bow down to him before whom offerings manifested themselves
On the ninth day: who extended his form until
It reached to the heaven of Brahma,
And showed all the virtues of saṃsāra and nirvāṇa.

I bow down to him from whose body shone a thousand rays of
light;
Reaching the height of saṃsāra, they formed a brilliant cloud
From which benefits and happiness rained on all beings
On the tenth day, when offered food by the four great kings.

I bow down to him who sat on the lion throne
Without manifesting his body
And taught the holy Dharma with the voice of Sarasvatī,
On the eleventh day, when Anāthapiṇḍika prepared a feast.

I bow down to him who, seated in the meditation of love,
Filled the three thousand worlds with golden light,

Causing all beings to love each other as parents their children,
On the twelfth day, when given offerings by the householder Tseta.

I bow down to him from whose navel two rays of light rose seven armspans high,
On the points of which were buddhas;
And from their navels came forth light and so on, filling all directions in the world,
When worshipped by King Shun Tsin on the thirteenth day.

I bow down to him who turned the clouds of flowers
Strewn by on the fourteenth day
Into twelve hundred and fifty jeweled carriages
That adorned the three worlds with their great beauty.

I bow down to him who, when Bimbisāra made offerings on the fifteenth day,
Satisfied all with the ambrosia of the gods
And sent forth purifying golden rays from his fingertips
That brought happiness to beings even in the lower hells.

I bow down to him who, conquering all darkness
By immeasurable, wonderful miracles,
Led countless living beings to the high state of human or god,
To emancipation and the path of perfect buddhahood.

I dedicate the merit I accumulate from having expressed
A mere atom of the miraculous deeds
From the jewel mountain of the Teacher's knowledge,
That I might obtain omniscience for the benefit of all.

The Tathāgata's body,
Attendants, life span, and sphere,

And his extraordinary marks—
Just these attributes may I and others obtain.

As the Teacher visited this world,
His teaching illumines like rays of the sun.
By brotherly accord between followers of the teaching,
May there be the good fortune that the teaching stays long.

THE MIRACULOUS DEEDS OF ŚĀKYAMUNI BUDDHA

At one time, Buddha was staying with hundreds of bhikṣus in the Bamboo Grove outside of Rājagṛha, the capital of Magadha. The ruler of that country, King Bimbisāra, was one of Buddha's greatest patrons. In loyalty and respect for Buddha and his bhikṣus he had led many of his subjects to the practice of the teaching. Six pandits were also staying in Magadha at the time, and their deceptive teachings were the cause of many sinful actions. King Bimbisāra's younger brother followed these six teachers and made great offerings to them, thinking that they taught the path to liberation. As a consequence he became defiled by error, so that even though Buddha's radiance was in the land, showing the glories of enlightenment, he did not see it. King Bimbisāra tried to persuade his brother to give up his erroneous ideas and to respect and listen to Buddha, but his brother replied, "I have my own teacher. Why should I listen to Buddha?"

Nevertheless, feeling that he should at least respect King Bimbisāra's feelings, the brother decided to give a feast, offering food and gifts to all who came. The six pandits came at once and sat in the highest seats. When Buddha and his disciples did not arrive, King Bimbisāra went to his brother and asked, "Why have you not invited Gautama?"

His brother replied, "I have done everything possible. I have even prepared the feast at noontime as Gautama does not eat after midday.

If he does not come, what more can I do?"

"Send someone to invite him," the king insisted, and finally a servant was sent to invite Buddha and his disciples.

They came at once and walked toward the few remaining seats, but before they could reach them the six pandits found themselves getting up from the highest seats and taking the lower. The six pandits tried three times to take the higher seats, but each time they found themselves in the lower. Finally, feeling shamed, they remained there. Before the food was served, water was brought to the guests so that they could wash their hands. As Buddha was in the highest seat, his host offered the water to him first, but he said, "Offer it first to your teachers." The water was then offered to the six pandits, but when the vessel was tipped nothing flowed into their hands. The host tried again and again, but still the water would not pour. He then offered it again to Buddha. The water flowed freely to Buddha, and after that to everyone.

Before they ate, the host asked Buddha to bless the food. He deferred again to the six pandits, saying, "Request the blessing from your own teachers." But when the six pandits tried to pray, they were unable to speak a word and gestured that Buddha should say the blessing. Buddha then prayed with a clear, beautiful voice, and the food was offered. It, too, was brought first to Buddha, but he said once more, "Offer it first to your teachers." The food was then offered to the pandits, but everything they tried to take flew up into the air. After food was taken by Buddha, everything came down into their hands.

After the meal, the host made the customary request for teaching. He asked Buddha to speak, but Buddha again deferred to the six pandits, saying, "Have your teachers speak of their doctrines." Again the six pandits, unable to speak a word, could only motion for Buddha to speak. He spoke out in a beautiful voice, and each listener heard what fitted his own needs. Everyone's understanding was greatly increased. Even King Bimbisāra's knowledge grew from high to higher. Many attained the first to the third stages of liberation; others expanded their bodhi-mind, and some attained the supreme bodhi-mind. A great number of people attained the stage of non-returning, and others, attaining the effects they prayed for, developed great faith in the doctrine of the Three Jewels. From that time on, the people of Rājagṛha followed the Buddha.

The six pandits went away angry at having lost their followers. They asked some of Māra's devils to help them curtail the Buddha's activities. Complying with their request, these devils manifested themselves in the bodies of the six pandits. They went to the market place and performed various miraculous deeds—shooting water, flames, and burning lights of many colors from their bodies. Many people marveled at these things and became their followers. To them the devils proclaimed, "Through the wickedness of Gautama we have fallen into misfortune. All the kings, brahmins, and great patrons who used to worship us and bring us offerings now no longer respect us. They used to give us all the necessities of food, dress, and medicine—everything we wanted. Now these same people are running after Gautama, giving him everything they used to give us. We therefore challenge Gautama, this great guru of everyone. For every one of his miracles we will do two; if he does sixteen, we will do thirty-two. People shall see for themselves who is more powerful."

Then the six pandits went to King Bimbisāra and asked him to deliver their challenge to Buddha. The king laughed at their arrogance. "You are foolish. Your miraculous deeds cannot begin to equal those of Buddha. Your challenge is like the light of a firefly compared with sunlight, like the water standing in an ox's hoofprint compared with the ocean. It is like the fox challenging the lion."

But the six pandits persisted and said, "You will see. What happened before is no indication of what will happen now. When we compete, it will be clear who is the greater."

King Bimbisāra visited Buddha and told him of the challenge. "These six pandits want to compare their miraculous deeds with those of the Tathāgata. I told them they were foolish, but they would not listen. Will you please show them your miraculous powers to reverse their wrong views and lead them to do virtuous work? When you do this, may I be there?"

Buddha replied, "The time will be known. Please prepare a suitable place."

So King Bimbisāra ordered his ministers to clean and prepare a broad field. There they put a lion throne and victory banners and the standard of the Conqueror Buddha. All the people eagerly awaited the sight of Buddha and the six pandits performing their miracles. However, to everyone's surprise, Buddha left Rājagṛha and went to the neighboring city of Vaiśalī.

All the people of Vaiśalī, the Licchavi, welcomed the Tathāgata. When the six pandits heard that Buddha had gone to Vaiśalī, they proudly proclaimed, "Gautama is afraid of us. He has run away to Vaiśalī," and they followed after him. King Bimbisāra with five hundred carriages, elephants, horses, provisions, and thousands of attendants and ministers also went to Vaiśalī.

The six pandits took their challenge to the king of the Licchavi, and he came to Buddha, saying, "Please show your miraculous powers and subdue these men."

Again Buddha answered, "All in good time," and told them to prepare a place.

But again he went to another country, Kauśambi, followed by a great multitude and the six pandits.

King Udrāyaṇa and the people of Kauśambi welcomed Buddha. Through King Udrāyaṇa, the six pandits again issued their challenge to Buddha, who again replied, "The time is known. Prepare a place." King Udrāyaṇa made great preparations, but Buddha went on to War, the land of King Shun Tsin. From War he went to Tigitsashiri, the country of King Indravarma and from Tigitsashiri to Vārāṇasī, which was ruled by King Brahmadatta. From there he went to Kapila, the country of his own people, the Śākyas, and finally he went to Śrāvastī, the land of King Prasenajit. He was followed there by the kings of the countries he had passed through, along with many thousands of their attendants, and by the six pandits with their ninety thousand followers.

The six pandits went to King Prasenajit, saying, "We have prepared our miraculous deeds. Much time has passed since we challenged Gautama, and he is still running away. It is time for us to compare our miraculous powers."

King Prasenajit replied, laughing, "You know nothing, yet you want to challenge the great king of Dharma. Such people as yourselves cannot be compared with him." But to quiet them, King Prasenajit visited Buddha and said, "Those six pandits are always wanting to challenge you. Please show your miraculous powers and subdue them."

Again Buddha replied, "The time is known. Prepare a suitable place."

King Prasenajit had his ministers clean and prepare a wide field, burning incense and placing there a lion throne and the standard and banners of the Conqueror.

On the first day of spring, Buddha went to this field that had been prepared for him and sat upon the lion throne before the great multitude that had assembled there.

After King Prasenajit had made great offerings to him, the Tathāgata took a toothpick in his hand and placed it in the ground. It grew at once into a marvelous tree. On its branches, which extended for miles, grew beautiful leaves, flowers, fruit, and jewels of every kind. The many-colored light emanating from the jewels was as brilliant as the light of the sun and moon combined. When the branches of the tree rustled in the wind, the sounds of the teaching were heard. Then Buddha himself spoke to the multitude assembled there. Many of the people listening progressed greatly—some attained arhatship and millions ripened the seeds for rebirth in the high states of humans or gods.

On the second day of spring King Udrāyaṇa made great offerings to Buddha. The Tathāgata then turned his head right and left, and on either side of the lion throne a jewel mountain emerged. Each of the mountains abounded in grass and flowers and fruit trees filled with beautiful birds, and on each mountain flowed a magical spring whose water had eight different tastes. One mountain was covered with lush grass to feed and satisfy animals, while the others was covered with special food to satisfy humans. Buddha then spoke the teachings according to each person's ability, and many freed their minds by listening. Some of those present generated the supreme bodhi-mind, and many established the inclination for rebirth as humans or gods.

On the third day of spring King Shun Tsin of War made offerings to the Tathāgata. After eating, Buddha rinsed his mouth with water. On the ground where the water fell, a great lake formed which extended for two hundred miles. The water had eight tastes, and the bottom of the lake was covered with seven kinds of jewels. Great quantities of lotus flowers of every color grew on its surface, and their fragrance filled the air; by the rays of light extending from them in all directions, the people could see everywhere. When they saw this, the people were very happy, and when Buddha spoke the teachings, some attained arhatship, some increased their bodhi-mind, and many others attained the seeds of rebirth in the worlds of humans or gods.

The next day King Indravarma prepared the offerings for Buddha. Buddha created a pool from which eight streams flowed outward in circular paths, and to which they returned. In the sound of the streams people heard the teachings of the five powers, the five strengths, the seven aspects of bodhi-mind, the eightfold path, the three principles of the path to liberation, the six kinds of omniscience, the six transcendences, the teachings of love and compassion, and the four immeasurables. From this statement of the Dharma, many attained understanding of the effects of reaching buddhahood and many attained the inclination to rebirth in the high states of humans or gods. Hundreds of thousands increased their virtuous work.

On the fifth day King Brahmadatta of Vārāṇasī prepared various offerings for Buddha. From the smiling face of the Tathāgata shone a golden light that filled the entire world. This light reached all living beings and purified the defilements of the three poisons: desire, hatred, and ignorance. All beings became peaceful in body and mind, and those assembled rejoiced greatly. When Buddha spoke, many increased their bodhi-mind, many planted seeds of rebirth as humans or gods, and a countless number increased their virtuous work.

On the sixth day the Licchavi people made offerings to Buddha. Buddha then let all who were there see into each other's minds, and each understood the others' good and bad thoughts. All experienced great faith and praised the knowledge of Buddha. When the Tathāgata then taught the holy Dharma, many people attained great understanding—some attained bodhi-mind, some arhatship, and an immeasurable number attained rebirth as humans and gods.

The next day Buddha's own clan, the Śākyas, made offerings to him. He blessed all the listeners, so that they became great *cakravartins*, each possessing seven magic jewels. Each ruled his own small country and had many respectful ministers. All were very happy with this, and when Buddha spoke, they had great faith. Having increased their bodhi-mind, many attained arhatship and others sowed seeds of rebirth as humans or gods.

On the eighth day of spring Indra invited Buddha and prepared a great lion throne. When the Tathāgata was seated upon it, Indra himself made offerings on Buddha's left while Brahma made offerings on his right. They both bowed down before him, while the people sat quietly. Buddha placed his right hand on the lion throne in the earth-touching mudrā, and there was a great sound of trumpeting elephants. Five fierce demons came roaring forth and the thrones of the six pandits were destroyed. After the demons came Vajrapāṇi, with flames shooting from the point of his vajra. The six pandits were terrified and jumped into the water and disappeared. Their teachers having deserted them, the ninety thousand attendants took refuge in Buddha and asked to become bhikṣus. Buddha welcomed them at once, and the matted locks and beards that had marked them as disciples of the six pandits miraculously disappeared. Buddha taught all of them according to their ability to understand. Freeing themselves from the fetters of desire, hatred, and ignorance, each attained arhatship.

Then the Tathāgata radiated eighty-four thousand rays of light from the pores of his body, so that the light filled the entire sky. On the point of each ray was a beautiful lotus, and on top of each lotus appeared a buddha along with his attendants. Each buddha was teaching the Tathāgata's doctrines. All the people felt joy at this sight, and their faith was greatly increased. Then Buddha spoke the holy Dharma and many increased their bodhi-mind, some attaining arhatship, and a countless number producing the inclination to rebirth as humans or gods.

On the ninth day Brahmarāja made offerings to Buddha. The Tathāgata extended his body until it reached to the highest heaven of Brahma. From this body rays of light shone in all directions, and from this great height he spoke the teaching.

On the tenth day the four great kings, protectors of the Dharma, invited Buddha to speak. Again he extended his body until it reached to the height of saṃsāra. Rays of light streamed from him, showing the teaching.

The next day the great patron Anāthapiṇḍika made offerings to Buddha, who was seated upon the lion throne in meditation. Though the assembly could not see his form, his body radiated golden light, while in a great voice he expounded the teaching.

On the twelfth day the householder Tseta invited Buddha to speak. The Tathāgata entered into the meditation of great love, and golden light radiated from his body, extending throughout the worlds. These rays of light cleared the three poisons from the minds of everyone they passed through. All living beings increased their compassion. They loved each other as a father and mother love their children, as a brother loves his sister.

The next day King Shun Tsin made offerings to Buddha. The Tathāgata sat on the lion throne, and two rays of light, rising fifty feet, radiated from his navel. On the point of each ray of light was a lotus, and on each lotus, a buddha. From the navel of each buddha extended two rays of light upon each of which was a lotus with a buddha, and so on, filling the worlds. All the buddhas were expounding the teachings.

On the fourteenth day King Udrāyaṇa made offerings to Buddha. He strewed flowers in front of Buddha, and they changed into twelve hundred and fifty carriages made of precious jewels. Buddha taught the Dharma to beings throughout the worlds as a doctor heals the sick.

On the fifteenth and final day of the spring celebration, King Bimbisāra brought gifts to Buddha. Buddha then told King Bimbisāra to bring vessels for food. The vessels, which the king himself brought forth, were miraculously filled with foods of a hundred different tastes. When the assemblage ate this food, their bodies and minds were completely satisfied. Buddha asked them, "Why is there such immeasurable misery in the world?" By his blessing, even the eighteen kinds of demons realized that their misery was caused by deeds they had done themselves. They felt great faith in Buddha. As on all the previous days, those assembled attained great advancement: some increased their bodhi-mind, some attained arhatship, some attained the stage of non-returning, many attained the seeds of rebirth as humans or gods, and countless others increased their virtue.

Then King Bimbisāra, bowing down with great respect before Buddha, asked him, "You have thirty-two extraordinary marks upon your body. Among them is the mark of a wheel on the soles of your feet. Please show us these wheels."

When Buddha showed them the wheel on the sole of one of his feet, those assembled asked him in great wonder, "What did you do in previous lives to be born with such an auspicious sign?"

"I have these signs because in former lives I practiced the ten virtuous actions and exhorted others to do the same."

"Please tell us of those deeds," Bimbisāra asked.

Buddha said, "Listen carefully and I will tell you. Many eons ago there was a great king in Jambudvīpa named Shingtanimi. He ruled over eighty-four thousand small countries and one hundred thousand cities. He had ten thousand ministers and twenty thousand queens, but he had no son. He was quite unhappy, as there was no one to continue his lineage, and he prayed to many gods to help him. Finally his favorite, Queen Sulipala, a very clever, honest, and virtuous woman, conceived a child. When her child was born, he was beautifully formed, and light radiated from his body. The king showed this wonderful child to the great seers, who, after examining the signs, predicted that he would be a great world sovereign, ruling over the four continents, and that he would be very honest and would influence his people to do virtuous deeds. They named him Prajñāprabha, and he grew up to be a prince of unequaled intelligence.

"When the great king died, all the ministers asked the prince to become king. At first he refused, but the ministers pleaded with him to reconsider. The prince said to them, 'These days people commit only sinful deeds. Killing and destroying each other, they do not respect virtue. Only if all the countries follow the ten virtuous actions will I become king.'

"The ministers agreed, saying, 'We want you to be king, so we ourselves will follow your advice and practice the ten virtuous actions. You, however, must instruct the people in how to live according to these virtues.' So Prince Prajñāprabha became king, and peace and harmony prevailed throughout the land.

"Māra, king of the demons, became jealous of King Prajñāprabha and wished to destroy his kingdom. He forged a proclamation in the king's name: 'Formerly I ordered you to live according to the ten virtuous actions. This was not correct, as they have only made me miserable and will not be helpful to you. From this time on all should follow the ten non-virtuous actions.' The people of all the kingdoms to which this letter was sent were very surprised and did not understand why their king should exhort them to do sinful deeds. They went to him, asking, 'Why did you send us this strange proclamation?"

"King Prajñāprabha went out into his country to see what had caused the confusion. While traveling, he came upon Māra, who had manifested himself in the middle of a huge bonfire and was crying out miserably. King Prajñāprabha asked him. 'Who are you? Why are you burning in such a hell?'

"Māra answered, 'In the past I told people to practice the ten virtuous actions, and therefore, I am now experiencing great misery.'

"The king said, 'You say your misery is the effect of telling people to do good? That is ridiculous. Do you also say that by telling people to perform non-virtuous acts, you get happiness?'

"Māra answered, 'Yes indeed. By telling people to do non-virtuous acts you obtain happiness, but by telling people to do virtuous acts you obtain only misery.'

"On hearing these words, the king was delighted, and said, 'I do not grieve at your present misery if it is the result of virtuous deeds, for only good comes from doing virtue.'

"When he heard the king's words, Māra disappeared. The king continued on his journey, visiting his people and exhorting them to practice the ten virtuous actions. All praised his knowledge, and there was happiness and peace throughout the land. As world sovereign, King Prajñāprabha traveled to the four continents and led all the people to virtue."

Buddha continued: "My father in this life was the great King Shingtanimi. My mother Māyādevī was the Queen Sulipala. I myself was King Prajñāprabha who practiced the ten virtues and exhorted so many others to do so. Thus, I have a wheel on the sole of each foot."

Again, King Bimbisāra asked the Tathāgata, "Why did those six pandits challenge you to a contest they could not win? And when they could not do anything to compare with your miraculous deeds, why did they run away and drown themselves? Please explain this."

Buddha answered, "Not only in this lifetime, but also in previous lifetimes these six have challenged me in order to obtain great name and wealth."

Then King Bimbisāra, bowing down with great respect, asked him, "How did these six challenge you in previous lifetimes?"

Buddha replied, "At one time there was a great king, Mahāshakuli. Although the king ruled over many small kingdoms, had many subjects, and was very rich, he was unhappy because he had no children to carry on his lineage. Indra, manifesting himself as a doctor, came to the king and said, 'Do not worry. I will help you.' The doctor went to the Himalayas and gathered many herbs, which he brought back and made into a medicine. He gave the potion to the king's favorite queen and told her it would help her conceive.

"The queen, however, did not believe that the medicine would work and so gave it to the four hundred and ninety-nine lesser queens. They drank it, and all of them became pregnant. Realizing her mistake, she had the bottle of medicine, which was now empty, brought to her, and, rinsing it with water, drank the washings. All the other queens had very beautiful sons, and the king was tremendously pleased. But when the son of Queen Tshenama was born, though his mind and body were sound, his face was so ugly that his parents named him Dongdum—'Burned Tree Trunk.' When the princes came of age, wives were found for all of them except Dongdum.

"It came to pass that another kingdom besieged the land of King Mahāshakuli, and the four hundred and ninety-nine princes went forth to defend their country. However, they were totally overcome and forced to retreat to the palace. Prince Dongdum came out of the palace and asked them, 'What has happened? Why are you running away?' to which they replied, 'We cannot stop our enemies.'

"Prince Dongdum remembered the bow and war horn that had been passed down in his family from his ancestors, the world sovereigns. These weapons had long lain unused in the palace, for no one had the strength to draw the bow or blow the horn. Armed with them, he went out alone to fight the enemy. When he drew the bow, it made a sound like a roaring dragon that could be heard for forty miles. When he blew the war horn, it made a sound like a thunderbolt crashing to earth. His opponents were so terrified that they turned and ran. Prince Dongdum returned to the palace victorious.

"Now, because of Prince Dongdum's newly acquired fame as a warrior, the king was able to arrange for him to marry the beautiful princess Rushibaza, daughter of King Lushipatsi. The marriage was performed at night so that she could not see his face, and it was arranged that she should never see him in the light of day. One day, however, when she was talking with the other four hundred and ninety-nine princesses, she praised her husband greatly, saying that he was very beautiful and unusually clever. The other princesses laughed at her and said, 'Your husband is so ugly that he looks like a burned tree trunk. If you were to see him in the daylight you would be surprised and afraid.' That night, while Prince Dongdum was asleep, the princess lit a candle and looked at him. Seeing his ugliness, she was very frightened and ran back to her own country.

"Prince Dongdum was very unhappy when he discovered she had gone, and taking his bow and war horn, he went to bring her back. When he got to the palace of King Lushipatsi, he found that the princes of six small surrounding countries were already competing for the princess. King Lushipatsi was afraid that if he gave the princess to one of these princes, the other five would destroy his country. Finally, one of his ministers suggested that the six princes should fight each other and the winner would get the princess. When Prince Dongdum heard this proclamation, he went to the camp of the princes and, with his bow and war horn, he conquered them. The six princes and all their attendant soldiers surrendered to him. King Lushipatsi was very pleased and returned the princess to Prince Dongdum.

"Taking the princess, he returned to his country with the ninety thousand soldiers of the other six princes. When they had reached the palace, he asked the princess why she had run away. She replied, 'When I saw that you were so ugly, I was afraid.' Prince Dongdum had never known that he was ugly; on hearing her words, he found a polished stone and was horrified to discover how ugly he was. He ran off into the jungle, determined to die there.

"Indra, the powerful king of the gods of the desire realm, appeared before him and asked why he had decided to die. Prince Dongdum said to him, 'My face is so ugly I cannot bear it myself. How can I impose it upon my beautiful wife?' On hearing this, Indra gave the prince a magic jewel. When he wore it, his face became as beautiful as Indra's.

"The prince returned to the palace. As he was putting up his bow and war horn, his wife saw him and, not recognizing him, said, 'Please don't touch these things. When my husband returns, there will be great trouble.' 'I am your husband,' Prince Dongdum said. She did not believe him, so he took off the magic jewel for a moment and was as ugly as before. He never took it off again, and he became known as Sulashen—Most Beautiful of All.

"He decided to build a great palace for his princess. The king of the nāgas came to him and opened wellsprings of jewels, gold, silver, and crystal. From each one of the wellsprings Prince Dongdum built one wall of the palace: the east wall of the blue vaiḍūrya jewel (lapis lazuli), the south wall of yellow gold, the west of white silver, and the north of crystal. His fame and fortune were such that he became world sovereign of the four continents."

Buddha continued, "In a past life, my father King Śuddodhana was the great King Mahāshakuli. My mother Māyādevī was his queen. My stepmother Prajāpatī was the princess Rushibaza. Kāśyapa was the father of the princess, King Lushipatsi. I myself was the ugly prince. The six pandits were the six princes. In that life they fought against me to get the princess, and in this life they have challenged me to a contest of miraculous deeds. From then until now they have wanted only fame and profit, and they would still rather die than correct themselves and bear their shame."

King Bimbisāra asked the Tathāgata, "What had Prince Dongdum done in the past to be so powerful and yet so ugly?"

Buddha replied, "This is the cause and effect of karma. Innumerable eons ago there lived near Vārāṇasī a rishi who was a *pratyekabuddha.* He was highly developed in meditation, but he had a certain nervous disorder caused by his environment, and the only thing that would soothe it was clarified butter. He went into Vārāṇasī and stopped at the house of a butter-maker to ask for some ghee. The man said to him angrily, 'You have a head and face like the trunk of a tree and hands and feet like its bark. People like you have nothing to give and live only by begging. Of what use are you?' Yet he gave him a little butter.

"As the rishi was going out the door, he met the owner's young wife. She had immediate faith in him, and asked, 'From where do you come, and what will you do with this small bit of butter?' When he told her, the young wife asked him to come back in and completely filled his begging bowl with clarified butter. She said to her husband, 'You offered this holy man such a small portion and spoke such harsh words to him. Please ask his forgiveness.' Hearing this, her husband was immediately very sad and told the pratyekabuddha to come any time and take as much ghee as he needed.

"From then on the pratyekabuddha came often to get ghee to cure his sickness. To return their kindness, he showed them the miracles of flying in the sky and shooting water and fire from his body. Seeing these miracles, the faith of the butter-maker and his wife was greatly increased. The butter-maker said to his wife, 'Let us dedicate together whatever virtuous work we have done, so that in the future we may always be born as husband and wife.'

"His wife replied, 'Alas, even though we pray together and dedicate our merit, because you spoke so harshly to this holy man, your face will be ugly as a burned tree trunk, and when we are married, I will run away from you during the night.'

"Her husband answered, 'I will follow you and get you back.'

"Then the husband and wife offered all their deeds of body, speech, and mind to the pratyekabuddha and confessed all their wrong deeds. The pratyekabuddha said to them, 'You have been very helpful to me. Tell me what you desire and I will help you to obtain it.'

"The husband and wife knelt down together and requested, 'May we have the opportunity to be husband and wife in the future and to have good fortune.'

"The butter-maker became Prince Dongdum. His wife became the Princess Rushibaza. Because he had spoken such harsh words to the pratyekabuddha, he was born with an ugly face, but because he repented and confessed, his appearance changed. By offering butter freely to the rishi, he became very strong and able, a world sovereign who extended his power over the four continents and enjoyed, according to his wish, the five kinds of desire objects. The effect of any action, virtuous or sinful, is never destroyed. Therefore, always act properly in body, speech, and mind."

Hearing this speech of the Tathāgata, King Bimbisāra and all the other kings, ministers, attendants, gods, and nāgas were very pleased. Their bodhi-mind increased and they attained the states of stream-winner, once-returner, non-returner, and arhat.

THE STORY OF PRINCE GENDUN

One day when Buddha was staying with his disciples on Vultures' Peak, Ānanda asked him, "Although Devadatta has attempted to harm you in many ways, you treat him as you treat your son Rāhula. Why do you show him such loving-kindness?"

Buddha replied, "Devadatta's harmfulness extends far beyond this life." And the Buddha told the following story:

> Once there was in Jambudvīpa a great king, Rinpoche Gocha. Though he ruled over five hundred small kingdoms, he was unhappy, for none of his five hundred queens had borne a child, and he feared that if he died without a successor, there would be war

among the kingdoms. For many years he prayed to the worldly gods for a son, but without success. One day, however, one of the gods noticed him musing on his misfortune and took pity on him.

He appeared before King Rinpoche Gocha and said, "Outside the city gates are two rishis. If you pray to the one with the golden face named Kanakavarṇa, a son will be born to you." The king at once sought out the two rishis and prayed to Kanakavarṇa for an heir. The rishi agreed to help him, promising to be reborn as a child of the royal family.

When the rishi died, he fulfilled his promise by entering the womb of the foremost queen. When the king and queen realized she had conceived, they performed many ceremonies for a safe birth, and after nine months a boy was born, golden in color and with many special marks upon his body. At the great banquet that was held to celebrate the birth, the special seer of the kingdom marveled at the child's markings and named him Gendun *(dge 'dun)*—He of Virtuous Purpose.

Soon after this another queen became pregnant, for the second rishi had also died and entered her womb. When the second son was born, the special seer was again summoned, and to this child he gave the name Dikdun *(sdig 'dun)*—He of Sinful Purpose.

The king built four palaces for his two cherished sons, one for each season. He educated his sons with great care, and Prince Gendun became a great scholar in all eighteen branches of learning.

For this reason, when Prince Gendun came of age, King Rinpoche Gocha made him heir to his kingdom. The prince then requested permission to see the kingdom he would rule, and so his parents made preparation for a great journey. Banners and ornaments were cleaned and polished; incense and flowers were strewn everywhere. Elephants decorated with seven kinds of jewels led the great procession of the prince and his one hundred thousand attendants forth from the city amidst the music of drums and bells. Amazed at Prince Gendun's beauty, the people proclaimed him as glorious as Brahma.

The procession soon came upon a group of beggars dressed in rags and clutching broken bowls. When they came to him asking for food, Prince Gendun asked them, "How did you come to be in such a wretched condition?"

One old beggar replied, "I became like this because I have no parents, no family, and no relatives."

Another answered, "I became like this from months and years of sickness."

Still another replied, "I have no other way to sustain my life, as the property of my family was stolen."

On hearing their words, Prince Gendun became very sad.

Farther on, his procession came upon a group of butchers slaughtering animals. The beasts were wailing and bellowing as miserably as if they were in hell. The prince asked the butchers, "What are you doing? How can such misery exist in this country?"

They replied, "Slaughtering animals is our inherited trade. We have no other way to sustain our lives." Prince Gendun wept to see them in this condition.

A little farther on he saw villagers plowing their land, driving their oxen by beating them. The plowshares were turning up many insects, which the birds were busily eating. Prince Gendun, amazed at the sight of animals devouring other animals, asked the villagers what they were doing. "This is our inheritance," they answered, "planting seeds to grow food in order to maintain our lives and offer tribute to the kingdom."

Along the way Prince Gendun also saw hunters setting nets and snares, capturing birds and animals, who made pitiful sounds when caught. Feeling great compassion, he asked the hunters what they were doing. They told him, "By hunting we maintain our lives."

Sorrowfully traveling on, he saw fishermen catching fish, which were flopping pitifully on the ground all around them. When questioned they replied, "We sustain our lives by catching fish."

When Prince Gendun returned home from his journey, he contemplated all that he had seen. "Because they are poor, people must do sinful work to procure food and clothing. Sustaining their lives in such a way, they will easily fall to lower states of being, and going from darkness to still greater darkness, they will have no opportunity to free themselves from misery." Thinking this, he was constantly unhappy, until finally he approached his father to make a request. His father said that he would grant him anything he wished, and so Prince Gendun said, "I feel sad to see the bad karma people accumulate by the things they must do to maintain their lives. May I give gifts to the poor from the wealth of the kingdom?"

His father was startled by his request, but said, "I cannot refuse you, as you are my own dear son. Give as much as you please."

Prince Gendun issued a proclamation that all who came to him would be given what they wished. People came from thousands of miles around, gathering like an assemblage of clouds, to receive the prince's gifts. He gave to each whatever he requested. Some asked for clothes, some for food, some for jewels, some for gold, some for horses, and some even asked for pleasure gardens; each received whatever he desired. After this had been going on for some time, and the treasury of the kingdom was one-third gone, the treasurer went to the king to ask what should be done. The king told him that he would not reverse his promise, but that the treasurer could himself speak to Prince Gendun if he wished. When the treasury was two-thirds gone, the treasurer finally went to the prince and told him the treasury would soon be emptied. Filled with remorse, Prince Gendun said, "I should honor my father. It is wrong to give away all that he has," and he ordered the doors of the treasury closed.

Realizing that the desires of the common person are endless, the prince consulted many sages, asking, "Is there any way that I can give gifts endlessly?" One sage told him to start a good business.

Another told him to cultivate land, another to raise animals. Still another said he should travel across the ocean and find the wish-fulfilling jewel. Having heard all the advice, Prince Gendun realized, "Business, farming, or raising animals will not bring me enough to give gifts endlessly. I have no choice but to go in search of the wish-fulfilling jewel."

Accordingly, the prince went to the king and queen for permission to seek the wish-fulfilling jewel. Fearful, they replied, "Empty the treasury completely if you will, but please do not go on such a dangerous journey. You could be killed by crocodiles, or poisonous dragons, or great rakṣas. Any number of terrible things could happen to you. It is better for us to become poor than for you to lose your life. Please stay at home with us."

Prince Gendun would not make the journey without his parent's blessing, so he said to them, "My dear father and mother, I will lie here before you and not get up until you give me your blessings to go in search of the wish-fulfilling jewel."

They begged him for many days to change his mind, but finally they saw that they would have to give in to him, and so they said, "Since we cannot prevent you from going, we will give you good advice and many attendants and pray to the gods and nāgas for your safe return. Get up now. Though you will undergo great difficulties, we are sure that you will be able to withstand them and that you will return to see your old parents again."

Prince Gendun was very happy and thanked his parents. They prepared a great fleet and arranged for many people to accompany him: five hundred traders and numerous experienced captains. At that time there lived in the city an old captain who was famed for his knowledge of the ocean. Prince Gendun went to him and asked for his help, but the captain replied that he was blind and too old to travel. Finally, the king went to the captain and asked him to accompany his son. The old man then replied, "I am very old and blind, but as my lord himself requests this of me, I cannot refuse."

When preparations for the journey were nearly completed, the king announced to his court, "My son needs an able companion. Is there anyone here who will go with him?"

At once, Dikdun, the prince's younger brother, said, "I would like to go with my brother. Let me go."

Feeling that a brother would be a better friend than anyone else, the king agreed, and the two brothers started out together. The king and queen accompanied them as far as their ship, which, according to custom, was moored with seven ropes. Each day, with the offering of prayers for a safe return, one rope was cut. In his farewell speech to the travelers, the king advised them, "Even though you might feel that the quest is impossible, do not be attached to your friends or relatives or value your own life. Earnestly seek the wish-fulfilling jewel." When at last they cut the seventh rope, the ship flew before the wind like an arrow shot from a bow.

After many months at sea, they finally reached the continent of the wish-fulfilling jewel. Leaving the others to wait for them, Prince Gendun and the blind old sea captain went on alone up a river, with the prince rowing their small boat.

When they had traveled a short distance, the captain asked, "Can you see a white mountain from here?"

"Yes," the prince replied.

"That is the mountain of silver," the captain said. "We must go on."

After they had traveled for several more hours, he asked, "Can you see a blue mountain?"

"Yes," replied the prince.

"That is the jewel mountain. Still we must go on."

The prince continued to row until the captain asked, "Have we come to the golden mountain?"

When the prince answered, "Yes," the captain told him to stop.

After they had landed, the blind old captain said, "I am too old to go on; you must go alone. On the other side of the mountain you will see a palace made of seven kinds of jewels. Its door will be closed and locked, but in front of it on a jeweled stand you will find a vajra. Knock with that and the door will open by itself. Once inside, you will be in a great jade courtyard with five hundred goddesses. Each will offer you the jewel she holds in her hand. Accept the jewels, but go on to a golden room behind them. There you will see another goddess holding with an ivory handle a jewel, which she will offer to you. This is the wish-fulfilling jewel. Take it and hold it very carefully. Keep your eyes on it at all times, and do not speak. Go now. I am a poor old man and I will die here." With these words, the old captain died.

Following his instructions, Prince Gendun found the palace of the seven jewels and knocked on the door with the vajra. When it opened, he went inside and found the five hundred goddesses in the jade courtyard, each of whom offered him the jewel she held in her hand. He accepted them and went on to the golden room, where another goddess offered him the wish-fulfilling jewel. As soon as he took it, it flew out of his hand, but finally he was able to seize it and hold it tightly. Once he had it, he flew swiftly to the place where his companions were waiting. He gave them the five hundred jewels but said nothing about having obtained the wish-fulfilling jewel.

They began the journey home, but in the middle of the ocean they were caught in a violent typhoon. The ship quickly sank, and all the crew with their jewels were swept away. As he was falling into the ocean, Prince Dikdun called out to his brother, "Take me under your refuge, deliver me." Prince Gendun was under the protection of the wish-fulfilling jewel, and when he put out his hand to his brother, Dikdun too came under its protection and was saved. As none of the others had had a chance to ask for refuge, they all drowned, but by the power of the wish-fulfilling jewel, Prince Gendun and Prince Dikdun eventually reached shore.

After they recovered, they set out on foot in the direction of their own country. Prince Dikdun suspected that his brother had the wish-fulfilling jewel. Hoping to find out, he said, "All our companions and all the jewels have been lost. We are the only survivors and we have nothing. It is shameful to return home like this."

Prince Gendun replied, "We have not failed in our quest. At least we have the wish-fulfilling jewel."

When he heard this, Dikdun thought, "When my parents see that he has found the wish-fulfilling jewel, he will gain great fame, and they will honor him even more. I must get rid of the wish-fulfilling jewel." But he said to his brother, "We must be very careful now to guard the stone. At night only one of us should sleep and the other should keep watch." Prince Gendun, who was very good to his brother, usually stood watch. One night however, he let his brother watch and fell into a sound sleep.

Dikdun quietly removed the wish-fulfilling jewel from around Prince Gendun's neck and then, suddenly afraid that Gendun would realize he had stolen it, put thorns in his eyes and ran away. With the thorns in his eyes, Prince Gendun cried out to his brother for help, thinking that thieves were attacking him; when Dikdun did not respond, he was afraid that something had happened to his brother. Finally, one of the gods of the earth, feeling pity for Gendun, came to him and told him that the evildoer was none other than Dikdun.

Though Prince Gendun was sightless and in great pain, he continued on his way. After many days of walking, he came to the country of Lekshiwa. There, along the road, he came upon a herd of five hundred cows. The leading cow, seeing the thorns in his eyes, came to Prince Gendun and licked his eyes with her tongue, while all the other cows gathered around him. Observing his cows acting so strangely, the cowherd discovered Prince Gendun and, seeing the thorns in his eyes, carefully pulled them out and led Prince Gendun to his home. There he put butter and milk on

Prince Gendun's eyes to soothe them, and cared for him for many days until he was better.

As soon as his pain lessened a little, Prince Gendun wanted to continue his journey, but the cowherd would not let him go until the wounds were completely healed. When the cowherd finally said he was well enough to go, Prince Gendun asked him for a musical instrument that he could play along the way. The cowherd gave Prince Gendun a lute and led him toward the city. When they had almost reached the city, the cowherd turned back and Prince Gendun went on alone, playing the lute and singing. Many people came to hear his beautiful voice and songs, and wherever he stopped, they brought him food and drink. What he did not need he gave to others and so was able to help five hundred beggars on his way.

One day when he was near the pleasure garden of the kingdom of Lekshiwa, some villagers heard his singing and asked him to play for the king. He went into the pleasure garden, and the king, hearing his songs, said to him, "Your voice is very beautiful. Please stay on as keeper of the garden."

Prince Gendun humbly replied, "I cannot even see. How can I possibly protect your garden from the birds and animals?"

The king replied, "You don't need to see. Just stay and sing. We will put bells here and there, and when you pull the ropes, the birds and animals will run away." And so Prince Gendun decided to stay there for a while.

Meanwhile, Dikdun had arrived home. The king and queen asked him what had happened to Prince Gendun and the others. Dikdun told his parents that, having obtained the wish-fulfilling jewel, they were returning home when they were shipwrecked and everyone had perished. When they heard this, the king and queen and all the people of the land went into a great mourning. The king, however, asked Dikdun if he had actually seen Prince Gendun perish; when Dikdun said he had not, his father decided secretly to send a certain goose to search for him. This goose had been Prince Gendun's special pet when he lived in the palace. Around the neck of the goose the king put a letter that told what Prince Dikdun had reported and asked for word of Prince Gendun. The bird flew far and wide, searching everywhere. Finally, one day, it recognized the voice of its master singing in the pleasure garden in Lekshiwa and immediately flew down to him. Since the prince could not see, the goose removed the letter with its beak and read it to him. Prince Gendun took a feather from the goose, and with it he wrote that he was well but could not return home as Prince Dikdun had put thorns in his eyes and he was blind. He then sent the bird back to the king.

One day soon after, the daughter of the king of Lekshiwa, a princess of great beauty, visited the pleasure garden and saw Prince Gendun sitting under a tree singing. Although the prince's face was disfigured and unshaven and his clothes filthy, she was very much attracted to him and stayed near him all day long, talking to him. When it was time to eat, she asked that food be brought for both of them. Prince Gendun protested, "I am a beggar and very ugly. How can I sit and eat with you?" The princess replied, "I will eat no food at all unless you eat with me." Finally, Prince Gendun agreed to share her food.

When it was nearly sunset and she still had not returned home, the king sent a message to the princess ordering her return to the palace at once. But she sent a message back saying that she would not leave the keeper of the pleasure garden. The king again ordered her to come home but still she refused and said that she would not return except as the wife of the blind singer. The king, though very surprised, did not refuse his daughter, for he felt there must be some valid reason for her attraction. He decided to invite them back to the palace as husband and wife, and so the two returned together.

After they had lived together for some time, the princess began to go out early every morning, not returning until late in the evening. Finally Prince Gendun asked her if she had a lover. "When you first asked me to become your husband," he said, "I refused to do so as I was only a blind beggar. But you insisted, and so we were married. Why do you act in this way now? It is not right."

The princess answered, "I have no one else."

As he did not seem to believe her, she continued, "If what I say is true, may sight return to one of your eyes." When she had spoken these words, Prince Gendun immediately regained the sight in one eye.

With great joy she asked him, "Who are you really?" He replied, "Have you heard of King Rinpoche Gocha? He is my father. I am Prince Gendun."

"I have heard of you," she answered. "But how did you come to such a miserable condition?"

When he told her the story of his misfortune, she asked him, "What will you do now if you meet with your brother Dikdun?"

Prince Gendun replied, "Though my brother Dikdun put out my eyes, I do not feel the least enmity toward him."

The princess said, "How can I believe that you feel no dislike for one who harmed you so? It is not possible."

At this, Prince Gendun repeated, "I have not the slightest feeling of enmity toward my brother. If this is true, may sight return to my other eye." At once he regained the sight of his other eye. Upon the restoration of his sight, the propitious signs on his body returned, also and he appeared once again a prince among men.

The princess ran happily to her father. "Do you know King Rinpoche Gocha?" she asked him.

"Yes," he replied, "I know him very well. Why do you ask?"

The princess answered, "The beggar that I married is his son, Prince Gendun."

The king laughed. "What has happened to you? Are you crazy, or just ill? Prince Gendun perished on his journey, yet you tell me now that the beggar you married is the prince."

"If you do not believe me," she said, "please come and see for yourself."

The king went with his daughter and when he saw the transformation that had taken place, he knew that it really was Prince Gendun who stood before him. He was very sorry that he had not recognized the prince before. Then he took him to another palace and established him there. He proclaimed that Prince Gendun had not perished on his voyage, but had returned and was alive and well. Thereupon, all the ministers of state called on Gendun and invited him to come in a great procession to the palace of the king. Prince Gendun was received at the palace, and it was proclaimed that he had married the princess.

Meanwhile the goose had returned to King Rinpoche Gocha with Prince Gendun's letter. When the king learned that Dikdun had brought such disaster on his brother, he had him imprisoned. Then he sent a procession of five hundred attendants to the kingdom of Lekshiwa to ask the prince to return home. When Prince Gendun received his father's message, he and the princess started out, accompanied by his father's five hundred attendants and by five hundred of the princess's attendants. As they approached, the king and queen rode out to welcome them, and when they met, Prince Gendun dismounted and bowed down at the feet of his father. With great rejoicing the whole procession returned to the palace.

Prince Gendun asked at once where his brother was. When he heard that Prince Dikdun had been imprisoned, he asked that he be immediately released. The king at first refused, but granted his son's request when Prince Gendun declared that he would not stay in the palace unless his brother were set free. Upon his release Prince Dikdun bowed down at the feet of his older brother, who welcomed him with great affection.

Prince Gendun very gently asked Dikdun what he had done

with the wish-fulfilling jewel. Dikdun told him, "I buried it on the way, as I realized I could not use it myself." Then he gave directions as to where the wish-fulfilling jewel could be found, and servants were sent for it. They could not find it and returned empty-handed. Finally, Prince Gendun and Prince Dikdun went together and recovered the wish-fulfilling jewel.

With the wish-fulfilling jewel in his possession, Prince Gendun prayed that the treasury he had depleted would again be filled and would remain full from that time on, though gifts be given from it day and night. By his prayers and the power of the wish-fulfilling jewel his wish was granted, and everything that anyone desired fell like rain. When their desires had been satisfied by the gifts of Prince Gendun, the people of the kingdom gave up all wrong actions of body, speech, and mind. By practicing the ten virtues taught them by Prince Gendun, all were reborn in the happy states of humans or gods.

Having finished this story, Buddha said to Ānanda, "My father in this life, King Śuddodhana, was King Rinpoche Gocha in the past. My mother was his queen. My disciple Kāśyapa was King Lekshiwa, and my stepmother Prajāpatī was the princess of Lekshiwa. Devadatta was Prince Dikdun, and I myself was Prince Gendun. You should help those who harm you, as did Prince Gendun. That is the way to attain buddhahood."

The Nun Utpaladok

At one time Buddha was staying in the grove of his patron Anāthapiṇḍika, located in Śrāvastī, the land of King Prasenajit. In that country lived many high-born women of unusual virtue who had become nuns. These nuns were given all the necessities of life, yet they were dissatisfied, as they felt they were not fulfilling their vow to free themselves from saṃsāra. They went to a great arhat, the nun

Utpaladok (She Who Is Beautiful As a Blue Lotus), to seek the teaching of emancipation. Bowing down at her feet, they prayed, "Please help us by showing us the holy Dharma, so that we may free ourselves from the influence of the passions."

The nun Utpaladok asked in return, "Do you wish to hear the teaching of the buddhas of the three times—past, present, and future?"

The five hundred nuns replied, "Please give us the teaching of the present and speak of the past and future some other time, for we wish to free ourselves from present doubts."

And so Utpaladok began.

Attachment is like fire; it burns all that exists, even the mountains. By the power of attachment, we harm each other greatly, causing hatred and rebirth in lower states of being, from which it is very difficult to find emancipation. Those who live a worldly life, attached to attractive things, only increase the miseries of old age, sickness, and death, and being born and reborn, they suffer great mental and physical misery. By married life they tie themselves completely to worldly things.

I myself was born a Kundugyuba, and my parents were respected people of high position. When I was old enough, my marriage was arranged with another of my caste, a clever person who was well known in our country. I had one son by him, and when a second child was soon to be born, I told him I wished to go to my parents' home to have the child, according to the custom of my country. He agreed, and we started out with our small son.

One night when we were halfway there, I suddenly began to give birth. I called to my husband who was sleeping a short distance away, but he did not come to me as he had been bitten during the night by a poisonous snake and was already dead. The child was born, another son. In the morning I looked for my husband, but his body had disappeared, having been dragged off by wild animals. Realizing what disaster had befallen me, I fell senseless to the ground.

Later I was reawakened by the weeping of my elder son, who had been sleeping beside his father. Moaning with pain and in great sorrow, I began to travel, carrying the baby and leading the small child by the hand. There was no one to help me, for we were in very isolated country. After a time we came to a great river. I was too weak to take both children across at one time, and so I took the baby first and laid him on the far bank. I returned for my other child. As I came close to him he became excited and jumped toward me, but I was too weak to reach him before the current swept him away. I crossed back to get my small baby, but where I had left him there was only blood. He had been eaten by wolves. Once again I fell senseless to the ground. When I revived, I continued my journey to my parents' home.

On the way I met a distant relative, who saw my miserable condition and asked what had happened. I told him, and he wept at my words. Then I asked him about my parents. Alas, my parents' house had burned in a great fire, and all my family was dead. Again I fainted, and my relative revived me and took me to his own house, where he and his family cared for me like their own daughter.

After a time I married again and soon became pregnant. One night when the time of birth was near, my husband was invited to the house of a friend. He didn't return until very late, as they had been drinking and enjoying themselves. Suddenly the child was born. I had closed the door and locked it from the inside, and when my husband returned and pounded on it I was too weak to get up and open it. He knocked many times and then, in a drunken rage, broke down the door. Seeing me lying there he began to beat me. I cried out, "I have a baby. I can't walk. I'm going to die," but still he beat me. Then he killed the child and threw it on the fire, and insane with drink, he forced me to eat the flesh of my own child.

After that disaster I could not stay with him, and I ran away toward Vārāṇasī. Sitting under a tree near the city, I heard a young man weeping with great sorrow. He had just buried his wife. After we talked together about our misfortunes, the young man led me to his home and asked me to marry him. Shortly after our marriage, however, my young husband became sick and died, and according to custom, I was buried, alive, with him. That night thieves came and broke open the grave, searching for gold. They found instead a young and beautiful woman. The leader of the band of thieves married me, but right after our marriage the thieves were captured and put to death. Again, according to custom, I was buried alive with my husband, but after three days wolves dug up the grave and I came out.

At this point I began to wonder: what kind of person must I be, that such disasters should befall me? How many times had I been all but dead and yet had had to start my life all over again? I had heard of a Śākya Prince who had become a buddha—one who knows everything of the past, present, and future—so I decided to go to him for refuge. With this purpose, naked though I was from the grave, I walked to the grove of Anāthapiṇḍika, the place where Buddha was staying. There I saw the Tathāgata, who is like a beautiful flowering tree, moving among the people like a moon among the stars. With his immeasurable wisdom, Buddha understood that this was the time when I would be able to subdue myself, and from his seat he called me to come toward him. Feeling very ashamed of my nakedness, I covered myself with my arms and fell to the ground. Buddha then told his disciple Ānanda to give me some clothes. Having covered myself, I bowed down at the feet of the Tathāgata and said to him, "By your mercy and compassion, please let me renounce the world and become a nun." The Tathāgata agreed, and Ānanda led me to Gyigandakmo, who ordained me and taught me the Four Noble Truths.

After great effort I attained arhatship and the understanding of all acts, past, present, and future.

The nuns were amazed at this story and asked, "What could you have done in your previous lifetimes to earn such misery?"

The nun Utpaladok told them, "Long ago there was a very wealthy man who took a second wife after his first had produced no children. By this wife he had a son. The parents loved the child very much and the older wife feared for her position, feeling that the child would inherit all and that she would get no share. Therefore, she killed the child, but in such a way as to leave no mark. However, the child's mother realized what the older wife had done and accused her of murder. To defend herself, the older wife swore that she had not killed the child, saying, 'If I killed your son, may my husband be killed by snakes. May any son I may have be carried off by water or eaten by wolves. May my parents burn to death and my relatives with them. May I myself have the misfortune to eat my own child's flesh and to be buried alive.' The one who swore this was myself. For this reason, I underwent such misfortune in this life."

Then the other nuns asked her, "Having incurred such terrible karma, what virtuous act did you do that you should have had the great good fortune to meet and be welcomed by the Buddha, and to reach the final goal of emancipation?"

"Long ago in Vārāṇasī there lived many great rishis—śrāvakas, pratyekabuddhas, and also many non-Buddhists who had great skill in religious practice. One day as one of the pratyekabuddhas was begging for his daily food, he stopped in front of the house of a merchant. The merchant's wife was very pleased to see him and came forth to worship him and make offerings. To increase her faith, the pratyekabuddha rose up in the sky and performed many miracles. The merchant's wife prayed to him that by her virtuous work she might obtain such a life herself. I was the merchant's wife, and by this dedication of virtuous work in the past I had the opportunity to meet the Tathāgata and to attain arhatship. And indeed, though I have undergone immeasurable misery for things I did in previous lifetimes, I will have to suffer still more retribution, for I have not yet completely purified myself from the effects of wrong deeds."

Upon hearing this, the five hundred nuns realized that all desires of body and mind are indeed like burning fire and that a householder is more miserable than a prisoner. By eliminating all defilements and attachments of mind, the five hundred nuns attained arhatship in one session of meditation.

Buddha said to the nun Utpaladok, "You have done very well. Because of this teaching, these five hundred nuns will attain the final goal. You have accomplished the deed of a bodhisattva."

4

Kadampa Precepts

This chapter is a collection of precepts of the Kadampa (Preceptors) lineage, founded in the eleventh century by "Teacher" Dromtönpa, Atīśa's chief disciple. This lineage was introduced in chapter 2. The title of the collection is Kadam Thorbu, *or* Precepts Collected from Here and There. *These precepts, which concern subjects relative to the understanding and practice of Buddhism, begin with dialogues between Atīśa and his closest disciples and are followed by teachings of Drom and his successors. The precepts were assembled and written down by Tsunba Jegom.*

The book was written primarily for monks. However, for the most part, the teachings in the book are applicable to lay people as well.

When Atīśa arrived in Tibet, his three disciples, Ku, Ngok, and Drom asked him, "For attaining the high states of liberation and omniscience, which is more important, to follow the precept of the lama or to follow the scriptures and commentaries?"

Atīśa replied, "The precept of the lama is more important than scriptures and commentaries."

"Why is that?" they asked.

"Even if you know that the primary characteristic of all phenomena is voidness and can recite the *Tripiṭaka* as well, you and the teaching will be completely separate if you do not apply the precept of the lama at the time of practice."

Again the disciples asked, "Please define the practice of the precept of the lama. Is it simply striving to do virtuous deeds in body, speech, and mind and acting in accordance with the three vows: the vow of individual liberation, the bodhisattva vow, and the tantric vow?"

"Both of these are insufficient," Atīśa answered.

"But why?"

"Although you keep the three vows, if you do not renounce the three realms of saṃsāra, your activities will only increase your worldliness. Although you strive to perform virtuous deeds in body, speech, and mind, both day and night, if you do not dedicate this work to the enlightenment of all, you will end up with numerous wrong concepts. Though you meditate and are considered a holy and wise teacher, if you do not abandon your interest in the eight worldly concerns, whatever you do will be only for the purposes of this life, and in the future you will not find the right path."

❧

At another time Atīśa was asked by Ku, Ngok, and Drom, "What is the highest teaching of the path?"

Atīśa replied, "The highest skill is in the realization of egolessness. The highest nobility is in subduing your own mind. The highest excellence is in having a mind which seeks to help others. The highest precept is continual mindfulness. The highest remedy is in understanding the naturelessness of everything. The highest activity is not to conform with worldly concerns. The highest siddhi is the lessening and transmutation of the passions. The highest giving is found in non-attachment. The highest moral practice is a peaceful mind. The highest patience is humility. The highest effort is to abandon attachment to activities. The highest meditation is the mind without pretension. The highest wisdom is not to grasp anything as it appears."

"And what is the final goal of the teaching?" the three disciples asked.

Atīśa replied, "The final goal of the teaching is possession of the essence of voidness and compassion. Just as in the world there is a panacea for all sickness called the solitary heroic medicine, there is the realization of voidness, which remedies all the fettering passions."

"But many say they have realized voidness. Why do their anger and attachment remain?"

"They are speaking empty words, for when you fully realize the meaning of voidness, your body, speech, and mind react with pleasure, like slipping fresh butter into barley soup. The great sage Āryadeva said:

> The nature of existence—
> Is it empty or not?
> Merely feeling this doubt
> Tears saṃsāra asunder.

"Therefore, when you realize the correct meaning of voidness, it is just like the solitary heroic medicine, for all the path is included in that realization."

"How do you include the entire path within the realization of voidness?" the disciples asked.

"All the path is included in the six transcendences (*pāramitā*). When you realize the correct meaning of voidness—and lose your blind lust for all things, material and spiritual—your life becomes one flowing act of transcendent giving. In the absence of attachment, you are no longer defiled by non-virtuous deeds, and you enter the ever-flowing harmony of transcendent moral practice. In this freedom from defilement, you also liberate yourself from the passionate domination of 'I' and 'mine' and attain the ever-flowing transcendent patience. As you take great pleasure in the realization of voidness, your life becomes one ever-flowing transcendent effort. Through this, you lose all attraction to objects and enter the ever-flowing transcendent meditation. And finally, when your mind is freed from the habit of seeing everything through the prism of three aspects,[13] you will attain the ever-flowing transcendent wisdom."

"Is it possible for one who realizes the meaning of voidness to attain buddhahood with only the wisdom and meditation of voidness?" a disciple asked.

Atīśa replied, "Whatever you perceive, whatever you proclaim—there is nothing that has not come from your own mind. Understand that this realization of mind is empty. Understanding the non-duality of the realization of mind and of voidness is *wisdom. Meditation* is the continuous concentration on this wisdom without any distraction. *Deeds* are the accumulation of merit and wisdom while you realize from the viewpoint of this meditation that everything is like an illusion. Once you are under the influence of these three, their practice will come even in dreams. Once it has come in dreams, it will come at the moment of death. When it comes at the moment of death, it will be present in the *bardo.* Once it is present in the bardo, there is certain to be accomplishment of the superior siddhi, and you will become a buddha."

❧

Once the venerable Atīśa was staying at Nyeythang, southwest of Lhasa. He was asked by the teachers of Shangnachung, Kyur, and Lhangtsang, "What are the teachings of logic (*pramāṇa*)? "

Atīśa replied, "There are many, both Buddhist and non-Buddhist, all of which are endless chains of ideation. They are not necessary, and there is no time to be wasted on them. It is time to condense the essential meaning of the teaching."

One of the teachers then asked, "How do you condense the essential meaning of the teaching?"

"Practice love, compassion, and bodhi-mind toward all sentient beings. Make effort to accumulate merit and wisdom on behalf of them all. Dedicate all roots of virtue to attain buddhahood together with all sentient beings, whose number would fill the sky. Understand that all these things are empty of self-nature, like a dream or a magician's illusion."

❦

When the venerable Atīśa first visited Tibet, he stayed in the western province of Ngari. He gave many precepts to the assembled disciples, who were under the guidance of Lha Jangchub Öd. Then, after two years had passed, Atīśa decided to return to India. Just as he was departing, Lha Jangchub Öd asked, "Even now as you are leaving, could we have one more precept?"

Atīśa answered "What I have already taught you is enough." But Lha Jangchub Öd persisted in his request, so Atīśa gave this precept:

> How wonderful! Dear friends, you have clear realization and great knowledge, while I have small worth and am not very intelligent. Yet, since you who are close friends and dear to my heart request me, I give you this advice from my childish knowledge.
>
> Friends, until you have obtained enlightenment, the lama is needed; therefore, depend upon the holy spiritual teacher. Until you fully realize the nature of voidness, you must listen to the teaching; therefore, listen closely to the precept of the lama. Merely understanding the Dharma is not enough to be a buddha; you must practice constantly.
>
> Go far away from any place that is harmful to your practice; always stay in a place that is conducive to virtue. Clamor is harmful until you obtain a firm mind; therefore, stay in an isolated place. Abandon friends who increase your fettering passions; depend on friends who cause you to increase virtue. Bear this in mind. There is never an end of things to do, so limit your activities. Dedicate your virtue day and night, and always be mindful.
>
> Once you have obtained the precept of the lama, you should always meditate on it and act in harmony with his speech. When you do this with great humility, the effects will manifest without delay. If you act according to the

Dharma from the depths of your heart, both food and necessities will come naturally.

Friends, there is no satisfaction in the things you desire. It is like drinking sea water to satisfy thirst. Therefore, be content. Annihilate all forms of pretentiousness, pride, and conceit; be subdued and peaceful. Abandon all that some call virtue, but that is really an obstacle to the practice of Dharma. As if they were stones on a narrow slippery path, you should clear away all ideas of gain and respect, for they are the rope of the devil. Like snot in your nose, blow out all thoughts of fame and praise, for they serve only to beguile and delude.

As the happiness, pleasure, and friends you have accumulated are of but a moment's duration, turn your back on them. Future life is longer than this life, so carefully secure your treasure of virtue to provide for the future. You leave everything behind when you die; do not be attached to anything.

Leave off despising and deprecating others and generate a compassionate mind toward those who are your inferiors. Do not have deep attachment to your friends and do not discriminate against your enemies. Without being jealous or envious of others' good qualities, with humility take up those good qualities yourself. Do not bother examining the faults of others, but examine your own faults. Purge yourself of them like bad blood. Nor should you concentrate on your own virtues; instead, concentrate on the virtues of others and respect those others as a servant would. Extend loving-kindness to all beings as though they were your own children.

Always have a smiling face and a loving mind. Speak honestly and without anger. If you go about saying many senseless things, you will make mistakes; thus, speak in moderation. If you do many senseless things, your virtuous work will cease; give up actions that are not religious. It is useless to make effort in unessential work. Because whatever you do comes as a result of your karma from long ago, results never match your present desires. Therefore, be calm.

Alas, it is far better to die than to cause a holy person shame; thus, ever be straightforward and without deceit. All the misery and happiness of this life arise from the karma of this and previous lives; do not blame others for your circumstances. Remember to repay the kindness of the lama, as all happiness is his blessing.

Until you subdue yourself, you cannot subdue others; therefore, first subdue yourself. As you are unable to ripen others without clairvoyance, make a great effort to achieve clairvoyance.

You will surely die, leaving behind whatever wealth you have accumulated, so be careful not to gather defilements due to wealth. As distracting enjoyments are without substance, adorn yourself with the virtue of giving. Always keep pure moral practice, for it is beautiful in this life and ensures happiness in future lives. In this world age of the *kaliyuga* where hatred is rampant, don the armor of patience, which nullifies anger. We remain in the world by the power of sloth; thus, we must ignite like a great fire the effort of achievement. Moment after moment your life is wasted by the lure of worldly activities; it is time to meditate. Because you are under the influence of wrong views, you do not realize the nature of voidness. Zealously seek the meaning of reality!

Friends, saṃsāra is a vast swamp in which there is no real happiness. Hurry to the place of liberation. Meditate according to the precept of the lama and dry up the river of saṃsāric misery. Always keep this in mind. Listen well to this advice, which is not mere words but comes straight from my heart. If you follow these precepts you will make not only me happy, but yourselves and all others as well. Though I am ignorant, I urge you to remember these words.

When the venerable Atīśa was staying on Yerpadrak, near Lhasa, he gave the following precept to Yeshe Barwa of Olgud: "I bow down to the Blessed One and to Ārya Tārā. I bow down to the holy lamas."

"Noble sons, reflect deeply on these words. In the kaliyuga the human lifespan is short, and there is much to be understood. The duration of life is uncertain; you do not know how long you will live. Thus, you must make great effort now to fulfill your right desires.

"Do not proclaim yourself a bhikṣu if you obtain the necessities of life in the manner of a layman. Though you live in a monastery and have given up worldly activities, if you fret about what you have given up, you have no right to proclaim, 'I am a bhikṣu living in a monastery.' If your mind still persists in desire for pretty things and still produces harmful thoughts, do not proclaim, 'I am a bhikṣu living in a monastery.' If you still go about with worldly people and waste time in worldly, senseless talk with those with whom you live, even though you are living in a monastery, do not proclaim, 'I am a bhikṣu living in a monastery.' If you are impatient and go about feeling slighted, if you cannot be even the least bit helpful to others, do not proclaim, 'I am a bodhisattva-bhikṣu.'

"If you speak thus to worldly people, you are a great liar. You may get away with saying such things. However, you cannot deceive those who have the boundless sight of clairvoyance, nor can you deceive those who have the Dharma-eye of great omniscience. Neither can you deceive yourself, for the effects of karma follow after you.

"Moreover, when generating bodhi-mind, remember the vows you have taken before the lamas and deities. Do not say, 'It is too difficult to be patient,' when you meet with someone who gives you the opportunity for special patience. Remember that even if it is very difficult, there is always something that can be done. Prior to taking a vow, consider carefully whether it is too difficult for you to keep. For if you do not keep a vow once you have taken it, you will be deceiving the lamas and deities. And again, always remember that even though a thing seems to be difficult, there is always something that can be done.

"To stay in a monastery, it is necessary to give up worldly ways and attachment to friends and relatives. By renouncing these, you are getting rid of all the cooperating causes of attachment and longing. From then on you must seek the precious bodhi-mind. Not even for an instant should you allow your past obsession with worldly concerns to arise. Formerly, you did not properly practice the Dharma, and under the influence of past habits that sapped your strength, you continually produced the concepts of a worldly person. Because such concepts are predominant, unless you make use of strong antidotes to them, it is useless to remain in a monastery. You would be like the birds and wild animals that live there.

"Do not think, 'It is too difficult to apply the antidotes right now.' If the wish-fulfilling jewel should happen to fall from the hands of a blind man, he may never find it again. As you practice, do not count the months and years, but continually examine the strength of your meditation and the extent of your realization. See whether or not your fettering passions are diminishing. Always be mindful. Do not make yourself miserable, nor should you ever even attempt to deceive yourself or the lamas and deities. Do not do anything that would bring disaster to yourself or others.

"When you diminish the activities of this life, you are only doing what is necessary. If there is a heap of filth in front of you, you have to get rid of it quickly. Should someone help you, why not be happy? In the same way you must get rid of all your habitual thoughts, using whatever antidotes are available to you. And, if the lama and your spiritual friends help you to do this, why not be happy?

"Having promised before the lamas and deities to work for the benefit of living beings, do not differentiate among those to whom you give gifts. Although there are differences in people, there is no differentiation in bodhi-mind.

"Do not be angry with those who would harm you. If you allow yourself to become angry, how can you cultivate patience? When fettering passions arise, you must remember their opposing practice. Otherwise, why bother with religious practice while increasing fettering passions? Constantly guarding your precious bodhi-mind, you should not have the slightest gap in your remembrance. If even a tiny gap should appear, the devil of fettering passions will enter. And when this devil enters, he will obstruct the bodhi-mind, and you will be unable to help others and will even fall into lower states of being. Think it over.

"Even if you have the thought, 'I have done religious practice,' you will go to your death empty-handed. Noble son, when you die, be careful that your lama and spiritual friends do not worry or despair. Do not bring doubt or despair to laymen who are faithful to the Dharma. You must check yourself again and again by comparing the teachings of Buddha with your own mind. If you do not do this, even though you think, 'I have done religious practice,' you will stray from the teaching. Because of this, at the time of death there will be no sign of your having practiced bodhi-mind, and when the sign that you will fall into lower states of being appears, others will feel great worry and despair. Therefore, do not be lazy in your practice of the Dharma or let yourself be deceived by the proud thought, 'I have spent my whole life devoted to religion,' and thus go empty-handed into the instant of death.

"In short, staying in a monastery will not be helpful if you do not reverse your obsession for fine things and do not renounce the activities of this life. For if you do not cut off these inclinations, thinking that you can work for the aims of both this and future lives, you will perform nothing but incidental religious practice. This type of practice is nothing but hypocritical and pretentious practice done for selfish gain.

"Therefore, you should always seek spiritual friends and shun bad company. Do not become settled in one place or accumulate many things. Whatever you do, do in harmony with the Dharma. Let whatever you do be a remedy for the fettering passions. This is actual religious practice; make great effort to do this. As your knowledge increases, do not be possessed by the demon of pride.

"Staying in an isolated place, subdue yourself. Have few desires and be contented. Neither delight in your own knowledge nor seek out the faults of others. Do not be fearful or anxious. Be of good will and have no prejudice. Concentrate on the Dharma when distracted by wrong things.

"Be humble, and if you are defeated, accept it gracefully. Give up boastfulness; renounce desire. Always generate the compassionate mind. Whatever you do, do in moderation. Be easily pleased and easily sustained. Run like a wild animal from whatever would entrap you.

"If you do not renounce worldly existence, do not say you are holy. If you have not renounced land and agriculture, do not say you have entered the priesthood. If you do not renounce desire, do not say you are a bhikṣu. If you are without love and compassion, do not say you are a bodhisattva. If you do not renounce activity, do not say you are a great meditator. Do not cherish your desires.

"In short, when you stay at a monastery, engage in few activities and just meditate on the Dharma. Do not have cause for repentance at the time of death."

❧

At another time, Atīśa stated, "This kaliyuga is not the time to display your ability; it is the time to persevere through hardship. It is not the time to take a high position, but the time to be humble. It is not the time to rely on many attendants, but the time to rely on isolation. Nor is it the time to subdue disciples; it is the time to subdue yourself. It is not the time of merely listening to words, but the time of contemplation on their meaning. Nor is it the time to go visiting here and there; it is the time to stay alone."

After Atīśa passed into parinirvāṇa, the teacher Drom became his successor. One time his three disciples, the brothers Potowa, Chengawa, and Puchungwa, asked Geshe Drom, "Please tell us the method of practice that includes the essence of all the paths to omniscient buddhahood."

Geshe Drom answered, "Although there are an inconceivable number of precepts, each of which is an entrance to the path of enlightenment, there is, for one who has the necessary foundation for practice, only one thing to be obtained."

"What is that one thing?" the three brothers asked.

"Possession of the essence of voidness and compassion. Let me explain this. Voidness is the *absolute* bodhi-mind: it is the realization that all phenomena are by nature without truly existent birth. Compassion is the *relative* bodhi-mind: it is great compassion extended to all living beings who have not yet realized this fundamental birthlessness.

"Therefore, those who practice the Mahāyāna path should first make effort in the method of generating these two aspects of bodhi-mind. Once this bodhi-mind has been attained, it should be diligently practiced. By doing this, one is certain to manifest the rūpakāya and the dharmakāya, the final effects of achieving both aspects of bodhi-mind.

"There are many methods of generating the two aspects of bodhi-mind, but condensed into a way of practice, there are no more than three root methods, and sprouting from these, nine principal branch methods. The three root methods are mind-practice, the accumulation of merit and wisdom, and the search for samādhi. Each root method has three principal branch methods.

"The three principal branch methods of mind-practice are the meditation on impermanence, the meditation of love and compassion, and the meditation on the egolessness of all persons and phenomena. Among the various methods of mind-practice, these three are the only important ones; all others are included within them.

"The principal branch methods for the accumulation of merit and wisdom are to honor the lama, to worship the Three Jewels, and to honor the Saṅgha. All other methods of the accumulation of merit and wisdom are contained in these three; thus, they are the only important ones.

"The principal methods of seeking samādhi are to maintain perfect moral practice, to pray to the lamas of the lineage, and to maintain continual solitude. These three methods are the only important ones in seeking the highest samādhi of abiding tranquility and intense insight; all others are included within them.

"By practicing these nine methods, you will naturally produce the two aspects of bodhi-mind. When you produce the absolute bodhi-mind, you will spontaneously realize that all phenomena, whether inner or outer, are empty of real existence, from the beginning without truly existent birth and totally free from ego-reflection.[14] In this realization, you will find boundless joy. When you produce the relative bodhi-mind, you will generate a deep love and compassion toward all those living beings who have not realized absolute bodhi-mind. Then, whatever you do will be for nothing other than the benefit of these myriad beings, and because you have achieved bodhi-mind, whatever you have done previously will be for their benefit also.

"There are two aspects to the conjoining of absolute and relative bodhi-mind. At the time you generate absolute bodhi-mind, you perceive the voidness of all existence. You must at this same moment of perceiving voidness, generate special compassion toward all living beings, who are not negated by your perception of voidness. At the time of generating relative bodhi-mind, deep compassion toward all living beings, you must also see the non-differentiation of self and others.

"Appearances are like a magician's illusions; actually, they are empty of self-nature. When you have successfully generated this unified realization of the two aspects of bodhi-mind, you have correctly entered the Mahāyāna path. By practicing that realization, you will come to the completion of meditation and will naturally obtain the rūpakāya and the dharmakāya. The dharmakāya arises from voidness, the absolute bodhi-mind; the rūpakāya arises from compassion, the relative bodhi-mind. From inseparable practice of the two aspects of bodhi-mind, you will obtain the inseparable dharmakāya and rūpakāya."

Again the three brothers questioned the teacher Drom: "In order to work perfectly for oneself and others, which is important, right view (*lta-ba*) or deeds (*spyod-pa*)?"

The teacher Drom replied, "One who has obtained the necessary foundation for practice and has entered the gate of the Mahāyāna must unify pure wisdom (right view) and pure deeds so that he may do perfect work for self and others. Wisdom alone or deeds alone is not enough."

"What, then, is pure wisdom, and what are pure deeds?"

"Pure wisdom, or right view, consists in the realization that all existents are fundamentally free from the two extremes—eternalism, the extreme of existence, and nihilism, the extreme of nonexistence. All phenomena have no *actual* existence; whether appearing inside or outside, their existence is merely relative. They are like dreams, illusions, and apparitions. Furthermore, pure wisdom is the understanding that all things are but a projection of your own mind. Understanding this, you do not seek out or have attachment to anything.

"Pure deeds are understanding the infallible effects of good and bad actions in this relative existence, which is illusory and dreamlike. Further, they are striving with deep compassion, while being careful of the cause and effect of karma, for the benefit of all living beings who do not understand the nature of existence.

"One who produces in himself the two aspects of bodhi-mind will naturally produce pure wisdom and pure deeds."

The disciples then asked, "Is it wrong to have pure wisdom alone or pure deeds alone?"

Geshe Drom replied, "If you have pure wisdom but do not have pure deeds and lose yourself in impetuous behavior, not being careful of the causes and effects of karma, you will be of no benefit to yourself and others, and even your pure wisdom will go wrong. Should you have pure deeds but lack the perception of the fundamental voidness of all things, you will not be able to benefit yourself and others and your pure deeds will begin to go wrong. If you do not unify pure wisdom and pure deeds, you will inevitably fall into mistaken paths. Therefore, you must learn both."

❧

At another time, the three brothers asked Drom, "Which is more important, to help living beings by means of the teaching, or to practice in an isolated place?"

The teacher answered, "A beginner who has no internal realization cannot help living beings with the teaching. His blessing is like pouring from an empty jar—nothing will come out. His advice is like unfermented beer—it has no essence.

"The person of admirable deeds who has not yet obtained the firmness of warmth[15] does not have the ability to act for the benefit of living beings. His blessing is like pouring from a full vessel—when it has filled another, it itself is empty. His advice is like a butter lamp held in the hand—it may illuminate others, but the holder remains in the shadows.

"However, when a person has entered the stages of the āryas,[16] whatever he does brings benefit to living beings. His blessing is like a magic vessel—though it fills countless vessels, it does not empty itself. His advice is like a butter lamp held by the base—it illuminates others and the one who holds it as well.

"Therefore, this kaliyuga is not the time for an individual to be of help to living beings unless he has cultivated love, compassion, and bodhi-mind in isolation. It is the time to guard against fettering passions. It is not the time to cut down the seedling of the magical medicine tree, but the time to cultivate it."

❦

A teacher from the district of Kham asked the teacher Drom, "What are the individual meanings of the two types of egolessness?"

Drom replied, "From the crown of your head to the soles of your feet, you cannot find anything which is 'I,' even though you search and make minute inquiry with your mind. This is the egolessness of person. Understand also that the mind of the seeker is without natural existence—that is the egolessness of phenomena."

❦

Lotsomo, from the Drom family of Penyulbay, once gave forty bushels of barley to the Radreng monastery. As she was in the presence of the teacher Drom, she said, "Geshe-la, I would like to talk with you. These monks are assembled for the purpose of attaining omniscient buddhahood. We lay people are also here for that purpose. As you have been filled with the precept of the venerable Atīśa as one vessel fills another, I would now like to ask you to give us, with nothing unmentioned, the true precept of obtaining buddhahood."

The teacher Drom told them, "First, meditate on the causes and effects of karma and on the imminence of death. Keep pure all the vows that you have taken. Meditate on love and compassion, and make firm your bodhi-mind. To do these things, use the methods to accumulate merit and wisdom and to purify yourself of sinful deeds. Integrate non-objectification with the three aspects of everything, so that your mind no longer discriminates between the perceiver, the object perceived, and the act of perceiving. Then, dedicate all your roots of virtue to attain perfect enlightenment together with all living beings.

"When you have done this, you will have no cause to regret that you did not meet the venerable Atīśa, for there is no other teaching than this. Nor, in the future, will anyone need be disheartened that they did not meet old Drom, for there is no higher teaching than this for the accomplishment of buddhahood."

❧

An upāsaka asked the teacher Drom, "Is it not true that abiding in love, compassion, and bodhi-mind is always the cause, whether by direct or indirect means, of accomplishing the purpose of others?"

Geshe Drom answered, "It is, without a doubt, the cause of accomplishing the perfect purpose of others and, thus, becomes the cause of your own perfected purpose. From the moment of abiding in love, compassion, and bodhi-mind, you can call yourself a 'non-returner,' for there is small possibility of your being born among the three lower states of being. At this point, it is only by the influence of very strong and sudden circumstances or very bad former activities that you can enter the lower states of being. Should this happen, by merely remembering for a fraction of an instant love, compassion, and bodhi-mind, you will immediately free yourself from the lower states of being and will certainly obtain the high state of a human or god.

"Furthermore, as Śāntideva stated in the *Bodhicaryāvatāra* (*Guide to the Bodhisattva's Way of Life*):

All happiness in the world
Comes from wishing others happiness;
All misery in the world
Comes from wishing your own happiness.

What need to say many things?
Children do things for themselves,
Buddha Śākyamuni does things for others—
Look at the difference.

"Therefore, love, compassion, and bodhi-mind are the causes of accomplishing the great purposes of self and others."

❧

One day an old gentleman was circumambulating the Radreng monastery. Geshe Drom said to him, "Sir, I am happy to see you circumambulating, but wouldn't you rather be practicing the Dharma?"

Thinking this over, the old gentleman felt it might be better to read Mahāyāna sutras. While he was reading in the temple courtyard, Geshe Drom said, "I am happy to see you reciting sutras, but wouldn't you rather be practicing the Dharma?"

At this, the old gentleman thought that perhaps he should meditate. He sat cross-legged on a cushion, with his eyes half-closed. The teacher Drom said again, "I am so happy to see you meditating, but wouldn't it be better to practice the Dharma?"

Now totally confused, the old gentleman asked, "Geshe-la, please tell me what I should do to practice the Dharma."

The teacher Drom replied, "Renounce attraction to this life. Renounce it now. For if you do not renounce attraction to this life, whatever you do will not be the practice of the Dharma, as you have not passed beyond the eight worldly concerns. Once you have renounced this life's habitual thoughts and are no longer distracted by the eight worldly concerns, whatever you do will advance you on the path of liberation."

❧

"What is the difference between Dharma and non-Dharma?" the teacher Drom was asked by Potowa.

"If something is in opposition to fettering passions, it is Dharma. If it is not, it is not Dharma. If it does not accord with worldly people, it is Dharma. If it does accord, it is not Dharma. If it accords with the teachings of Buddha, it is Dharma. If it does not accord, it is not Dharma. If good follows, it is Dharma. If bad follows, it is not Dharma."

Geshe Gonpapa said, "Omniscience is founded on merit and wisdom. Merit and wisdom are founded on bodhi-mind. Bodhi-mind is founded on love and compassion. The precepts of all these are founded on six transcendences.

"Further, giving is founded on non-attachment. Moral practice is founded on reliance on spiritual friends. Patience is founded on humility. Effort is founded on meditation on death. Meditation is founded on dwelling in isolation. Wisdom is founded on mindfulness. Blessings are founded on your faith and respect for the lama and the Three Jewels. Siddhis are founded on vows and obligations. Excellence is founded on hearing, thinking, and meditating. Being of service to others is founded on desirelessness. The progress of self and others is founded on meditation and devotion."

Yerbay Shangtsun said, "When we desire liberation from the depths of our hearts, we should, through continuous contemplation of the imminence of death, always abide in the thoughts and deeds of the four qualities of the āryas.

"These four qualities of the āryas are: to be satisfied with simple religious dress, to be satisfied with meager food, to be satisfied with a poor cushion, and to be satisfied with the minimum of medicine.

"Said in another way, these four are: to be desireless, to be content, to be easily sustained, and to be easily satisfied. To be desireless is to be unattached to all possessions and not to desire many or good things to maintain oneself. Contentment is to be happy with simple things. To be easily sustained means to subsist with meager and poor food, a poor cushion, and simple dress. To be easily satisfied means to be content with scant alms and recognition.

"A person who lives in this way is said to be abiding in the four qualities of the āryas, as all his practice of Dharma is directed toward enlightenment. A person who is completely taken up with worldly desires is not abiding in the four qualities of the āryas. Instead, he is said to be abiding in the qualities of the devil, for abiding in non-virtuous activities is the cause of rebirth in saṃsāra's lower states.

"If we do not give up the desires of this life now, we will come under the influence of attachment again in future lifetimes. To give up the desires of this life, the most potent countermeasure is continual meditation on impermanence. If you do not meditate on impermanence in early morning, by midday you will have many desires."

Again Yerbay Shangtsun said, "If you wish to obtain omniscient buddhahood, you must be free of three entanglements. You must not entangle virtue with prejudice. You must not entangle activities of body and speech with fettering passions. You must not entangle meditation with inclination toward your own liberation. In short, you must practice the path of transcendent realization.

"What is the definition of transcendent realization? Widening what should be widened, it is the widening of wisdom. Constraining what should be constrained, it is constraint in activities. Heroic when heroism is needed, it is heroic opposition to fettering passions. Cautious where caution is needed, it is the caution that provides patience in times of adversity."

Geshe Potowa was asked by an upāsaka, "To actually practice the Dharma, what is most important?"

"The most important thing is the meditation on impermanence. Meditate on impermanence, the imminence of death; it will cause you to begin practicing the Dharma. This will create conditions impelling you to do virtuous work, which will then assist you in realizing the equality of all things in their nature of existence.

"Meditation on impermanence will also cause you to decide to renounce the enjoyments of this life, which will create the conditions for ridding yourself of all worldly desire and thus assist you to enter the path of nirvāṇa.

"When you have meditated on impermanence and have gained some understanding, you will seek the Dharma. This will create the conditions for the achievement of Dharma and thus assist in its final accomplishment.

"Meditating on impermanence and finding some understanding of it will also cause you to commence armor-like effort, which will, in turn, create the conditions for commencing the effort of religious practice. This will assist you in commencing effort on the stage of non-returning."

❦

Kyang Chadotsul petitioned Geshe Potowa for a precept.

Geshe Potowa answered, "When you frequently contemplate impermanence and become conscious of the certainty of death, you will have no difficulty in abandoning sinful activities and doing virtuous work.

"In addition to that, when you frequently meditate on love and compassion and produce them in yourself, you will have no difficulty in working for the benefit of living beings.

"Finally, when you frequently meditate on voidness and produce some realization of it, you will have no difficulty in liquidating delusion."

❦

Another time Geshe Potowa spoke to a gathering of his students: "The blessed Buddha, knowing that the legacy of sentient beings consists of eighty-four thousand aspects of fettering passions, proclaimed the eighty-four thousand aggregates of Dharma as countermeasures. In short form, their content has been recorded in the precious Three Baskets (*Tripiṭaka*). Their subject matter is included in the three precious precepts: exceptional moral practice, exceptional meditation, and exceptional wisdom.

"Depend on exceptional moral practice and thus produce exceptional meditation; by depending on that, produce exceptional wisdom. By that exceptional wisdom, you will be able to eradicate the fettering passions and will certainly achieve buddhahood.

"Exceptional moral practice is the principal precept for beginners, for it is the basis of everything. Indulgence of desire is completely contradictory to it and is the root of all fettering passions. When you indulge in desire, you produce fettering passions and, by their influence, accumulate bad karma and remain lost in saṃsāra.

"As an antidote to desire, Buddha taught the meditation of repulsion. In that teaching there are five phases of meditation. The first is the meditation of mother or sister. At the time the figure of a desirable woman appears in your mind, meditate on her as your mother if she is older than you. When you feel desire for one of your own age, meditate on her as your sister. When you feel desire for one younger than yourself, meditate on her as your daughter in order to reverse the desire.[17]

"If you fail to reverse your desire by this meditation, another method is the meditation of shame and self-reproach. When you think improper thoughts, you have shamed and disgraced yourself in front of all the bodhisattvas and buddhas, who, with their wisdom-eyes, see and know all, and you will not be able to take refuge in them. When you act improperly, the gods of the earth and sky will proclaim your activities, and you will get a bad reputation in this life and birth in lower realms in future lives. Therefore, be mindful of this self-reproach and shame, for by this meditation you can reverse desire.

"If this meditation still does not reverse your desire, there is the meditation of filth and stench. Contemplate the body of the desired woman as a leather bag full of the thirty-six aspects of filth, or as a city of eighty thousand worms. Imagine that it is filled with larvae like the inside of a dead dog rotting in the summer heat. Meditate on the figure of the woman as successively bloody and raw, oozing pus, putrid, squirming with vermin, being eaten by maggots. Conceive of it as completely rotten, and reverse desire.

"If even by this method you do not reverse desire, contemplate the woman as enemy and murderer. This woman is the enemy who destroys your religious attitude, the killer who slays liberation, the hailstorm that ruins the crop of virtue, the thief who robs you of spiritual pleasure, the devil who saps the root of virtue, the warden who holds you in the prison of saṃsāric misery, the terrorist who incites all fettering passions, the furnace of hell that spews forth all misery. When you contemplate all this, you will certainly reverse desire.

"If by these means you still have not done so, the final method is the meditation of delusion. For example, when the magician manifests a beautiful form of a man, woman, horse, or elephant, most people are fooled. All phenomena are similarly without self-nature, false and delusive, and by attachment and desire for them, sentient beings suffer in saṃsāra. I, for one, have always been deluded by women's bodies, which are so diseased, useless, false, and beguiling. Mindful of this, think: 'Even now she comes to deceive me,' and reverse desire.

"If by all these methods of meditation you still cannot reverse desire, a devil has entered into you. You should then ask your spiritual teacher for the method to exorcise this devil."

Geshe Chen-ngawa, while speaking to a gathering of his disciples, said: "In brief, the Dharma can be divided into abandoning harmful activities and taking up helpful ones. All the teachings of the higher and lower vehicles as well as the teachings of the Three Baskets are included within this precept.

"To apply this precept, patience is most important. If you are without patience and someone harms you, you will feel vengeful. Should you act on that feeling, you will not cease from harmful activities, much less be helpful to others. Therefore, patience is necessary to begin religious practice.

"To meditate on patience, there are four methods: setting up the target for the arrow; love and compassion; teacher and disciple; and meditation on the nature of existence.

"First is meditation on setting up the target for the arrow: if you have not set up a target, it cannot be hit by an arrow. The arrow of harm strikes in this life because we have set up a target by the bad karma we accumulated in previous lives. Thus, it is not right to be angry with those who harm us. As Śāntideva said in the *Bodhicaryāvatāra:*

> If I had not done harm to others,
> No harm would come to me.
> I did harm living beings—
> It is fit that harm returns to me.

"Furthermore, if you have harmed others in the early part of your life, you will receive retribution in the later part of the same life. The harm done in the early part of the year will return in the later part. The same for the early and later parts of months and days. If you set up a target of bad activities and hateful speech, it will be struck by arrows of retribution. We set up the target ourselves; understand that the arrows come from our own harmful acts, and do not be angry with others.

"Next is the meditation of love and compassion. When a lunatic harms one who is sane, the sane person should not return the harm by fighting him but should say, 'How sad!' One who harms you is also insane, possessed by the madness of powerful fettering passions. Think, 'How sad!' and cultivate compassion for him.

"Actually, a lunatic is less crazy than the sane person who harms you, for he harms only the bodies of himself and others and, thus, his harm is not so great. He is crazy only for a while, a few days, months, or years, and so the duration of his harm is not great. The sane person who does harm, harms all sentient beings, and so he is the crazier. He is under the influence of fettering passions, which extend in the limitless world from beginningless time, and so the harm is of long duration. By carelessly committing non-virtuous deeds in body, speech, and mind, he produces the misery of the three lower states. Thus, his harm is very great. As this one has the greater need for compassion, cultivate love and compassion toward one who harms you, and do not be angry. As Śāntideva said in the *Bodhicaryāvatāra:*

> If one who is influenced by fettering passions
> Will even kill himself,
> How can it be
> That he will not harm others?
>
> Influenced by fettering passions
> He will destroy himself and others, too.
> If I am angry and have no compassion,
> I am worse than he.

"The third meditation of patience is on teacher and disciple. If there is no lama to impart instruction, there can be no vow. If there is no teacher to explain the Dharma, there can be no realization. Similarly, if there is no enemy who harms you, there can be no practice of patience. Thus, feel that those who abuse you are the teachers of patience. Be happy at this opportunity and concentrate on repaying their kindness. Meditating that you are a disciple being taught patience, do not be angry.

"To meditate on the nature of existence as voidness, contemplate that all three aspects of harmfulness—the agent of harm, the recipient of harm, and the act of harming—are all void of self-nature. As all these things that you now see opposing you are erroneous creations of your mind, like dreams and illusions, it is not right to be angry. As Śāntideva said in the *Bodhicaryāvatāra:*

> From being praised,
> What do you gain, what do you lose?
> In being despised,
> Why be happy, why be sad?

"When you wake from sleep, you understand that the enemies in your dreams have no self-nature and you are not angry with them. As your actual enemy is also without self-nature, do not be angry with him but cultivate patience."

❧

Geshe Chen-ngawa said, "In order to obtain omniscience and liberation, we must learn not to conform with worldly people. Such people value Buddha more than living beings, value self more than others, value those who are helpful more than those who are harmful, and value happiness more than misery.

"Those who practice Dharma must do the opposite. We should value living beings more than Buddha. Why is that? Not only is it not disrespectful to value living beings more than Buddha, there are four good reasons for doing so: all living beings in saṃsāra are our kind mothers; as these mothers suffer in saṃsāra, we must help them; by helping them, we will naturally achieve our own purpose; and by helping them, we respect and worship all the buddhas and bodhi-sattvas.

"Worldly people value themselves more than others, but we must value others more than ourselves. Why? From beginningless time we have created our own misery; it has not been created by others. Misery is brought about by our own fettering passions. As self-grasping and fettering passions are one, it is our own self-grasping that has created our misery. Therefore, we must oppose this enemy in every way, and value others more than ourselves, since it is in relation to other living beings that we accumulate merit and wisdom. Also, it is in relation to other living beings that we meditate on the two aspects of bodhi-mind, which lead to the attainment of nirvāṇa.

"Worldly people value those who help them more than those who harm them; we must do the opposite. Why? In this world, parents are considered to be the greatest help, for they give their children servants, wives, herds of horses, palaces, gold, turquoise, and land. Yet, according to the Dharma, there is no greater harm than that because, desiring these gifts, children accumulate and extend bad karma and fettering passions, and by this they may finally fall into hell. What appears now to be help has a final result of misery, and the kind fathers and mothers of this life can thus be considered our greatest enemies. We must instead value those who bring us harm. Why? When harmed by an enemy, we can meditate on patience, and from patience we obtain immeasurable merit. When harmed by devils, we begin to make effort, and traveling higher and higher paths, we obtain all siddhis. Thus, we must value those who harm us.

"Finally, worldly people value happiness more than misery; we must do the opposite. Why? Desire for the happiness of food and clothes, of idleness, of sex, of rest, and of sleep is finally the cause of despair. Therefore, we must value misery more than worldly happiness. Why? By the misery of work undertaken for the lama and the Saṅgha, by the misery of the hardships of moral practice, and by the misery undergone while doing virtuous work in body, speech, and mind, we purify defilements and accomplish merit and wisdom. By these we obtain states of great spiritual happiness; therefore, we must value misery. When troubled in mind and sick in body, we can turn from saṃsāra and produce the mind of renunciation. Therefore, we must value misery.

"If you have learned these four ways of not conforming with worldly people, you are like a good and clever woman; you do not need more explanation. If you do not have these four aspects, you are like a bad woman; no teaching will be helpful."

Geshe Chen-ngawa said, "Nowadays, even the best people mix their religious practice with worldly interests. Afraid of weakness, they seek patronage with families of great name. Afraid of devils, they recite mantras of wrathful deities. Afraid of starvation, they accumulate many possessions. Afraid of being criticized, they act hypocritically.

"Among such people do you think any will become a buddha? It isn't likely. Do you think a sheep can rise up when the butcher is grasping him for slaughter? Do you think he can free himself when he is already butchered? It isn't likely.

"What should be done? If someone harms you, do not retaliate, but cultivate patience. If you do that, you will not be overcome by even the most powerful person. Therefore, as the chief strength is meditation on patience, it is senseless to seek patronage.

"If devils come, seeking to trouble you, realize that, like the horns of a hare, an independent ego does not exist; if you give up life and body to the devils, even the demons of the three thousand worlds cannot harm you. Therefore, the principal power is the realization of egolessness, and it is senseless to recite mantras of wrathful deities.

"If you are completely impoverished, you will entrust yourself to the Dharma. As a final consequence of turning toward the Dharma, you will entrust yourself to the life of a beggar. As a final consequence of this, you will entrust yourself to death. Because of your holy life, after your death you will be revered by all those faithful to the teaching. Therefore, the greatest joy is found in non-attachment, and it is meaningless to accumulate possessions.

"If you are without hypocrisy, although some may criticize you, you will actually be the most admirable. Therefore, as the basis of a good name is to be without falsehood in thought or deed, it is useless to act hypocritically."

Again Geshe Chen-ngawa said: "Depending on the self of a person and the self of phenomena, the fettering passions and all else that is wrong are increased. Yet it is really the self of persons which harms us. Therefore, we should overcome or abolish this self of persons by the wisdom gained through hearing, thinking, and meditating on the teaching.

"But if through hearing, thinking, and meditating you feel disdainfully, 'I am holy,' while your patience becomes less than that of a fawn alone in the forest and your self-grasping increases, this is a sign that the wisdom of hearing, thinking, and meditating has gone wrong.

"Understanding that all external appearances are empty of true existence but still not subduing your inner self-grasping is like setting up a target and shooting the arrow away from it. It is like losing a thief in the forest and searching for his footprints in the meadow; like scattering offerings in the west to appease devils who abide in the east."

Geshe Puchungwa said: "Though we have obtained the indispensable human body with its leisure and opportunity, we do not have the power to stay in it—we have to die. Just as a tree sheds all its leaves, at the time of death, we cannot take with us any of the enjoyments or concepts of this life. At that time the measure of our knowledge, our strength, and the wisdom of our goals will be clear. When we face death happily and with joyful anticipation, we are wise, strong; our goals are noble, and we will enter death clearheaded. But if at that time the form of Yama and the distinct signs of lower states of birth appear, our goals were foolish, and we are without self-mastery.

"We, for the most part, follow the wrong path, seeking to fulfill the desires of this life. The perfect Buddha never spoke falsely. The authors of the commentaries, such as Nāgārjuna, never spoke falsely. The holy spiritual friends do not speak falsely. Then how do we enter the wrong path? By the desires of this life. Thus, we should always contemplate death, for by remembering the imminence of death we understand the need for non-attachment to this life. We should contemplate the perniciousness of all saṃsāra, for then we understand the need to be unattached to the whole of it. By remembering living beings in the cultivation of love, compassion, and bodhi-mind, we understand the need to be unattached to our selfish purposes. By remembering egolessness in the meditation on the voidness of all things, we understand the need to be unattached to objects and attributes."

Again Geshe Puchungwa said, "To practice Dharma earnestly, you must be like a small bird. As a sparrow is unable to mingle with hawks, you should not mingle with worldly people, for if you do so, you will be carried away by devils. When a worldly person dislikes you, it is just what you want, for then he will leave you alone. Because of his insults, others will leave you alone. Also, although you have nothing but an ounce of barley flour, if your mind is tranquil and happy, you can do virtuous work. If you increase your virtuous work, you will increase your knowledge and by that you will naturally benefit living beings."

Again, Geshe Puchungwa said, "The greatest happiness is the happiness of abandoning desire rather than the happiness of indulging desire. The most important realization is understanding properly the meaning of one thing, rather than understanding many words. The most important help is the help of the Dharma rather than the help of material gifts. The most important fear is to fear the misery of future lives rather than the misery of this life. The most important decision is to cease internal wrong concepts rather than merely to cease wrong concepts about external things."

Geshe Nyugrumpa said, "You who wish to obtain rebirth as a human or god and also wish to obtain perfect enlightenment must think of saṃsāra as a prison. You should see this life and body as a bubble of water, bad company as an enemy, the spiritual teacher as a wish-fulfilling jewel, the fettering passions as a poisonous snake, sinful activities as strong poison, the aspects of desire as the embers of a fire, sweet words and fame as an echo, respect and gain as an entangling snare, bad friends as a contagious disease, good friends as a beautiful and fortified palace, and all sentient beings as your mother and father. You should feel that giving is the wish-fulfilling cow, that moral practice is a precious jeweled ornament, that patience is strong armor, that effort is the wish-fulfilling wisdom-horse, that meditation is a great treasure, and that the wisdom of hearing, thinking, and meditation is a bright lamp."

Geshe Khampalungpa said, "As it is so very difficult to obtain a life of leisure and opportunity, guard moral practice as you would your eyes. As it is not certain when your illusory body will be destroyed, practice the Dharma with body, speech, and mind. As impermanent virtuous work is ineffectual until dedicated, make heartfelt prayers for the benefit of all living beings. As all that is impermanent is illusory, abandon attachment, not holding anything as truly existent."

Geshe Benjagpa advised himself: "As we do not have any influence over even today, do not count on living forever, venerable sir, and do not feel as 'mine' this illusory body. Reverend monk, do not hold as dual that which is without duality, and toward those who have not realized non-duality, generate love and compassion. Reverend monk, make valiant effort, for in this short life you sow the field for the crops of future lives."

When he was having an audience with Geshe Kharagomchung, the 'Victorious Teacher' Yeshe Sung asked, "What is the way to devote one's life to the practice of Dharma?"

Geshe Kharawa replied, "There are three stages in the practice of Dharma: the initial stage is to not harm living beings; the middle stage is to help living beings; the highest stage is meditation on the significance of birthlessness, which is that living beings and oneself are undifferentiated."

ᔕᔓ

Again, Geshe Kharawa said, "As a person who has no faith has no chance to develop excellence, one should rely upon the spiritual teacher and read the sutras. As a person who makes no effort has no chance to develop excellence, one should meditate on impermanence and abandon laziness. As a person who has pride has no chance to develop excellence, one should be self-effacing and humble. If one does these things, one has the suitable basis to become a śrāvaka, a bodhisattva, or a practitioner of the Mantrayāna—in short, one has the suitable basis for all excellence."

Again Geshe Kharawa said, "It is a mistake not to see that attachment is harmful, for it keeps us from rising from saṃsāra. It is a mistake not to see that anger is harmful, for anger destroys the root of virtue. It is a mistake not to see that pride is harmful, for pride stunts the root of virtue, preventing the growth of excellence.

"Do not despise giving; by giving we obtain the spiritual pleasures of humans and gods. Do not despise moral practice; by moral practice we obtain rebirth as a human or god. Do not despise compassion, for it is the source of all the Mahāyāna teachings. Do not despise the bodhisattva precepts, for the bodhisattva vow is the special method of achieving perfect omniscience. Do not despise the Mantrayāna vow, for through the Mantrayāna one can quickly obtain the ordinary and superior siddhis."

He also said, "The culmination of the wisdom of right view is freedom from all assertions. The culmination of meditation is freedom from all mental activities. The culmination of deeds is freedom from all discrimination. The culmination of practice is freedom from all superfluous experience."

❦

Geshe Dragyaba said, "If you wish to practice the Dharma sincerely, you must turn your back on the concerns of this life by constant meditation on impermanence. Though you may have happiness, pleasure, and fame in this life, if your mind is not directed toward the Dharma, you will be deluded in everything you do. Thus, you must quickly detach yourself from happiness, pleasure, and fame. If you totally renounce these things now, what you do in this life will be meaningful. If you do not renounce these things, though you may be known as a great meditator and teacher, holy and wise, your activities will only be worldly, and you will merely fill your surroundings with junk; non-virtuous and sinful deeds will arise naturally, and your life will gradually cease to accord with the Dharma. If you continue in this way, not thinking about death, you will die clinging to your enjoyments and will be reborn in a lower state of being.

"When you have achieved understanding of impermanence and have renounced worldly aims, you can achieve your purpose although you may not be renowned for cleverness or holiness. When you die, by the strength of having prepared for death beforehand, you will die with happiness and pleasure, unhindered by any attachment.

"Therefore, keeping impermanence in mind, look and see if what you have done previously, are doing now, and will do in the future is involved with concerns of this world. If your activities are entangled with these concerns, they are defiled by fettering passions; you must stop pretending that such activities are religious practice. To abandon such activities you must cultivate heedfulness, which consists of continuous, careful remembrance and watchful discernment.

"If you are motivated by desire for the things of this life, however much effort you make, in the tomorrow of death you will be empty-handed. Therefore, recognize that death is imminent and do actual religious practice.

"When you practice the Dharma, you cannot be certain which will come first, next year or your next life. Therefore, before next year, donate all your material goods to the Saṅgha. Confess and cease all wrong-doing. Focus your mind on your aim. Make great effort in your religious practice. Pray sincerely that whatever you do will be for the benefit of living beings. There is no other method of action.

"You cannot be certain which will come first, next month or your next life. Therefore, before next month, do as I have just said. You cannot be certain which will come first, tomorrow or your next life. Therefore, before tomorrow, do as I have just said. As we cannot be certain even of this evening, this very day give your material goods to the Saṅgha. Confess your sinful activities. Pray sincerely; meditate. There is no other method of action.

"From the time of birth, you move toward death. As you cannot know when death will come, you must always do religious practice as if you were going to die this evening."

Geshe Neysurpa said, "As you will not reach buddhahood by conceiving of others as your adversaries, you must realize that all living beings are your mother and father. As you will not obtain buddhahood by the habitual concepts of the ordinary mind, you must realize that all sentient beings are deities. As you will not obtain buddhahood by distinguishing attributes, you must realize that voidness is the nature of all living beings."

Geshe Langri Tangpa said, "As one person cannot truly take the measure of another, do not criticize anyone. As all Buddha's teachings are effective, do not discriminate between them, saying that some are good and some bad. As all the deeds of the Mahāyāna are for the benefit of all beings, do not weaken the armor of the bodhisattva path. As you cannot lead others until you have achieved stability yourself, make effort and meditate in isolation."

Geshe Sarba said, "As women are the root of the fettering passions, do not rely on them. As wine is the root of the fettering passions, do not drink. As travel is the root of the fettering passions, do not take many trips. As accumulation of possessions is the root of the fettering passions, abandon material attachments."

Geshe Chayulpa said, "Maintain pure moral practice, as it is the foundation of the path of liberation and enlightenment. Practice bodhi-mind, for it is the vital force of that path. Always make effort to accumulate merit and wisdom, for they are the ladder up that path. Always rely upon the spiritual teacher, as he is the guide on that path."

Geshe Chayulpa also said, "Object and subject are like sandalwood and its fragrance. Saṃsāra and nirvāṇa are like ice and water. Appearances and voidness are like clouds and sky. Voidness and habitual thoughts are like the ocean and its waves."

Geshe Tolungpa said, "If you desire liberation from the depths of your heart, you must follow the holy rather than the clever teacher. You must follow the one who devotes himself to the teaching rather than the one who explains it, the one who is humble rather than the one who has great position, the one of faith rather than the one famous for his intelligence. There is no harm if you do not know the teaching, but misfortune will come if you follow those whose actions are contrary to the Dharma."

He also said, "Do not accept as truly existent appearances that are only imputed designations. Do not be attached to impermanent phenomena; do not grieve over the destruction of such illusory things. Do not weaken your opposition to fettering passions and desires. Do not follow the eight worldly concerns. Do not associate with bad company. Do not have great longing for your relatives. Do not weaken your respect and faith in the lama and the Three Jewels. Do not be greatly attached to body and enjoyments. Do not weaken your one-pointed hearing, thinking, and meditating. Do not praise activity, gain, and renown. Do not weaken your resolute meditation. Do not lessen the compassion which unselfishly helps others."

Geshe Nambarpa said: "Without renouncing saṃsāra's three realms, you cannot direct your mind towards liberation; meditate on the perniciousness of all saṃsāra. Without controlling your desire, you will not cut off attachment to things; get rid of your belongings as you would empty a spittoon. You can not receive the blessings of the spiritual teacher if you do not conceive of your lama as Buddha; strengthen this concept."

Geshe Chimbupa, when asked for a precept by a yogi, said, "Appearances are illusory; do not hold them as truly existent. The five aggregates are flesh and blood; do not hold them as 'mine.' Possessions are accumulated by the effects of former karma; do not make so much effort to acquire things. What you have been doing makes you miserable; limit your activities. Saṃsāra is wretched; do not accept it as meaningful. Follow this precept now—do not say, 'I will do it in the future when the days are longer.'"

Geshe Shabogaypa said, "You have now obtained a human life that has leisure and opportunity and have found a spiritual teacher. At this time you have encountered the Mahāyāna teaching. Now you must prepare yourself for future lives and turn your steps toward liberation and buddhahood.

"To prepare yourself for future lives, you must despise the concerns of this life, abandoning the ten non-virtuous activities and taking up the ten virtuous activities. To obtain liberation, you must turn your mind from all of saṃsāra. To turn your steps toward omniscient buddhahood, you must practice bodhi-mind.

"To produce these attitudes, you must accumulate merit. If you do not accumulate merit, you cannot understand the teaching. Although you may understand something, it will not be absorbed, while even the little understanding you have will dwindle and not be helpful. Furthermore, it is because in the past you have not accumulated merit and instead have accumulated its opposite that you have wandered in saṃsāra. Even in this life, it is because you have not accumulated merit and have not abandoned non-virtuous actions that things are not working out as you desire. Therefore, the root of all the teaching is to accumulate merit and to eradicate sins."

❧

Geshe Shabogaypa also said, "As the desires of this life cause all the misery of this and future lives, we must not seek the fulfillment of our desires. When we try to fulfill our desires, we are not happy. We become unsure of the direction of our life, and wrong speech, wrong mind, and wrong actions all surface at once.

"Therefore, we must turn away from our many desires. When we are able to do this, we establish the beginnings of happiness and pleasure. The best sign of happiness in this and all future lives is not desiring or accumulating anything at all. When we do not desire gain, we have the greatest gain. When we do not desire reputation, we have the best reputation. When we do not desire fame, we have the greatest fame. When we do not desire companions, we have the best companions.

"If we are sincerely to practice the Dharma, we must entrust ourselves wholeheartedly to the life of a mendicant, for the ultimate mendicant is one who entrusts himself to death. When we can produce this feeling, not gods, not men, nor devils can conquer us. But when we indulge in the desires of this life, we lower ourselves and make ourselves completely miserable. We bring censure on ourselves in this life and rebirth in lower states in future lives.

"Therefore, when, not wishing our own happiness, we limit our criticism of others, humble ourselves, limit our desires, and avoid all activities that are not religious, we will then obtain enlightenment in the future.

"In short, we are always beginning what is not necessary to begin, realizing what is not necessary to realize, doing what is not necessary to do. Though we say all this, if we do not actually turn away from the desires of this life, there is no way of finding happiness now or in future lives. If we turn away from all desires, we do not need to seek happiness at all."

Geshe Shabogaypa further said, "Without controlling yourself, do not wish to control others. Without having knowledge yourself, do not wish to teach others. One who has great faith avoids wrongdoing. One who takes pleasure in voidness does not cling to ego. One who has great wisdom knows the difference between Dharma and non-Dharma. One who is wise understands the Dharma. One who is concerned about even the slightest sin is also concerned about the greater sins. One of benevolent mind has ceased from doing harm. One not able to live alone must be able to get along with others. One who wishes to be holy does not allow his patience to weaken. One who now gives many gifts does not give less when he has fewer means. One who is debased does not give lofty teachings. One who has a good teacher does not act badly. One who is happy to learn the Dharma is also happy to practice it. One living in isolation does not mingle with others. One who seeks goodness has few desires. One who wishes to obtain liberation is not addicted to the eight worldly concerns."

Finally, Geshe Shabogaypa chastised himself: "You old fool—you wish for high teachings, though your nature is low. You charlatan—you desire to improve others, but do not improve yourself. You sham—you act as if the Dharma were meant only for others to follow, and not for yourself. You blunderer—you have charged others to act correctly, but act incorrectly yourself. You shiftless bum—each rise precedes a greater fall. You politician—you make extensive promises, but abbreviated application. You rascal—you seek fettering passions, and at the same time pretend to apply their countermeasures. You coward—you are fearful of others seeing your faults, and hope that they will see only your good qualities.

"You involve yourself with your relatives instead of cultivating spiritual friends. You involve yourself with fettering passions instead of cultivating their antidotes. You leave practice for future lives instead of cultivating it in this life. You involve yourself with those who help you rather than cultivating those who harm you.

"You idiot—you harm others, not knowing you harm yourself. You do not know that to help others is to help yourself. You do not see that misery and harm that come to you are conducive to practicing the Dharma. You do not see that desire and happiness are non-conducive to the practice of Dharma.

"You say to others that practicing the Dharma is very important, yet do not follow the teaching yourself. You despise others who are sinful, yet do not stop your own wrongdoing. You see the slightest faults in others, yet do not perceive great faults in yourself. You soon stop helping others when you get nothing in return. You cannot bear to see other teachers receive respect. You are subservient to those in high position while contemptuous of those beneath you. Talk of future lives is not pleasing to your ears. You act holy and disdainful when corrected by others. You want others to see your virtues and are content when they do not see your faults. You are satisfied with a good façade though what is inside is not so good.

"You like to be given things. Not seeking happiness within yourself, you seek it externally. Having vowed to learn Buddha's teaching, you learn worldly affairs instead. Though you agree with the advice of the bodhisattvas, your actions are preparing you for hell. Though you have dedicated your body, enjoyments, and virtuous activities of past, present, and future for the benefit of all living beings, you refuse to give up your ego. You like sinful friends, forgetting that they lead to ruin. You do not know that the anger of a spiritual friend is helpful.

"Do not waste time in pointless debate. Do not build castles in the air, increasing your cravings. Do not delight in dangerous activities. Do not do many things that senselessly hinder virtuous work."

Feeling self-reproach, he scolded himself in this way.

This is the lineage of Atīśa's teaching, the heartfelt speech of many holy beings. These precepts were collected from here and there by the venerable Tsunba Jegom.

5

The Essence of Good Explanation: Praise of Munīndra

THESE LAST FOUR CHAPTERS are representative of the teachings of Tsongkhapa. The first, The Essence of Good Explanation: Praise of Munīndra, *praises Śākyamuni Buddha for his teaching of voidness as the import of dependent origination. This is followed by Tsongkhapa's short root text,* The Three Principles of the Path, *with a later commentary in the form of instructions for meditational practice. The third selection is Tsongkhapa's concise summary in verse of the teachings of the unified Sūtrayāna and Tantrayāna paths as brought to Tibet by Atīśa. The fourth presents the stages of this path from the viewpoint of reliance on the lama.*

At one time Tsongkhapa was studying the controversy between the Prāsaṅgika and Svātantrika tenets of the Madhyamaka, striving to obtain final insight into the nature of existence. He retreated to a hermitage, for he was not yet satisfied with his understanding of the intent of Buddha. There he made intense prayers, unifying the lama and Mañjuśrī. One night Nāgārjuna and his five principal spiritual sons—Āryadeva, Buddhapālita, Bhāvaviveka, Candrakīrti, and Śāntideva—appeared to Tsongkhapa in a dream. All were sitting and discussing the meaning of the teachings when one of the sages, who was of bluish color and slightly larger than the others, came forward, holding in his hand a volume on the Madhyamaka. With it, he made the gesture of blessing Tsongkhapa.

When Tsongkhapa awoke, he began to read Buddhapālita's commentary on the Mūlamadhyamakakārikā, *and as evidence of the blessing, he effortlessly obtained certain, pure realization of the Prāsaṅgika system. His realization was completely different from what it had been before, and by it, he completely destroyed all false objectification of phenomena and all habitual thoughts leading toward the extremes of eternalism or nihilism.*

Inspired by his realization, he composed in one morning The Essence of Good Explanation: Praise of Munīndra.[18] *In it is expressed the highest teaching of the equivalence of dependent origination and voidness.*

The Essence of Good Explanation: Praise of Munīndra

Namo Guru Mañjughoṣāya

I bow down to the highest of speakers,
The fully accomplished Buddha,
Who showed the truth of dependent origination:
No production, no cessation,
No eternalism, no nihilism,
No going or coming,
No sameness, no diversity,
Complete pacification of ego-reflection.[19]

I bow down to him who, by realization and speech,
Is the omniscient one and the peerless teacher:
The conqueror who from his realization
Has shown dependently linked origination.

Ignorance is the root
Of all worldly deterioration.
Buddha saw this and, to reverse it,
Spoke the truth of dependently linked origination.

At that time, how could intelligent ones[20]
Not understand
That very key of your teaching,
The path of the realization of dependent origination?

As this is so, as praise to
You, the Protector,
Who can find anything more wonderful
Than your speech of dependent origination?

"Whatever depends on conditions,
That is empty of self-nature."
What good precept is there that is
More amazing than this speech?

The immature who hold on to this[21]
Strengthen the bonds of extremism,
While to the wise this very thing is the way
To cut the net of ego-reflection.

As this doctrine is not seen in any other teaching,
You alone are called 'Teacher';
This word of praise used among the faithless
Is like calling a fox a lion.

Wonderful teacher, wonderful refuge,
Wonderful speaker, wonderful protector.
I bow down to the teacher
Who eloquently taught dependently linked origination.

You, the benefactor,
To help living beings,

Spoke out this incomparable proof
For the realization of voidness, the essence of the doctrine.

How can those who see
This system of dependently linked origination
As contradictory or unproved
Understand your teaching?

You, seeing that voidness
Is the import of dependent origination,
Saw that activity is correct and is
Not contradictory with voidness of self-nature.

If one sees the reverse of this,
Then there can be no action in voidness
And no voidness in that which has action;
Thus, one falls into a terrible abyss.

Therefore, highest praise is given
To the vision of dependent origination in your teaching;
There is neither absolute nothingness
Nor existence by self-nature.

Non-dependence is like a flower of the sky;
Therefore, non-dependence does not exist.
If something were to exist by self-nature,[22] that existence
Would contradict dependence on cause and condition.

As, therefore, there does not exist any thing
Other than that which has come forth dependently,
It is said that there does not exist any thing
Other than that which is void of self-nature.

Self-nature is unchangeable.
If things had any self-nature,
Ego-reflection would be unchangeable
And passing from sorrow[23] could not occur.

Therefore, 'free of self-nature'
Was spoken again and again with a lion's roar
Amidst the assembly of the wise.
Who could challenge such speech?

There does not exist a bit of self-nature,
And it is correct that the order of things is
That, dependent on 'this,' 'that' comes forth.
These two aspects are non-contradictory—there is no more
to say.

Thus, by reason of dependent origination
One does not rely on an extreme view.
This good speech by you, the Protector,
Is the reason you are the peerless speaker.

All is empty of self-nature,
And effects come forth dependently;
These two realizations are complementary—
They do not hinder, but assist each other.

What is more beautiful than this?
What is more wonderful than this?
There is no other praise
Than to praise you in this way.

Enslaved by ignorance,
Some challenge you;

It is not surprising that they are impatient
At the sound of no self-nature.

Others, though accepting dependent origination,
The valuable treasure of your speech,
Are impatient at the roar of voidness.
At them I am surprised.

Such people hold self-nature
By the very term
'Peerless dependent origination,'
The door which leads to no self-nature.[24]

By what method can they be led
To that good path that is so pleasing to you,
The unsurpassed entrance
Well traveled by superior āryas?

Self-nature, non-composed, non-dependent,
And dependently linked, composed, dependent;
How can these two come together
In one form, without contradiction?

Therefore, all things that come forth dependently
Are from the first completely free of self-nature;
Yet they appear to have self-nature,
And thus, you said, they are like a magician's illusion.

From this one can well understand
The statement[25] that even those
Who would oppose what you taught
Cannot find any reasonable fault in the teaching.

Why? This explanation
Puts far away the possibility
Of exaggerating or discrediting
Objects seen and not seen.

This path of dependent origination,
Which is the reason your speech is seen as peerless,
Also creates certainty
Of the soundness of your other statements.

Seeing the import of existence, you taught it well.
Learning what you taught,
One gets rid of all troubles
And transmutes the root of ills.

One who is disinclined to your teaching,
Though he wearily perseveres,
Invites one fault after another
By his firm belief in self-grasping.

Most wonderful! When the wise
Understand the difference between these two,[26]
How could they not respect you
From their hearts?

I do not mention many of your teachings,
For even a rough understanding
Of even a portion of what you spoke
Will bestow great bliss.

Alas, my mind is obscured by ignorance.
Though I have long gone for refuge,

I have not found even a portion
Of the great accumulation of your excellence.

Yet, when the flow of life is about to cease,
And I face the lord of death,
I will feel myself fortunate
To have this slight faith in you.

❧

Of teachers, the teacher of dependent origination,
Of wisdom, the wisdom of dependent origination:
In these, like a powerful conqueror in the worldly realms,
You are without peer in your perfect understanding.

All that you have spoken
Initiated from the view of dependent origination
And is for the purpose of passing from sorrow;
You have no actions that do not bring peace.

Wonderful your teaching!
All who listen
Can attain peace;
Who could disrespect upholding your teaching?

Victorious over all opponents,
Free of all internal contradiction,
Fulfilling the two purposes[27] of humankind—
In this system of yours my delight increases.

For this purpose you offered
Your body, your life,
Your precious family, your perfect enjoyments,
Time and time again throughout innumerable eons.

Seeing your excellence
I am like a fish drawn to the hook,
Drawn to that teaching that came from your heart;
What misfortune not to have heard it directly from you.

With the strength of that distress,
Like a mother's mind
Always dwelling on her precious child,
My mind is always with the teaching.

Then, as I contemplate your speech,
You, the teacher, completely surrounded by a net of light
And shining with the glorious marks and signs,[28]
Speak out with the beautiful voice of Sarasvatī.

Contemplating what was thus spoken,
The image of Śākyamuni in my mind,
Though only a reflection,
Helps me as moonlight soothes the torment of heat.

Although this good system
Is so wonderful,
People who are unskilled in it
Vie among themselves like tangling vines.

Having seen this, I myself
Followed after the skillful
With manifold effort,
Seeking again and again the intent of your teaching.

At that time I studied many canons
From my own sect and from the sects of others;
My mind was tormented
Again and again by a web of doubt.

You predicted that the commentator
On the system of the peerless vehicle[29]
Which abandons the extremes of existence and non-existence
Would be Nāgārjuna, whose commentaries are a lotus garden.

Increscent sphere of undefiled knowledge
Traversing unimpeded across the sky of scriptures,
Dispelling the darkness of the heart of extreme views,
Eclipsing the stars of wrong speech—

All is illumined by the rosary of moonbeams
Of good explanation of the Eminent Moon;[30]
When by the kindness of the lama I beheld this,
My weariness was relieved.

Of all actions,
The highest is that of speech;
As this is so, it is from this viewpoint
That the wise should follow Buddha.

Following the Teacher, I became a monk
And my practice of his teaching was not so bad;
I, a bhikṣu making effort in a yogi's deeds,
In this way respect the greatest Sage.

As I met with the doctrine of that peerless teacher
By the kindness of my lama,
I dedicate this virtue that all beings
Might be upheld by a spiritual teacher.

May the teaching of the Benefactor be undisturbed
By the wind of false concepts until saṃsāra's end.
Having understood the nature of the teaching,
May all be filled forever with belief in the Teacher.

May I not for even an instant be remiss
In upholding in all my lives, though it cost my life and body,
This good system of Śākyamuni,
Which illumines dependent origination.

May I spend day and night considering
The way to propagate this achievement,
Accomplished with great effort
And immeasurable hardship by that superior guide.

When I make effort in this system with pure high resolve,
May Brahma, Indra, and the world protectors,
Mahākāla and the other guardians,
Assist me always without fail.

May I and others attain
The Tathāgata's body,
Attendants, life span, and sphere,
As well as his extraordinary signs.

As the Teacher visited this world,
His teaching illumines like rays of the sun.
By brotherly accord between followers of the teaching,
May there be the good fortune that the teaching stays long.

6

The Three Principles of the Path

The second work of Tsongkhapa translated here is a short root text, The Three Principles of the Path. *These three principles are renunciation, bodhi-mind, and right view. The root text, presented first in its entirety, is followed by a commentary containing instructions for meditation written in the early nineteenth century by the Fourth Panchen Lama, Tenpe Nyima.*

This use of root text and commentary is integral to the Tibetan system of transmission of the teaching. Root texts are usually relatively short poems, difficult to understand but easily memorized. Although the author of a root text will sometimes write a commentary on his own text, most commentaries have been written by later scholars. They usually follow the root text line for line or verse for verse, explaining and clarifying the meaning.

This commentary gives comprehensive instructions for meditation, from the six preparatory practices to the final dedication. Following each relevant section, the author has quoted the verses of the root text.

The Three Principles of the Path

I bow down to the venerable lamas.

I will explain as well as I am able
The essence of all the teachings of the Conqueror,
The path praised by the Conqueror's offspring,
The entrance for the fortunate ones who desire liberation.

Listen with clear minds, you fortunate ones
Who direct your minds to the path pleasing to Buddha,
Who strive to make good use of leisure and opportunity
And are not attached to the joys of saṃsāra.

Those with bodies are bound by the craving for existence.
Without pure renunciation, there is no way to still
Attraction to the pleasures of saṃsāra.
Thus, from the outset seek renunciation.

Leisure and opportunity are difficult to find.
There is no time to waste: reverse attraction to this life.
Reverse attraction to future lives: think repeatedly
Of the infallible effects of karma and the misery of this
world.

Contemplating this, when you do not for an instant
Wish the pleasures of saṃsāra,
And day and night remain intent on liberation,
You have then produced renunciation.

Renunciation without pure bodhi-mind
Does not bring forth the perfect bliss
Of unsurpassed enlightenment;
Therefore, bodhisattvas generate excellent bodhi-mind.

Swept by the current of the four powerful rivers,
Tied by strong bonds of karma, so hard to undo,
Caught in the iron net of self-grasping,
Completely enveloped by the darkness of ignorance,

Born and reborn in boundless saṃsāra,
Ceaselessly tormented by the three miseries—

All beings, your mothers, are in this condition.
Think of them and generate bodhi-mind.

Though you practice renunciation and bodhi-mind,
Without wisdom, the realization of voidness,
You cannot cut the root of saṃsāra.
Therefore, strive to understand dependent origination.

One who sees the infallible cause and effect
Of all phenomena in saṃsāra and nirvāṇa
And destroys all false perceptions
Has entered the path that pleases the Buddha.

Appearances are infallible dependent origination;
Voidness is free of assertions.[31]
As long as these two understandings are seen as separate,
One has not yet realized the intent of the Buddha.

When these two realizations are simultaneous and concurrent,
From a mere sight of infallible dependent origination
Comes certain knowledge that completely destroys all
modes of mental grasping.
At that time the analysis of the profound view is complete.

Appearances clear away the extreme of existence;
Voidness clears away the extreme of non-existence.
When you understand the arising of cause and effect from
the viewpoint of voidness,
You are not captivated by either extreme view.

Son, when you realize the keys
Of the three principles of the path,
Depend on solitude and strong effort,
And quickly reach the final goal!

ଓଃଓ

THE THREE PRINCIPLES OF THE PATH: INSTRUCTIONS FOR MEDITATION BY THE FOURTH PANCHEN LAMA

Oṁ svasti. Compassionate, holy, and reverend lamas, I bow down at your feet and go to you for refuge. By your great mercy, may I follow you always.

Herein is the practice of the three guiding principles of the path, the special precepts that the protector Mañjuśrī gave directly to the great Tsongkhapa, King of Dharma of the three realms. These three principles condense the essence of all the teachings and their commentaries into stages of practice for an individual. The instructions for practice have two parts: what should be done in the actual session, and what should be done between sessions. The actual session consists of preparation,[32] subject matter, and dedication.

Clean and dust the room in which you are practicing, and place an image of Buddha or some other religious object before you. Make pure offerings. Sit in meditation posture, and repeat the refuge prayer three times:

> I go for refuge to the lama.
> I go for refuge to the Buddha.
> I go for refuge to the Dharma.
> I go for refuge to the Saṅgha.
>
> To the Buddha, the Dharma, and the Superior Assembly,
> I go for refuge until enlightenment is reached.

As you say this, visualize rays of light and nectar of five different colors streaming from the objects of refuge. This light and nectar are antidotes; they enter the minds and bodies of all living beings and purify defilements, sins, madness, and sickness, as well as their latent tendencies, which have accumulated from beginningless time. Feel that you are under the protection of the Three Jewels (Buddha, Dharma, and Saṇgha). Then generate bodhi-mind by repeating:

> Through whatever merit I have accumulated
> By giving, moral practice, patience, effort, meditation, and wisdom,
> May I attain buddhahood for the sake of all living beings.

And pray:

> By the roots of virtue that come from giving, moral practice, and meditation that I have done, had others do, or rejoiced at others' doing, may I obtain complete perfect buddhahood for the sake of all living beings. I will do this. For this purpose I will learn the deeds of the bodhisattvas. Bless me, lamas and gods, that I may be able to do this.

By strongly requesting this, you please the assembled lamas and deities; a duplicate image separates from each of their bodies, and by dissolving into you, transforms you into the body of lama and Buddha. Rays of light radiate from your body purified into lama and Buddha. This light shines upon all living beings and purifies them. You should have the intense feeling that you are establishing all beings in the high position of lama and Buddha. This is said to be the special precept of the oral lineage of *Wensa* (*dben sa*), the meditation that generates bodhi-mind through actualizing the path and its final goal.

Then, contemplate the four immeasurables—equanimity, love, compassion, and joy:

> All living beings, our aged mothers, are wandering helplessly in saṃsāra. What is the cause of this? They wander in saṃsāra because of desire and hatred, and therefore they are miserable.

> If all beings were in a state of immeasurable equanimity, free from desire and hatred, how wonderful it would be! May they achieve this state. I will establish them in this state of immeasurable equanimity. Lamas and gods, enable me to do this.
>
> If all living beings possessed happiness and the causes of happiness, how wonderful it would be! May they possess them. I will cause them to have happiness and the causes of happiness. Lamas and gods, enable me to do this.
>
> If all living beings were free from misery and the causes of misery, how wonderful it would be! May they be free from these. I will free them from misery and the causes of misery. Lamas and gods, enable me to do this.
>
> If all living beings dwelt continually in the happy lives of humans or gods and in the bliss of liberation, how wonderful it would be! May they never separate from these happy states. I will cause them never to separate from this great happiness. Lamas and gods, help me to do this!

Praying very strongly, imagine a rain of nectar falling on all living beings, purifying their defilements.

To generate bodhi-mind as it is specifically taught here, think, "For the benefit of all living beings, my aged mothers, no matter what happens to me, I will attain as quickly as possible the precious position of a completely perfected buddha. With this aim, I will enter into meditation on the three guiding principles of the path."

Repeat this prayer again and again.

The objects of refuge then dissolve gradually into light, merging inward from the outer limits of the holy assembly. This light dissolves into Tsongkhapa, who is seated in the center. Tsongkhapa then melts into light and dissolves into your forehead between your eyebrows. Feel intensely that you have been blessed by all the objects of refuge.

In order to visualize the field of assembly, clearly imagine in the vast space in front of you the extensive wish-fulfilling jewel tree, its branches laden with leaves, flowers, and fruit. On its top are one hundred thousand lotus petals; upon them, eight magnificent lions hold up a magnificent and resplendent throne. Your own kind root lama, appearing as Tsongkhapa, King of Dharma, is seated on a cushion of sun and moon and lotus. His clear white face is smiling with pleasure. He is wearing the three religious robes and a golden pandit's hat, and his hands, at his heart, form the mudrā of turning the wheel of Dharma.

Each hand holds the stem of a blue lotus. Upon the blossoming blue lotus at his right shoulder, the wisdom of all the buddhas is embodied in the form of a flaming sword. Its light fills the world, and the flame that burns from its tip consumes all ignorance. Upon the blossoming blue lotus at his left shoulder is a volume of the *One Hundred Thousand Verse Prajñāpāramitā Sūtra,* the sole mother of all buddhas of the three times. On its sapphire pages are glowing letters of burnished gold, from which shine rays of light, clearing away the ignorance of living beings. These letters are not just shapes, but speak out in a clear tone the stages, path, and final goal. They proclaim the way of acting for the benefit of all living beings, beginning from the first arising of bodhi-mind to the twenty-seven great deeds of a buddha. Merely by holding this image in mind, you are awakening your inclination to the Mahāyāna path.

Seated in the heart of Tsongkhapa is the conqueror Śākyamuni, and seated in his heart is the conqueror Vajradhara. In each pore of Tsongkhapa's body are countless buddha-fields, and from each of these, innumerable rays of light shine in the ten directions. On the tip of each ray appear an inconceivable number of buddhas, equal to the number of beings in saṃsāra. The actions of each buddha are for the benefit of all living beings.

Tsongkhapa is seated in the middle of a five-colored rainbow in the full lotus position, and upon a ray of light that radiates upwards from his heart are many lamas, beginning with the root lama who actually revealed this teaching to you through the conqueror Vajradhara at the top. Except for the conqueror Vajradhara, all are actually your own root lama, yet they appear in the form of Mañjuśrī, orange in color, whose right hand holds aloft a flashing sword and whose left hand holds at his heart a book that has as its nature radiant light. From Tsongkhapa's heart a ray of light emanates to his right. Upon it are seated, on moon-lotus cushions, the lamas of Maitreya's lineage of the extensive deeds of love and compassion. Upon a ray of light emanating to his left are seated the lamas of Mañjuśrī's lineage of the profound view of voidness. On a ray of light extending directly in front of Tsongkhapa are seated the lamas with whom you have actual dharmic connection.

Surrounding Tsongkhapa, a multitude of yidams, buddhas, bodhisattvas, ḍākinīs, and protectors of the Dharma are seated on lion thrones. On jeweled stands in front of each of them, their own teachings appear as books that have radiant light as their actual nature. On the crown of the head of each in the holy assembly is a white *Oṃ*; on the throat of each is a red *Āḥ*; and at the heart of each a blue *Hūṃ*. From the *Hūṃ*, light radiates in the ten directions. This light invites wisdom beings, like those on whom you have been meditating, to come from their dwelling places. These wisdom beings dissolve into those of the holy assembly. Feel intensely that by this, your lama has the nature of the three refuges—Buddha, Dharma, and Saṅgha.

Then, generating yourself as a deity, make offerings of pure water, fine cloth, and so on to the field of assembly. Having done this, when you meditate on the path, your mind will become clear, and you will be purified of defilements.

Then, offer the seven acts of worship[33] and the *maṇḍala*. These are the keys to accumulation and purification, which increase merit and clear away sins. In this way meditation is furthered and obstructions disappear.

Begin with obeisance. Bow down and recite whatever names you know of the buddhas, bodhisattvas, and lineage lamas. Then say:

I bow down to all spiritual teachers,
Who, moved by compassion and by skillful means, illumine
This best gate for the fortunate traveling to liberation,
This eye through which all the glorious scriptures are seen.

Then continue with the seven acts of worship:

I bow down with pure body, speech, and mind
To those lions among humans,
The tathāgatas of the three times
In the ten directions of the world.

By the power of the enlightenment wish in the deeds of
 Samantabhadra,
I mentally manifest all the buddhas,
And with images of myself as numerous as bits of dust in a
 field,
I humbly bow down to all those conquerors.

Upon each speck of dust sit countless buddhas,
Each surrounded by buddhas and bodhisattvas.
I feel that all spaces
Are filled by buddhas in this way.

Expressing the wisdom of all the buddhas,
By oceans of sound, all the music of speech,
And by inexhaustible oceans of praise,
I glorify all the *sugatas.*

I offer to the buddhas
Fragrant incense, fine butter lamps,

Aromatic balms, ornate umbrellas, and sounds of cymbals,
Beautiful flowers, and precious rosaries.

I offer to these conquerors
Fine silks and rare perfumes
And mounds of fragrant, colored powder equal in size to
    Mount Meru,
In a specially formed arrangement.

By the power of faith in the deeds of Samantabhadra,
I lay before all the conquerors
Extensive and unsurpassable offerings;
I bow down and make offerings to all the buddhas.

Recite this softly and bow down. At this time confess the sins you have committed against each of the three vows,[34] and, bowing down as many times as possible, recite this prayer from *Confessions of Sins:*

> I bow down to the thirty-five buddhas of confession. May they and all the tathāgatas, arhats, and fully accomplished buddhas, who are enjoying well-being in all the realms of the ten directions of the world, show compassion to me.
>
> I confess without withholding or concealing all sins great or small that I committed myself, had others commit for me, or welcomed others doing, in all births in endless saṃsāra—in this life, in former lives, and in lives to come. I confess these before the blessed buddhas—those who have wisdom, the all-seeing eye, power, valid insight, omniscience, and understanding. Henceforth, I will be bound by this confession.
>
> I dedicate toward the perfect enlightenment of all beings all virtuous deeds great or small that I have done or will do

in all births in endless saṃsāra—in this life, in former lives, and in lives yet to come. As the blessed buddhas who came previously, as those who have not yet come, and as those abiding in the present completely dedicate their virtuous work, so I completely dedicate mine.

Continuing with the seven acts of worship:

I confess individually
All the sins I have done
With body, speech, or mind
Because of desire, hatred, and ignorance.

I rejoice at and will follow
All virtuous deeds done by any living being,
By the buddhas of the ten directions, by bodhisattvas,
By pratyekabuddhas, by those still learning, and by those
with no more to learn.

I request those lights of the ten directions,
All those who, through the stages leading to enlightenment,
Have gained a buddha's freedom from attachment,
To turn the peerless wheel of Dharma.

I pray with folded palms
To all those desiring to enter parinirvāṇa
To remain with us for innumerable eons
And bring happiness and benefit to all living beings.

I dedicate to the perfect enlightenment of all
Even the smallest virtue accumulated
By this obeisance, offering, confession,
Rejoicing, entreaty, and prayer.

Imagine the field of assembly before you, and repeat this softly. Then offer the following maṇḍala:

> Golden land, filled with incense and strewn with flowers, Mount Meru and the four continents ornamented by sun and moon—imagining all this as a buddha-field, I offer it. May all living beings find enjoyment in this pure land.
>
> Imagining myself as a world ruler, I offer all virtues of the three times, all enjoyments of body, speech, and mind of myself and others, and the precious and glorious maṇḍala like that offered by Samantabhadra, to the lama, yidam, and the Three Jewels. By the power of their great compassion, may they accept this and bestow on me their blessings.
>
> *Idaṁ Guru Ratna Maṇḍalakaṃ Niryatāyami*

Saying this, offer the maṇḍala. Then recite this prayer of the three great purposes, which was taught by Tsongkhapa himself:

> May I put an end to all mistaken states of mind, from not respecting the spiritual teacher to apprehending an ego in persons or phenomena.
>
> May I easily produce all right states of mind, from respecting the spiritual teacher to apprehending the truth of egolessness.
>
> May I surmount all inner and outer obstacles.

Recite this three times. Then recite the following prayer to the lamas of this lineage:

> I pray to the conqueror Vajradhara, protector of saṃsāra
> and nirvāṇa,
> Who does not abide in the extremes of either.

By his wisdom he has cut the bonds of saṃsāra;
By his compassion he has thrust aside the joy of nirvāṇa.

I pray to the protector Mañjuśrī,
Whose wisdom-body encompasses
All the treasure of wisdom of buddhas
More numerous than particles in a miraculous buddha-field.

I pray to the feet of Pawo Dorje
Who, after years of deep wishing-prayer,
Cleared away his web of doubt
When Mañjuśrī appeared to him.

I pray to the feet of the glorious lama Tsongkhapa,
Who understood by reasoning the reality of the two truths
And, by the power of unified method and wisdom,
Manifested the three kāyas of a buddha.

I pray to the feet of the sage of Jambudvīpa,
To Gendun Drup, lion of the excellent path.
With resplendent mane of one hundred thousand teachings,
He dwells in the garden of the scriptures of Buddha.

Bless me always and without effort
To generate faith by merely remembering
The kind lamas, who are the root of all excellence,
Of all worldly and spiritual well-being.

May I attain the pure mind that unquestioningly
Depends on the spiritual friend, who strives for awareness,
Who speaks honestly, who desires liberation from his heart,
And who, having subdued himself, lives peacefully with few
desires.

May I achieve non-attachment,
Turning my mind completely from honor and gain,
Thinking, "The time is short," for it is not mere words
That death is certain but its hour unknown.

May I naturally produce compassion,
Turning from pursuit of selfish joy
To contemplate the pain of all wretched beings,
Each of them my own kind mother.

May I understand the thought of those holy men,
Nāgārjuna and Āryadeva, father and son,
Who expounded the meaning of profound dependent
  origination,
The only medicine for the illness of the two extremes.

Having set forth this prayer, may all roots of virtue
Past, present, and future, of myself and others
In birth after birth
Cause only supreme enlightenment.

May they not ripen for even an instant
As those things not conducive to enlightenment:
As desire for fame or advantage,
For companions, enjoyments, honor, or gain.

By the blessings of the conquerors and their wondrous offspring,
By the truth of infallible dependent origination,
And by the power of my strong high resolve,
May I accomplish the objective of this wishing-prayer.

Pray strongly that you may quickly realize the three principles of the path.

❧

There are two parts to the subject matter of the teaching. The first is to increase understanding of the path and to resolve to meditate on it; the second is the actual way to meditate.

Continuing to visualize the assembly of lamas and deities in front of you, contemplate as follows:

> Faith in the lama is the foundation of all excellence. It is the fundamental root of all present and future good and the basis of the common and superior siddhis. Reliance on a holy spiritual teacher is the way to produce, maintain, increase, and accomplish all the stages and paths. Therefore, in the beginning learn to rely on the spiritual teacher, for this is the root of the path.

Rely on the spiritual teacher in thought and deed. To rely on the spiritual teacher in thought, clearly visualize in the space in front of you those who have shown you the teaching, and think:

> These spiritual teachers of mine are actually buddhas, for the completely perfect Buddha proclaimed in the tantras that in this degenerate age the conqueror Vajradhara would appear in the form of the spiritual teacher and act for the benefit of all living beings. Thus, my spiritual teachers are all the conqueror Vajradhara manifesting himself in different embodiments. He appears as the spiritual teacher in order to guide those who did not have the good fortune to see and hear Śākyamuni Buddha.
>
> Not only are my kind root lamas actually buddhas, but their kindness surpasses that of all the buddhas; for the buddhas and bodhisattvas who came previously left me behind, unable to subdue me. My kind root lama, unable to bear

> this, because of his compassion took up the deeds of the Conqueror; even those buddhas who came previously did not express any teachings that were more profound.
>
> In order to obtain a single verse of the Dharma, it was necessary for the teacher Śākyamuni to undergo inconceivable hardships. At one time he put one thousand iron nails into his body, and at another time he used his body to burn a thousand lamps. He gave up all enjoyments without regret: his son, his queen, his body, whatever he had. By the kindness of my root lama, I need not undergo such hardships. If I am able to meditate on the Mahāyāna, which is complete and without error, these profound precepts are able to bestow quickly upon me rebirth as a human or god, liberation, and full enlightenment. My lama has taught me these precepts as freely as a father instructs his son. I can never repay his kindness.

Meditate in this way until tears pour forth from your eyes and the hairs of your body stand on end.

Also, rely on the spiritual teacher in your deeds: learn the three ways to please him. Bring him offerings, respect him in body and speech, and do as he instructs. As the last is the most important, firmly resolve, "In order to do as my lama has taught, I will practice the three principles of the path in which are included the meanings of all the scriptures and commentaries."

How can the meaning of all the scriptures and commentaries be included within the three principles of the path? The main concern of all the scriptures and commentaries is to free disciples from saṃsāra and establish them in buddhahood. To obtain buddhahood, it is necessary to learn method and wisdom. The guiding principle of method is bodhi-mind, and the guiding principle of wisdom is right view. To produce bodhi-mind and right view, you must renounce saṃsāra, for if you do not desire to liberate yourself from saṃsāra, you cannot produce the love, compassion, and bodhi-mind that desire to liberate other living beings.

The guiding principle of method, by which the rūpakāya is attained, is accumulation of merit. The key, root, and essence of all accumulation of merit is bodhi-mind. The guiding principle that is the cause of attaining the dharmakāya, the mind of Buddha, is accumulation of wisdom. The key, root, and essence of all accumulation of wisdom is right view. Thus, all the keys of the path are included within renunciation, bodhi-mind, and right view. This is the teaching that the protector Mañjuśrī delivered with great care to the renowned Tsongkhapa, King of Dharma.

As the foundation of all merit is reliance on the spiritual teacher, you must experience this from the first. The root text states:

I bow down to the venerable lamas.

This line indicates all the practices of preparation that have been previously outlined. Think: "Before I meditate on the path, I will first produce some understanding of its entirety and then meditate systematically on its levels and categories." One should firmly resolve to keep to this meditation.

As the root text states:

I will explain as well as I am able
The essence of all the teachings of the Conqueror,
The path praised by the Conqueror's offspring,
The entrance for the fortunate ones who desire liberation.

Listen with clear mind, you fortunate ones
Who direct your minds to the path pleasing to Buddha,

Who strive to make good use of leisure and opportunity
And are not attached to the joys of saṃsāra.

✣

There are three parts to the actual way of meditation. These are the meditation of renunciation, the meditation of bodhi-mind, and the meditation of right view.

The meditation of renunciation reverses the attraction to this and future lives. Concerning this life, the root text states:

Leisure and opportunity are difficult to find.
There is no time to waste: reverse attraction to this life.

Contemplate the importance and difficulty of obtaining leisure and opportunity, the uncertainty of the time of death, and the misery of the lower states of being.

Continue to visualize the lamas and deities in front of you, and contemplate the importance of leisure and opportunity. Think:

> To have leisure is to have the time to practice the holy Dharma; to have opportunity is to have all the favorable conditions for practicing the Dharma. Thus, this life of leisure and opportunity is to have all the favorable conditions for practicing the Dharma. Therefore, this life of leisure and opportunity is very important. Relying on it, I can achieve giving, moral practice, patience, and so forth, which will cause my future happy rebirth as a human or god. In particular, by the three vows, I can quickly obtain perfect buddhahood in one short lifetime, even in this degenerate age. Therefore, having obtained this life of leisure and opportunity, which is so important and so difficult to find, I will utilize its essence without wasting it senselessly. Lamas and gods, enable me to do this.

Continue to visualize the assembly of lamas and deities before you, and contemplate the difficulty of obtaining leisure and opportunity.

> Most humans and other living beings are usually involved in the ten non-virtuous activities, which are obstacles to obtaining leisure and opportunity. Very few accomplish those things that are necessary to obtain a lifetime of leisure and opportunity. Those are: to lay a foundation of moral practice, to assist it with the practice of giving and the other transcendences, and to dedicate it with stainless prayer.
>
> For lower beings—animals and such—even to obtain rebirth in the happy states of humans or gods seems almost impossible. Even among beings who have been reborn in those happy states, to have obtained leisure and opportunity is as rare as a star in the daytime. Therefore, as I have obtained such a life, which is so difficult to come by, I will make good use of it without wasting it senselessly. I will rely continually on the lama and Buddha, and practicing the essence of the Mahāyāna teachings as taught by him, I will obtain perfect buddhahood in a single lifetime. Lamas and gods, enable me to do this.

Concerning future lives, the root text says:

Reverse attraction to future lives: think repeatedly
Of the infallible effects of karma and the misery of this world.

First consider the infallible effects of karma, and then consider the miseries of saṃsāra. Continuing to visualize the assembly of lamas and deities, contemplate as follows:

> Buddha has said, "Virtuous actions as causes give rise only to happy effects; they do not give rise to misery. Non-virtuous

activities as causes give rise only to misery; they do not give rise to happiness. Furthermore, even very small virtuous or sinful deeds give rise to extremely great happiness or misery. Without virtuous or sinful deeds as causes, there will be no experience of happiness or misery. If virtuous or sinful actions as causes meet no obstruction, happiness or misery will certainly come forth, as the force of actions done will not have been exhausted."

Thus, I will have firm faith and confidence in the teaching that actions done have great force depending on their field, motivation, substance, and context.[35] I will learn to accept what is good and reject what is not; I will avoid defiling the three doors of body, speech, and mind even slightly by the ten non-virtues, and will strive to the utmost to achieve the ten virtues. Lamas and gods, enable me to do this.

Then consider the general misery of saṃsāra. Continuing to visualize the assembly of lamas and deities before you, contemplate as follows:

Once I have taken rebirth in saṃsāra by the influence of karma and fettering passions, I will not be free of suffering. As friends become enemies and enemies become friends, I cannot be sure whether someone will help or harm me. No matter how much I indulge in the joys of saṃsāra, I am never satisfied. Instead my attachment increases and brings unbearable misery. No matter how fine my body, I must give it up; this happens again and again, for we are enveloped in the womb over and over with no apparent limit to our births. As, in the end, I must certainly give up whatever good things of saṃsāra I have obtained, there is no security in obtaining anything. There is no security in companions, for I must go alone from this life to the next. Having obtained this life of leisure and opportunity, I will achieve, no matter what occurs, the excellent position of lama and Buddha, who have abandoned the misery of saṃsāra. Lamas and gods, enable me to do this.

Now consider the particular miseries of saṃsāra. Continue to visualize the assembly of lamas and deities and contemplate as follows:

Once I have taken compulsive embodiment,[36] I will not be free from misery. What need even to mention the three lower states? If I take embodiment as a human, I face the misery of hot and cold, hunger and thirst; of separation from friends and contact with enemies; of seeking but not finding the things I desire; and having what I do not desire descend upon me; and I face the miseries of birth, old age, sickness, and death.

If I take embodiment as a demigod, I will be unable to bear the glorious prosperity of the gods. I will feel the torment of jealousy, and as I war with them, physical misery will descend upon me.

If I take embodiment as a god of the desire realm, I will fight with the demigods and experience the misery of dismemberment, killing, and being killed. Also, when struck by the five portents of death,[37] I will experience the misery of knowing that I must lose this prosperity and return to lower states of being.

Even if I take embodiment as a god of the higher realms of form and formlessness, I will not have the power to remain there once the impetus of good karma is exhausted, and I will experience the misery of falling into a lower state of being.

In short, taking compulsive embodiment is the framework for birth, old age, sickness, and death in this life, and for the misery of misery and the misery of change in both this and future lives. Merely by taking compulsive embodiment through the influence of former actions and fettering passions, I find myself in a state of conditioned embodiment.[38] Therefore, no matter what occurs, I will obtain the high position of my lama and the buddhas, who have freed themselves from the misery of saṃsāra and compulsive embodiment. Lamas and gods, enable me to do this.

When you no longer desire the enjoyments of saṃsāra and are nauseated by them as a prisoner is nauseated by his prison, you will produce a strong and ceaseless longing for liberation. This is the indication that you have attained the mind of renunciation. The root text says:

When you do not for an instant
Wish the pleasures of saṃsāra,
And day and night remain intent on liberation,
You have then produced renunciation.

Renunciation without pure bodhi-mind
Does not bring forth the perfect bliss
Of unsurpassed enlightenment;
Therefore bodhisattvas generate excellent bodhi-mind.

❦

To generate bodhi-mind, you must first achieve equanimity toward all living beings and then meditate on the seven causal precepts. Begin by picturing in front of you a living being who has neither helped nor harmed you. Think:

> From his own point of view, he desires happiness and does not desire misery. Therefore, I will be free from attachment and aversion; I will not feel close to some and help them while feeling distant from others and harming them. I will learn to have equanimity toward all living beings. Lamas and gods, enable me to do this.

When you feel equanimity toward that person, picture a living being who is attractive to you. Try to feel equanimity toward that person. Think: "My partiality is due to the influence of attachment. It is because I have previously desired attractive beings that I have again been born in saṃsāra." Control your desire and meditate.

When you feel equanimity toward that attractive person, picture a living being who is unattractive to you. Try to feel equanimity toward that person. Think: "Because there has been discord between us, I have generated aversion to him and so lack equanimity." Thinking that without equanimity there is no way to generate bodhi-mind, control your aversion and meditate.

When you feel equanimity toward that unattractive person, picture both a being who is very attractive to you and a being who is very unattractive to you. Think:

> These two are the same in that each from his own viewpoint desires happiness and does not desire misery. From my viewpoint, even this one to whom I now feel close has been my enemy countless times. This one toward whom I now feel hostility has been my mother countless times and has protected me with mercy. Which one should I desire? Which one should I hate? I will have equanimity and be free from attachment and aversion. Lamas and gods, enable me to do this.

When you feel this equanimity, extend it to all living beings.

> All living beings are the same, in that each from his own viewpoint desires happiness and does not desire misery. From my viewpoint, all living beings are my relatives. Therefore, I will learn to have equanimity and be free from attachment and aversion; I will not feel close to some and help them while feeling distant from others and harming them. Lamas and gods, enable me to do this.

❧

Once you have developed the mind of equanimity, begin the first of the seven causal precepts for generating bodhi-mind. Continue to visualize the lamas and deities in front of you, and contemplate as follows:

> Why are all living beings my relatives? As there is no beginning to saṃsāra, there is also no beginning to my births. In passing through these lives, there is no form of living being that I have not taken countless times, and there is no country or region where I have not been born. Of all beings, there is no one who has not been my mother innumerable times. Each has been my mother in human form countless times and will become my mother again.

❧

When you have fully experienced this truth, contemplate the kindness extended to you by living beings when they were your mother. Continue to visualize the lamas and deities in front of you and picture the clear form of your mother, both when she was young and when she was old.

> Not only is she my mother in this life, but she has cared for me in lives beyond number. Specifically, in this lifetime, she mercifully protected me in the womb, and when I was born, she put me on soft pillows and cradled me in her

> arms. She held me to the warmth of her breast. She welcomed me with compassionate smiles and looked at me with happy eyes. She cleaned my snotty nose and wiped away my excrement. Even my slightest ailment gave her greater misery than the thought of losing her own life. Scorning all affliction, torments, and abuse, not considering herself at all, she provided me as well as she could with food and shelter. She gave me infinite happiness and benefits and protected me from measureless misery and harm.

Contemplate her very great kindness , and then, in the same way, contemplate the kindness of your father and others close to you, for they have also been your mother countless times.

⁂

When you have fully experienced this truth, meditate on living beings toward whom you feel impartial. "Though it now seems that they have no relation to me, they have been my mother times beyond number, and in those lives they protected me with kindness."

When you have experienced this truth, meditate on those living beings who are now your adversaries. Picture them clearly in front of you, and think:

> How can I now feel that these are my enemies? As lifetimes are beyond number, each has been my mother innumerable times. At the times when they were my mother, they provided me with immeasurable happiness and benefits and protected me from misery and harm. Without them I could not have lasted even a short time, and without me they could not have endured even a short time. We have felt this strong attachment times without number. That they are now my adversaries is due to bad karma; at another time they will be my mother who protects me with kindness.

When you have fully experienced this truth, meditate on the kindness of all living beings.

Then meditate on repaying the kindness of all living beings, your mothers. Continuing to visualize the lamas and deities in front of you, contemplate as follows:

> From beginningless time these mothers have protected me with kindness. Yet as their minds are churned by the demons of fettering passions, they have not obtained independence of mind, and are crazed. They lack the eye to see either the path to the high states of humans and gods or the path to nirvāṇa, the assuredly good. They are without a spiritual teacher, one who can lead the blind. Continually pummeled by the discord of wrong acts, they slip toward the edge of the terrifying abyss of rebirth in saṃsāra, especially its lower states. To ignore these kind mothers would be shameful. In order to return their kindness, I will free them from the misery of saṃsāra and establish them in the bliss of liberation. Lamas and gods, enable me to do this.

Then, cultivate love. Picture a person to whom you are strongly attached, such as your mother.

> How can she have undefiled happiness when she does not even have the defiled happiness of saṃsāra? What she now boasts of as happiness slips away, changing to misery. She yearns and yearns, strives and strives, desiring a moment's happiness, but she is only creating causes of future misery and birth in lower states of being. In this life as well, weary and exhausted, she creates only misery. She definitely does

> not have real happiness. How wonderful it would be if she possessed happiness and all the causes of happiness! May she possess them. I will cause her to possess happiness and all its causes. Lamas and gods, enable me to do this.

When you have gained experience of this, continue to meditate, first picturing other persons who are close to you, such as your father, then picturing a person toward whom you feel impartial, then an adversary, and finally all living beings.

❧

Then cultivate great compassion and high resolve:

> My kind fathers and mothers, whose number would fill the sky, are helplessly bound by karma and fettering passions. The four rivers—of desire, existence, ignorance, and dogmatism—sweep them helplessly into the currents of saṃsāra, where they are battered by the waves of birth, old age, sickness, and death. They are completely tied up by the tight and difficult-to-remove bonds of various kinds of karma. From beginningless time, they have entered into the iron trap of holding the concepts "I" and "mine" in the center of the heart. This trap is very difficult for anyone to open. Enshrouded by the great darkness of ignorance, which obscures judgment of good and bad, they do not even see the path leading to the happy states of being. Much less do they see the path leading to liberation and enlightenment.
>
> These wretched beings are ceaselessly tortured by the misery of misery, the misery of change, and the pervasive misery of conditioned activities. I have seen all beings, my mothers, wretched, engulfed in the ocean of saṃsāra. If I do not save them, who will? If I were to ignore them, I

> would be shameless, the lowest of all. My desire to learn the Mahāyāna would be only words, and I could not show my face before the buddhas and bodhisattvas. Therefore, no matter what, I will develop the ability to pull all my kind, wretched mothers from the ocean of saṃsāra and to establish them in buddhahood.

Think this, and generate a very strong and pure high resolve.

❧

Finally, cultivate bodhi-mind. Ask yourself whether or not you can establish all living beings in buddhahood, and reflect:

> I do not know where I am going; how can I establish even one living being in perfect buddhahood? Even those who have attained the positions of śrāvaka or pratyekabuddha can accomplish only the minor purposes of living beings and cannot establish beings in buddhahood. It is only the perfect Buddha who can lead beings to full enlightenment. Therefore, no matter what, I will obtain peerless and completely perfect buddhahood for the sake of all beings. Lamas and gods, enable me to do this.

❧

Once you have produced bodhi-mind, there are limitless ways to practice the activities of the bodhisattvas. In brief, be motivated entirely by bodhi-mind, and with pure and exact reasoning, generate deep realization of the nature of the two truths. Then develop in your mind each of the six transcendences: giving, moral practice, patience, effort, meditation, and wisdom. When you have gained experience of them and thus increased your strength of mind, practice all six transcendences within each transcendence (i.e., the giving of giving, the moral practice of giving, the patience of giving, the effort of giving, the meditation of giving, the wisdom of giving, and so forth). In this way all the meanings of the Mahāyāna sutras and commentaries are included in the six transcendences. The deeds of the bodhisattvas are not other than these.

Bodhisattvas must first learn to subdue their own nature by practicing the six transcendences. Then in order to benefit others, they practice the four ways of assembling. Thus, these four are taught separately from the six transcendences. These four are: giving gifts to the disciple, kind speech, acting for the benefit of the disciple, and behaving in accord with one's own teaching. However, these four are at the same time included among the six transcendences. Giving gifts is included in the transcendence of giving. Kind speech is included within the giving of Dharma. Activities for the benefit of the disciple and oneself acting according to one's teachings are included within the moral practice of working for the benefit of living beings.

Thus, decide: "In order to quickly obtain perfect buddhahood for the sake of all living beings, I will practice the precepts of bodhi-mind, having generated the mind that *wishes* for enlightenment in order to free all living beings from saṃsāra and establish them in buddhahood." Then, generating the mind that actually *enters* this path: "I will practice the deeds of the bodhisattvas, these six transcendences, and the four ways of assembling. Lamas and gods, enable me to do this."

❧

During the actual session, develop bodhi-mind and its precepts as much as possible. Between sessions, having learned to conjoin all activities of the three doors—body, speech, and mind—with bodhi-mind, clearly reflect love, compassion, and bodhi-mind in all that you do. If all activities are conjoined with bodhi-mind, even if it is only a contrived bodhi-mind, whatever you do will become the means of perfecting the accumulation of merit and wisdom.

In former times, King Prasenajit asked Buddha: "I desire to be able to practice the Mahāyāna without neglecting the administration of my kingdom. However, as I have many duties, I am not able single-mindedly to practice virtue. What should I do?"

Buddha answered, "As kings have many duties and are not always able single-mindedly to practice virtue, generate bodhi-mind in all that you do. If you carry out your duties motivated entirely by bodhi-mind, not only will your royal duties not fail, but whatever you do will be the means of attaining buddhahood."[39]

When physical illness and mental anguish arise, cultivate taking and giving. Think: "May the physical illness and mental anguish of all living beings, whose number would fill the sky, be added to my own suffering."

When joy and fortune arise, meditate on giving and taking. Think: "I give this joy and fortune of mine to all living beings."

At the time of eating, generate bodhi-mind. Think: "I eat this food to sustain my body for the sake of all living beings. Inside my body there are eighty-four thousand organisms. I assemble them now by the gift of food; in the future I will assemble them by the gift of Dharma. Not succumbing to purposeless eating and drinking, I will conjoin whatever I do with bodhi-mind."

At the time of sleeping, think: "I sustain this body of mine for the sake of all living beings. Whatever things inside my body are replenished by sleep, by sleep I will replenish and sustain." Go to sleep in that hopeful state of bodhi-mind.

At the time of cleaning your room, generate bodhi-mind, thinking: "I clean away the dust of karma and fettering passions of all living beings."

At the time of bathing or washing your hands, generate bodhi-mind, thinking: "I wash away the defilements of the fettering passions of all living beings."

When opening a door, generate bodhi-mind, thinking: "I open

the door of liberation for all living beings, taking them from lower states of being and leading them to buddhahood."

When offering light to an object of worship, generate bodhi-mind, thinking: "I will clear the darkness of ignorance from all living beings throughout all space."

From these examples learn to conjoin whatever you do, all activities of body, speech, and mind, with bodhi-mind. Read in detail the Mahāyāna sutras and learn from the speech of the lineage lamas, for the precepts of bodhi-mind are boundless, limitless, and vast as space.

The root text says about cultivating bodhi-mind:

Renunciation without pure bodhi-mind
Does not bring forth the perfect bliss
Of unsurpassed enlightenment;
Therefore, bodhisattvas generate excellent bodhi-mind.

Swept by the current of the four powerful rivers,
Tied by strong bonds of karma, so hard to undo,
Caught in the iron net of self-grasping,
Completely enveloped by the darkness of ignorance,

Born and reborn in boundless saṃsāra,
Ceaselessly tormented by the three miseries—
All beings, your mothers, are in this condition.
Think of them and generate bodhi-mind.

This is the way of practice, as it has descended from the precepts of the oral lineage.

❧

The cultivation of right view includes the ways to become convinced of the egolessness of persons and of the egolessness of phenomena. To do this, one should analyze the ego by means of the four keys, for it is said in the scriptures, "There are countless methods of reasoning by which one can become convinced of egolessness. Yet, if one uses the four keys for beginners, understanding arises easily."

Concerning the egolessness of persons, consider the following: even in a deep sleep we hold the feeling "I" in our hearts. This feeling is innate self-grasping. When someone accuses you, "You did such and such," and actually you did not do it, you think, "He accuses me falsely. I didn't do anything." At that time, the thought "I" arises very strongly. This is clearly innate self-grasping holding "I" as its object. At that time, you should analyze with a subtle portion of your mind what that object "I" is and in what way it is held.

At the time of analyzing innate self-grasping, if the analyzing mind becomes very forceful, the ego-holding mind vanishes, leaving nothing to be analyzed. When this occurs, bring forth the submerged mind that clings to "I" and again analyze it with the subtle portion of your mind.

Once you have identified innate self-grasping, you can begin with the first of the four keys. This is the key recognizing how we perceive the object to be negated, the "I" held as the object of innate self-grasping. We feel that there exists an indivisible "I" that, from the beginning, is changeless and independent, and is not merely a designation imputed on the five aggregates taken as a whole or the mind and body taken as a whole.[40] We do not feel that this "I" exists completely apart from the five aggregates, the mind and body. Nor do we feel that it exists just in the mind or just in the body or just in any one of the five aggregates alone.

The "I" that is held in this way by innate self-grasping is the object to be negated. Recognize this nakedly within yourself, not just as general words or from the understanding of others.

The second key is to realize the extent of the logical possibilities. If we feel that there is an "I" that exists in connection with the five aggregates, it must be either the same as or different from those five aggregates. It must exist in one of these two ways. Decide definitely that this is so, that there is no third way for it to exist. The last two keys are the application of this logic.

The third key is to recognize that there can be no truly existent sameness. Suppose you feel that the "I" is the same as the five aggregates. A person made up of five aggregates is felt to have one "I." If that indivisible "I" and the five different aggregates truly were the same, then there would have to be either five different "I"s or only one indivisible aggregate. As both of these possibilities are clearly absurd, understand that the "I" is not the same as the five aggregates.

The fourth key is to recognize the lack of truly existent diversity. Since the "I" is not the same as the five aggregates, suppose that it is different from them. If this were the case, just as you are able to indirectly identify the fifth aggregate after separating out the other four, you should be able to identify, "This is the 'I,'" after separating out each of the aggregates. However, you can not do this. Therefore, understand that an "I" that is different from the five aggregates does not exist.

Through this analysis by means of the four keys, realize that the "I" conceived by innate self-grasping to be an independent entity is completely non-existent. Sustain this realization in one-pointed meditation that is free from listlessness and excitement. Should your understanding diminish, repeat the analysis of the four keys as before and renew your realization. Those of sharp intellect can come to the same realization by directly analyzing whether or not the "I" exists as it appears.

At the time of determining the lack of true existence of the "I," there are two perspectives to your understanding. From the perspective of realization, there is a deep understanding of the lack of true existence of anything; from the perspective of perception, there is clear emptiness that is merely the absence of a truly existent "I," the object of negation. When you sustain these two aspects in one-pointed meditation, you are practicing contemplative equipoise like space; following this, in the after-attainment, meditate that the ego, as well as all other phenomena, are merely diverting forms. Then, in subsequent meditation of contemplative equipoise like space, increasingly strong realization of the lack of true existence is drawn forth. Depending on that, in after-attainment, learn to view whatever you see as not truly existent, even though it appears to be so. View everything as false, as diverting forms that are like a magician's illusions.

❧

Meditation on the egolessness of phenomena consists of two parts. One must become convinced that both non-compounded and compounded things have no true existence. Take your body as an example of a compounded thing. We feel sure that our body exists independently and is not merely an imputed designation. This "body" is the object to be negated by meditation, for the body is nothing more than a conglomerate of five limbs made up of bones, flesh, and fluid.[41]

The argument used to negate the truly existent body is the same as that used to negate the truly existent "I." The body that is felt to be a truly existent entity must be either the same as or different from the combination of five limbs made up of bones, flesh, and fluid. Consider that it is the same: a body develops from the semen of the father and the ovum of the mother, which, coming together, provide a basis for the entrance of consciousness. If the truly existent body really were the same as the combination of five limbs, then, since a truly existent body is unchanging, that drop of semen and ovum would have to be, from the moment of conception, a combination of five limbs. This is clearly absurd.

Consider that the truly existent body is different from the combined five limbs. If this were the case, you should be able to show, "This is the 'body,'" after separating out each of the five limbs. You cannot.

Thus, as the truly existent body is neither the same as nor different from your combined five limbs, draw forth and sustain the definite realization that such a truly existent body does not exist at all.

The second aspect of the meditation on the egolessness of

phenomena is to become convinced that non-compounded things have no true existence. Take as an example the sky. As the sky has many different directions, analyze whether the sky is the same as or different from those directions. Draw forth and sustain the definite realization that there is no true existence. Meditate as before.

Single-mindedly sustain the definite realization that not even an atom of all the phenomena of saṃsāra and nirvāṇa—the ego, the aggregates, mountains, houses, tents, and so forth—exists in and of itself. Know that all are merely imputed designations. This is the yoga of contemplative equipoise like space. Following this, in the after-attainment, realize that all objects of perception are by nature false, not truly existent, as they arise in dependence upon cause and circumstance. This is the yoga of illusoriness. When, depending on these two yogas, contemplative equipoise is joined by the bliss of well-practiced mind and body, which is drawn out by the power of analysis, one obtains actual intense insight.

Concerning the meditation of right view, the root text says:

One who sees the infallible cause and effect
Of all phenomena in saṃsāra and nirvāṇa
And destroys all false perceptions
Has entered the path that pleases the Buddha.

Appearances are infallible dependent origination;
Voidness is free of assertions.
As long and these two understandings are seen as separate,
One has not yet realized the intent of Buddha.

When these two realizations are simultaneous and concurrent,
From a mere sight of infallible dependent origination
Comes certain knowledge that completely destroys all modes of mental grasping.
At that time the analysis of the profound view is complete.

Appearances clear away the extreme of existence;
Voidness clears away the extreme of non-existence.
When you understand the arising of cause and effect from the viewpoint of voidness,
You are not captivated by either extreme view.

The last part of the actual session is the dedication of merit. Having gained experience of the three principles of the path through focusing meditation and analytical meditation, you should conclude the session by saying: "I bow down, worship, and go for refuge to the feet of the lama, who is indistinguishable from Mañjuśrī." As you make this strong prayer to the assembly of lamas and deities, repeating it many times, the entire field of assembly gradually dissolves into light, merging from the outer limits of the field into Tsongkhapa and Mañjuśrī, who are seated in the center of the holy assembly. As Tsongkhapa, together with Mañjuśrī, dissolve into you, the individual meditator, all impurities and ailments of body and all defilements and sins of mind are purified, and you yourself are transformed into Mañjuśrī. Rays of light emanate from your body. They strike all living beings throughout space and establish them in the high state of Mañjuśrī. The vessel of existence that surrounds you is also purified; feel intensely that it has become a crystal palace of the gods. To the extent of your ability, meditate that all animate beings and inanimate objects are perfectly purified. Then establish a catena of mantras in your heart and in the hearts of all living beings. Repeat as much as possible, *Oṃ āḥ ra pa tza na dhi.* (The last time you repeat it, say, "*Dhi, dhi, dhi, dhi, dhi, dhi, dhi, dhi, dhi...*" at the end of the mantra until you run out of breath.)

To dedicate the merit, say:

By the virtue done here,
May I quickly become Mañjuśrī

And establish all beings, without exception,
In his high state.

I dedicate the pure white virtue I have accomplished
That I might uphold the Dharma of instruction and
 understanding
And accomplish all the wishing-prayers and deeds
Of the buddhas and bodhisattvas of the three times.

By the power of this virtue,
May I in all lives not part from the four wheels of the
 Mahāyāna.[42]

May I complete the paths of renunciation, bodhi-mind,
 and right view,
And the two stages of the Vajrayāna.

I will follow my lama as a son follows his father, striving to accomplish the essence of the three principles of the path, the keys that include the essence of all Buddha's teaching.

❧

The root text says:

Son, when you realize the keys
Of the three principles of the path,
Depend on solitude and strong effort
And quickly reach the final goal!

Tsongkhapa with great mercy gave this teaching to us, his followers.

❧

When your mind has become well practiced in the general path of the Mahāyāna, enter the path of the Vajrayāna, the unsurpassed path by which buddhahood is attained not in three immeasurable eons, but in one short lifetime of the degenerate age. When you have pleased a qualified Vajrayāna teacher in the necessary three ways, your nature will be ripened by initiation.

Guard more dearly than your life the vows and obligations taken at this time. Seek the key realizations of the two stages of the Vajrayāna, for their deep meanings are the essence of the ocean of tantras. When you have found unmistakable realization of these, make effort in the yoga of four sessions. There is no practice greater than learning the path of both sutra and tantra in its entirety. This is the final key to the precepts that manifest the quintessence of the heart and mind of Tsongkhapa. Tsongkhapa himself said in *The Concise Meaning of the Stages of the Path:*

> Having produced the general path needed for the two
> Mahāyāna paths,
> Both Sūtrayāna—cause—and Mantrayāna—effect—
> Depend on a protector, a skillful pilot,
> And enter the great ocean of tantras.
>
> Then, through reliance on the complete and perfect
> precepts,
> Make good use of this lifetime of leisure and opportunity.
> I, a yogi, practiced like this;
> You who desire liberation, please do likewise.

Experience in yourself all these things, from relying on the holy spiritual teacher in thought and deed through all the forms of practice up to learning the two stages of the profound path. Each day practice in four sessions, or at least in one. If you do this, you will have used well this life with its opportunity and leisure, and you will be able to extend in yourself and others the precious teachings of the Buddha.

7

The Concise Meaning of the Stages of the Path

The third section is Tsongkhapa's Concise Meaning of the Stages of the Path. *It was written as a companion piece to Atīśa's* Lamp of the Bodhi-Path (Bodhipathapradīpa), *and together they form the core of Tsongkhapa's comprehensive work on the unified path teachings,* The Great Stages of the Path (Lam-rim Chenmo).

This work sets forth in brief but concise form the lam-rim *teaching, first formulated and taught in Tibet by Atīśa, which unifies the Theravāda, Mahāyāna, and Tantrayāna traditions. Rather than regarding the varied teachings of Buddhism as disparate systems, it integrates them into a gradual process of liberation for an individual with one of the three levels of motivation: concern for status in future lives, desire for freedom from saṃsāra, and dedication to enlightenment in order to free all beings.*

Thus, we can see how the main teachings of the three traditions of Buddhism can be integrated into a unified system of practice wherein each element of practice is taken up or discontinued with the most effective timing and productive relationship to the individual's course of development. If anything can be indicated as the major contribution of the Tibetans to Buddhism, it is their uniquely characteristic, lofty overview of the practice of religion embodied in this teaching, its development, experiential verification, and preservation to this present day.

The Concise Meaning of the Stages of the Path

I bow down to the prince of the Śākyas,
Whose body was formed by a million perfect virtues,

Whose speech fulfills the hopes of all beings,
Whose mind perceives all to be known.

I bow down to Mañjuśrī and Maitreya,
Whose emanations dance in innumerable fields.
Having assumed the burden of the Conqueror's deeds,
They are superior sons of that peerless teacher.

I bow at the feet of Nāgārjuna and Asaṅga,
Who are the ornaments of Jambudvīpa;
Renowned throughout the three realms, they composed
commentaries
On the 'Mother of Conquerors' [43] so hard to fathom.

I bow to Dīpaṃkara,[44] who, from these two great vehicles,
Received the treasure of precepts
That comprise the key complete and without error
To the two lineages, the paths of extensive deeds and
profound view.

I respectfully bow down to the spiritual teachers
Who, moved by compassion and skillful means,
Illumine this best gate for the fortunate traveling to
liberation,
This eye through which all the glorious scriptures are seen.

This teaching of the stages of the bodhi-path
Is the legacy handed down from Nāgārjuna and Asaṅga,
Who are crown ornaments of the wise of Jambudvīpa
And banners of fame resplendent among humans.

This precept is a wish-fulfilling jewel,
Fulfilling all desires of humankind;

Receiving a thousand rivers of good teaching,
It is an ocean of glorious explanation.

Through it one can realize that all the teachings are without contradiction
And understand all of the doctrines as precepts;
One can easily find the intention of Buddha,
And avoid the abyss of wrongdoing.

Thus, this precept is relied on by many of good fortune,
The wise of India and Tibet.
What sensible mind would not be captivated
By the path of stages for the three levels of beings?

Contemplate the significance of this way,
Which gathers the essence of all the scriptures;
Even hearing or teaching it in a single session,
You gather the glorious benefits of hearing or explaining the teaching.

Depend, with effort, in thought and deed
On the holy spiritual friend, the teacher of the path,
Who is the root of the good arrangement of dependent origination
Giving all excellence in this and future lives.

Having seen this, retain it though it cost your life,
And please your guide by accomplishing as he instructs.
The reverend lama practiced like this;
Those desiring liberation should do likewise.

This life, which has leisure,
Is more precious than the wishing-jewel;

So difficult to find, it is as quickly gone as lightning in the sky.
Thus, realize that all worldly activities

Are like chaff in the wind
And seize the essence of leisure and opportunity day and night.
The reverend lama practiced like this;
Those desiring liberation should do likewise.

You cannot be certain that after death
You will not be born in lower states of being.
To protect you from this fear, firmly take refuge in the
Three Jewels
And do not lapse from their precepts.

Knowing well the effects of black and white karma,
Accept what is good and reject what is not.
The reverend lama practiced like this;
Those desiring liberation should do likewise.

Unless you attain a human life with its requisites,
You will not succeed in achieving the highest path;
Learn that cherishing dependence on the four powers[45]
Is the way to ensure attainment of such a life.

For those powers are the special key to purify sinful karma,
The defilement from falling into sins of body, speech, and
mind.
The reverend lama practiced like this;
Those desiring liberation should do likewise.

If you do not try to contemplate the truth of suffering—
the afflictions of saṃsāra—

You will not produce desire for liberation.
If you do not contemplate the cause of suffering—
the stages by which saṃsāra is entered—
You will not know how to eradicate saṃsāra's source.

Value the knowledge of what binds you,
And from world-weariness, renounce saṃsāra.
The reverend lama practiced like this;
Those desiring liberation should do likewise.

Producing bodhi-mind is the king post of the Mahāyāna path,
The base and support of bodhisattvas' great deeds,
A philosopher's stone transmuting all into merit
and wisdom,
A treasure of merit assembling glorious virtue.

Understanding this, the heroic offspring of Buddha
Hold the precious bodhi-mind as their central meditation.
The reverend lama practiced like this;
Those desiring liberation should do likewise.

Giving is the wishing-jewel that fulfills the hopes of living
beings.
The excellent weapon that cuts the knots of greed,
The deed of the bodhisattvas that strengthens courage,
And the basis of fame extending in the ten directions.

Understanding this, bodhisattvas rely on the good path
Of giving up everything, their fortune and even their bodies.
The reverend lama practiced like this;
Those desiring liberation should do likewise.

Moral practice is water that cleanses the defilement of
wrongdoing;
It is moonlight cooling the hot torment of passions.
As lofty as Mount Meru in the midst of humankind,
It assembles all beings with no threat of force.

Understanding this, bodhisattvas guard this moral practice
As they would their eyes.
The reverend lama practiced like this;
Those desiring liberation should do likewise.

Patience is the finest ornament of powerful beings
And the best restraint for the torment of passions.
It is garuḍa, enemy of the snake of hatred;
It is the armor not pierced by weapons of harsh speech.

Having understood this, develop in many ways
The armor of great patience.
The reverend lama practiced like this;
Those desiring liberation should do likewise.

When you don the mantle of effort steady and
unswerving,
The excellence of instruction and insight grows like the
waxing moon.
All actions become significant,
And whatever is begun is accomplished as desired.

Understanding this, bodhisattvas put forth
Great waves of effort, dispelling lethargy.
The reverend lama practiced like this;
Those desiring liberation should do likewise.

Meditation is the majesty that subjugates the mind:
It means to be as immovable as Mount Meru when sitting;
When rising, to undertake all virtuous aims,
Thus drawing forth great joy of supple mind and body.

Understanding this, powerful yogis rely
On meditation, which subdues the enemy, wandering
mind.
The reverend lama practiced like this;
Those desiring liberation should do likewise.

Wisdom is the eye that sees profound voidness,
The path that completely uproots saṃsāra,
The treasure of knowledge praised in all the scriptures,
The illustrious lamp dispelling dark ignorance.

Having understood this, the wise who desire liberation
With great effort generate that path.
The reverend lama practiced like this;
Those desiring liberation should do likewise.

In one-pointed meditation alone
You do not find the power to cut saṃsāra's root;
And by wisdom set apart from abiding tranquility,
Though you analyze intensely, you do not expel
the passions.

Having placed wisdom that resolves the meaning of existence
Upon the horse of unwavering tranquility,
Cut off all mental inclination to either extreme
With the sharp weapon of Madhyamaka, the logic free of
extremes.

By wisdom that deeply analyzes in this way,
Increase the understanding that realizes voidness.
The reverend lama practiced like this;
Those desiring liberation should do likewise.

The samādhi achieved by one-pointed meditation
Is not enough; by proper analysis
Distinguish the pattern of existence
While increasing the samādhi that rests firm and unmoving.

Seeing this, understand how wonderful is the effort
That conjoins intense insight and abiding tranquility.
The reverend lama practiced like this;
Those desiring liberation should do likewise.

Contemplative equipoise is void like space;
In the after-attainment, all is void like a magician's
illusion.
By meditation on both, method and wisdom are joined—
Thus, transcendent bodhisattva deeds are praised.

Realizing this, fortunate ones[46]
Are not satisfied by either path alone.
The reverend lama practiced like this;
Those desiring liberation should do likewise.

Having produced the general path needed for the two
Mahāyāna paths—
Both Sūtrayāna—cause—and Mantrayāna—effect—
Depend on a protector, a skillful pilot,
And enter the great ocean of tantras.

Then, through reliance on the complete and perfect
precepts,
Make significant the attainment of leisure and opportunity.
The reverend lama practiced like this;
Those desiring liberation should do likewise.

In order to develop my mind
And also to help others of good fortune,
By the virtue that comes from explaining in clear words
The complete and perfect path pleasing to the Buddha,

I set forth this wishing-prayer that all beings
May not be separate from the pure, good path.
The reverend lama set forth this prayer;
Those desiring liberation should do likewise.

As I met with the doctrine of the peerless teacher
By the kindness of my lama,
I dedicate this virtue that all living beings
Might be upheld by a holy spiritual teacher.

First, seek to listen to the extensive teachings;
Then, consider as precepts all the doctrines;
Finally, practice day and night
And dedicate all to extend the teaching.

8

The Foundation of All Excellence

THE FINAL SELECTION is The Foundation of All Excellence, *which presents the stages of the path from the viewpoint of reliance on a spiritual teacher and the mind-practice of the three levels of beings. Tsongkhapa's poem, presented first in its entirety, serves as the root text for the commentary that follows, written by Kushri Kabchu Sudhi.*

In this case the commentator has made a line-for-line commentary on the root text, quoting sutras as scriptural authority at the end of each section. In order to make this process clear, we have inserted the lines of the root text in italics. Also, many of the sutra citations have been omitted to limit the length of this selection.

The Foundation of All Excellence *is usually recited last during the chanting of prayers, as it is a prayer to achieve the object of one's meditation or prayer. When the text is recited in this way, the last line of each verse is repeated.*

THE FOUNDATION OF ALL EXCELLENCE

The kind reverend lama is the foundation of all excellence.
Seeing that dependence on him is the root of the path,
May I rely on him
With great respect and continuous effort.

A human life with leisure is obtained this once.
Understanding that it is very important and hard to find,
May I produce unceasingly
The mind that takes up its essence day and night.

The fluctuation of life is like a bubble of water;
Remember death, for we perish so quickly.
After death, the effects of black and white karma
Pursue us as the shadow follows the body.

Finding certainty in this,
May I always be careful
To do only virtuous deeds
And abandon even the slightest non-virtuous actions.

The door to all misery is seeking satisfaction in pleasure.
Having realized that there is no security
In the pernicious perfections of saṃsāra,
May I be strongly intent on the bliss of liberation.

That pure thought produces
The great heedfulness of remembrance and discernment.
May I accomplish by this means the essence
Of the individual vow, which is the root of the doctrine.

Having seen that all beings, my kind mothers,
Have fallen like myself into the ocean of saṃsāra,
May I practice pure bodhi-mind,
Which assumes the obligation to free all living beings.

Bodhi-mind alone, without cultivation
Of the three moral practices, does not lead to enlightenment.
Having realized this, may I practice
With intense effort the bodhisattva vow.

By quieting attraction to objects that are false
And analyzing the meaning of reality,
May I quickly produce within myself
The path that unifies tranquility and insight.

When, by this practice, I become a vessel of the general path,
May I soon enter
The great gateway of the fortunate ones:
The Vajrayāna, supreme of yānas.

The basis of achieving the two siddhis
Is the pure vow one takes on entering this path.
Having found real understanding of it,
May I keep this vow though it cost my life.

Having realized the significance of the two stages,
Which are the essence of the Vajrayāna,
By unswerving effort in the four sessions of yoga
May I achieve what the holy lama has taught.

May the spiritual teacher who has shown me the good path
And all my spiritual friends who practice it have long lives.
May I at last completely surmount
All inner and outer obstacles.

May I in all births enjoy the glorious Dharma
Inseparable from the perfect lama;
Having completed the stages[47] and paths,[48]
May I quickly obtain the high stage of Vajradhara.

COMMENTARY BY KUSHRI KABCHU SUDHI

Namo Guru Mañjughoṣāya

This teaching joins opening the door to the stages of the path to liberation with the precious scriptures of the Tathāgata. In it is explained the practice that begins with reliance on the spiritual teacher, and then proceeds through the stages of mind-practice. The root text states:

The kind reverend lama is the foundation of all excellence.
Seeing that dependence on him is the root of the path,
May I rely on him
With great respect and continuous effort.

The kind reverend lama is the foundation of all excellence:

As the kind holy spiritual teacher shows us the actual path, he is the foundation of all worldly and spiritual excellence that can be derived from hearing, thinking, and meditating on the teaching.

Seeing that dependence on him is the root of the path:

When you rely on the spiritual teacher, whatever excellence you have achieved so far will not degenerate; instead, it will increase, and you will finally accomplish all excellence of the stages and paths of the Mahāyāna.

May I rely on him
With great respect and continuous effort:

Having realized that the spiritual teacher is the root of all excellence, by continuous effort of body, speech, and mind, develop great faith that perceives his knowledge and does not perceive in him even the slightest fault. Remember his great kindness with deep gratitude, and honor him; make offerings to him, respect him in body and speech, and strive to do as he instructs.[49]

❧

The *Gaṇḍavyūhasūtra* says:

> Serve the spiritual teacher with a mind that is like earth, never tired of its burdens; with a mind immutable as a diamond; with a mind like a dog, never angered at misery; with a mind like a young prince who never contradicts the edict of a king of the Dharma.

Conceive of yourself as a sick person, of the spiritual teacher as a doctor, and of his precepts as medicine. Become convinced that earnest practice will heal your sickness.

~

After you have come to rely on the spiritual teacher, you must proceed through the various stages of mind-practice. The next verse of the root text is an exhortation to make good use of this human life with its leisure:

A human life with leisure is obtained this once.
Understanding that it is very important and hard to find,
May I produce unceasingly
The mind that takes up its essence day and night.

Mind-practice on the difficulty of obtaining leisure and opportunity is very important, for it increases the inner inclination to accomplish the holy Dharma.

A human life with leisure is obtained this once:

For beginningless lifetimes we have wandered in a leisureless condition in the three lower states of being because of the influence of our karma and fettering passions. Now, this one time, because of the convergence of a great deal of virtuous karma, we have obtained this human life, which has the ten aspects of opportunity and the eight aspects of leisure.

Understanding that it is very important and hard to find:

When we consider the obstacles to obtaining a human life, the actual nature of this life, its causes and effects, and the allegories concerning it, we see how very rare it must be. This life is more precious than a universe full of wish-fulfilling jewels, for it enables us to accomplish the ten virtues, which cause birth as humans or gods, and beyond that, can even cause attainment of the adamantine body. It also enables us to produce bodhi-mind, to achieve the six transcendences, and to fulfill the three precepts (moral practice, meditation, and wisdom), which lead to omniscience and the assured good of liberation.

May I produce unceasingly
The mind that takes up its essence day and night:

Understanding the importance of this, do not senselessly ruin yourself by laziness or by heedless involvement in the eight worldly concerns. Always practice mindfulness. Hearing, thinking, and meditating on the doctrine of the Buddha by day and by night, generate the mind that desires to take up the essence of the holy Dharma of instruction and understanding. If you apply such thought to practice, you will strive to use the methods to make meaningful this human life with its leisure and opportunity.

❧

The actual way of utilizing the essence of human life with leisure and opportunity is found in the three levels of mind-practice: the path of lower beings; the path of middle beings; and the path of higher beings. Concerning the first level, the root text says:

The fluctuation of life is like a bubble of water;
Remember death, for we perish so quickly.
After death, the effects of black and white karma
Pursue us as the shadow follows the body.

Finding certainty in this,
May I always be careful
To do only virtuous deeds
And abandon even the slightest non-virtuous actions.

After experiencing the desire to utilize this human life with its leisure, you must learn how to do so, stage by stage. In this, begin with the realization of impermanence and the truth of suffering, and continue through the great wave of the bodhisattva's deeds. After you have ascertained, through listening and thinking, the levels, enumerations, and nature of the path, meditate on them without confusing their stages. This is the great key to practice.

The fluctuation of life is like a bubble of water:
This human life, with its leisure, is not dependable, for inner and outer circumstances do not allow us to stay as we are, and in each moment the life-flow fluctuates, moving toward death. We perish as quickly as the bubbles in a puddle of rain water.

Remember death, for we perish so quickly:
Again and again contemplate impermanence, remembering that we have no power to remain forever and no certainty as to when we will die. The way to achieve final happiness is to be unattached to worldly activities or to this life's bodily enjoyments, for these are like chaff in the wind and will be of no benefit in the future.

After death, the effects of black and white karma
Pursue us as the shadow follows the body:
After death, nothing except our inclinations residing on our stream of consciousness remains, and we must take rebirth. As a result, the karma accumulated by good and bad deeds pursues us as a shadow follows the body. Therefore, decide to practice only Dharma from this time on. The three grades of virtuous karma—small, middling, or great—lead respectively to rebirth in a human life, as a god of the desire realm, or as a god of the higher realms. They also have the conditioning effects of long life and good health, and the positioning effects of abiding in a place of great beauty. In short, they result in happiness, which increases until perfect omniscience is obtained.

The three grades of non-virtuous karma—small, middling, or great—lead respectively to rebirth as a hungry ghost, an animal, or a being in hell. They have the conditioning effect that even when you rise out of these inferior births and are reborn as a human, you will, for example, have a short life with much illness and will enjoy killing others. The positioning effect of such karma is that wherever you live will be very disagreeable. In short, you must face the wretched results of non-virtuous karma, for the deeds done will not decay, and there is no way to avoid their effects. These effects will, in fact, multiply. You must firmly believe in these true words of the compassionate Teacher.

If you assembled in palpable form all your non-virtuous actions accumulated from beginningless time, the mass would be greater than Mount Meru or the ocean. If, in this life, you heedlessly heap up more wrong actions, you will surely be reborn in lower states of being. Born in a hot hell, you will burn in a fire of molten iron that is forty-nine times hotter than the ordinary fire of men. Like the wick of a butter lamp, your body will become indistinguishable from flame; you will be cooked in boiling molten copper. Born in a cold hell, your body, cracking and blistering, will be embedded in a glacier surrounded by snow-covered mountains. Born as a animal, you will undergo the wretched necessity of killing and eating other animals. Born as a hungry ghost, you will find nothing to eat or drink, and even if you should find something, it will burn like fire in your stomach.

Finding certainty in this,
May I always be careful
To do only virtuous deeds
And abandon even the slightest non-virtuous actions:

Beings in the three lower states experience misery that lasts for hundreds of thousands of human years. Contemplating this, produce great faith in the lama and the Three Jewels, who are able to protect you. Completely absorb yourself in the thought that your lama is the one who knows, and from now until enlightenment, take refuge in him. Do not engage in even the subtlest form of any of the ten non-virtuous actions. Repent and confess any wrong you have done.

Constantly increase the feeling, "I will never do it again," and from this time on, give up all wrongdoing. With strong determination and prayer, think, "As much as I can, I will perform virtuous actions. I will not give up the effort to do those things that are now too difficult, for at some future time I will do them." To bring this about, you must, with remembrance and discernment, remain heedful day and night.

❦

The *Guhyācittavyaptisūtra* says:

> How do humans and gods avoid degenerating the root of virtue? They abide in heedfulness. What is heedfulness? Heedfulness consists in guarding the mind; giving up wrong things; abandoning worldly pleasures and depending on the pleasure of the Dharma; not giving way to harmful or desirous mental constructs; not giving way to non-virtuous mental activities, such as desire, hatred, or ignorance; not performing injurious actions with body, speech, and mind; in short, not degenerating the root of virtue in any way. This, monks, is heedfulness.

❦

From heedfulness you progress to the second stage of mind-practice, the general path for the middle being. By making effort, beginning with the remembrance of death and continuing through the cultivation of right actions and the rejection of wrong, you will attain rebirth in happy stages of being. Yet, at this stage, you have not passed beyond the misery of conditioned activities, for you are still constrained by the bonds of karma and fettering passions, and in the future you will certainly fall back into lower states of being. In the prison of the three realms of saṃsāra, you will continue to be tortured on the rack of the three miseries.[50] Therefore, you must first produce the desire for release, and then you must travel the path to liberation. Thus, there are two parts to the practice of the middle being: to engender the desire for liberation, and to ascertain the path that leads to it.

Concerning the former, the root text says:

The door to all misery is seeking satisfaction in pleasure.
Having realized that there is no security
In the pernicious perfections of saṃsāra,
May I be strongly intent on the bliss of liberation.

The door to all misery is seeking satisfaction in pleasure:

Though you seek happiness in saṃsāra, you will never find satisfaction: it is like drinking salt water to satisfy thirst. Instead of being satisfied, your attachment will increase and become the door to great and long-lasting misery that far outweighs any happiness you might have found.

Having realized that there is no security
In the pernicious perfections of saṃsara,
May I be strongly intent on the bliss of liberation:

There is not the slightest security in worldly happiness; it is as momentary as a flash of lightning. Just as someone lost in the desert pursues a mirage, thinking it is water, so we in saṃsāra pursue that which has the nature of suffering, thinking it is happiness.

Even the most perfect enjoyments of saṃsāra bring forth only wretchedness: karma, fettering passions, sickness, and pain. Through hearing and contemplating the teachings, learn to realize that these pernicious perfections are the basis from which all undesired things arise. Consider this again and again with the mind of renunciation, which sees all saṃsāra as a burning fire and desires unceasingly the perfect, irreversible bliss of liberation. This mind of renunciation is indispensable for entering either the Hīnayāna or Mahāyāna path.

You should next examine the causes of the misery of saṃsāra.

The chief causes of misery are the karma of non-virtuous deeds, of virtuous deeds, and of immovable actions.[51] All these arise because of the fettering passions and shoot you into saṃsāra like an arrow from a bow. The fettering passions, in turn, are caused by misconceptions that arise from our distorted mental activities. Remain constantly aware of the perniciousness of these misconceptions, for they project happiness upon misery and permanence upon impermanence. Remember the perniciousness of attachment to desirable objects in general, and specifically to wine and women. Remember the perniciousness of hatred, mental turmoil over harm to yourself or those close to you and of ignorance, which is confusion about the cause and effect of karma and about the nature of "just-thatness" (voidness-). Remembering the perniciousness of all these, abandon them.

❧

Also contemplate the twelve links of dependent origination as set forth in the *Gaganagañjaparipṛcchanāmamahāyānasūtra:*

> The way of profound dependent origination is as follows: ignorance conditions conditioned activities; conditioned activities condition consciousness; consciousness conditions name and form; name and form condition the six senses; the six senses condition contact; contact conditions feeling; feeling conditions craving; craving conditions grasping; grasping conditions existence; existence conditions birth; birth conditions aging and death, sorrow, lamentation, suffering, misery, anguish, unhappiness, and agitation. In this way there come forth only great masses of misery. The sublime wisdom of the bodhisattvas has penetrated to what the causes and conditions are by which a living being is completely fettered by the passions. This is called the way that all existence comes forth, dependently linked origination.
>
> What is the way of reversing dependent origination? By

the cessation of ignorance, there is cessation of conditioned activities; by the cessation of conditioned activities, there is cessation of consciousness; by the cessation of consciousness, there is cessation of name and form; by the cessation of name and form, there is cessation of the six senses; by the cessation of the six senses, there is cessation of contact; by the cessation of contact, there is cessation of feeling; by the cessation of feeling, there is cessation of craving; by the cessation of craving, there is cessation of grasping; by the cessation of grasping, there is cessation of existence; by the cessation of existence, there is cessation of birth; by the cessation of birth, there is cessation of aging and death, sorrow, lamentation, misery, anguish, unhappiness, and agitation. Thus, there is cessation of the great masses of misery. This is called the way of stopping the process of dependent origination. The sublime wisdom of the bodhisattvas has penetrated to the causes and conditions by which a living being is purified. This is called penetrating to the profound way of Dharma. This is not the way of śrāvakas and pratyekabuddhas.

❧

The next step is to ascertain the path that leads to liberation. Concerning this, the root text says:

That pure thought produces
The great heedfulness of remembrance and discernment.
May I accomplish by this means the essence
Of the individual vow, which is the root of the doctrine.

That pure thought produces
The great heedfulness of remembrance and discernment:

When you have fully realized the perniciousness of saṃsāra and desire to escape from it, then, motivated by desire for liberation, take the excellent individual vow, which is the root of the doctrine. You should cultivate great heedfulness, which consists of remembrance, discernment, self-reproach, shame, and cautiousness: remembrance of what is to be done or not done; discernment, which constantly examines body, speech, and mind and discriminates between right and wrong actions; self-reproach, which causes you to shrink from wrongdoing; shame, which causes you to shrink from the censure of spiritual friends; and cautiousness, which causes you to fear the karmic effect of wrong actions.

May I accomplish by this means the essence
Of the individual vow,[52] *which is the root of the doctrine:*

By this heedfulness you can attain the essence of pure moral practice. Guard it more dearly than your life, for moral practice is the source of the precepts of meditation and wisdom—the source of all excellence.

As long as you have desire and attachment, you must wander in saṃsāra. Fearing this, renounce saṃsāra and enter the actual path. You will be able to do this by making good use of this life with its leisure and opportunity, but as the excellent life of a monk is especially helpful, the wise take pleasure in monkhood.

You can obtain liberation by following the three precepts of the path (moral practice, meditation, and wisdom),[53] but you will only be able to fulfill the minor purposes of yourself and others. Therefore, Buddha taught that one must finally enter the Mahāyāna path. Indeed, it is best to enter the Mahāyāna from the beginning, for that vehicle by its nature abounds in skillful means and is thus able to bring incalculable benefits and happiness to all living beings. Therefore, we say that the Mahāyāna path includes the three great purposes.[54]

Bodhi-mind is the gateway to the Mahāyāna, the basis of all Buddha's teaching, and the method of rapidly reaching buddhahood. In order to produce this bodhi-mind, Buddha taught that in each living being there is the potential for attaining buddhahood. This is called the buddha-essence (*tathāgatagarbha*), the lineage abiding within. This buddha-essence is the nature of mind, which in itself is not spoiled by any defilement and exists pure from the very beginning in the midst of fettering passions. Concerning this, he taught that to learn the lineage of the extensive deeds of the bodhisattvas is essential, for by producing bodhi-mind through the mind-practice of the highest type of being, one accomplishes those practices that lead to buddhahood.

❧

From the *Tathāgatagarbhasūtra*:

> Until you reach the path, you wander in the world
> With the precious form of the Sugata
> Completely wrapped, as in a bundle of rags,
> By things degrading and dirty.
> The omniscient gods saw this
> And spoke of it to others.
>
> Here it is. You have this precious tathāgata
> Wrapped in rags. Unwrap it quickly.
> I have also seen with my omniscient eye
> That, wrapped in the fettering passions,
> All beings suffer,
> Always troubled by the misery of saṃsāra.
>
> I have seen within the wrapping of fettering passions
> That which is not seen by those who think they are free:
> The meditating form of Buddha—pure,
> Not moving, not changing.
> Having seen this, I make this exhortation;
> Whoever would strive for the highest enlightenment, listen.
>
> This is the voidness of living beings,
> Like a buddha seated in the midst of fettering passions .

When you pacify all fettering passions
And free the sublime wisdom of the Sugata,
You obtain the name of buddha
And bring joy to humans and gods.

Mind-practice for the highest beings consists of first producing bodhi-mind, the entrance to the Mahāyāna, and then learning the deeds of the bodhisattvas. Concerning the former, the root text says:

Having seen that all beings, my kind mothers,
Have fallen like myself into the ocean of saṃsāra,
May I practice pure bodhi-mind,
Which assumes the obligation to free all beings.

Having seen that all beings, my kind mothers,
Have fallen like myself into the ocean of saṃsāra:

First develop equanimity toward all living beings. Then think, "By the influence of karma and fettering passions, I myself have fallen into the immeasurably deep ocean of saṃsāra, and I am tortured ceaselessly by the crocodiles of the three miseries. With my mind's eye I can also see that all living beings, who have been my infinitely kind mother again and again, are also tortured by the misery of saṃsāra."

May I practice pure bodhi-mind,
Which assumes the obligation to free all beings:

"In return for their kindness may all beings meet with undefiled happiness. May they be free from all misery. May I myself cause this to happen."

Thinking this, produce the high resolve to assume the obligation to free all beings. To the extent of your ability you must continually develop the precious aspiration for enlightenment that is the vital force of the Mahāyāna, thinking, "I will obtain perfect buddhahood in order to free all beings from misery."

ଓଡ଼ୃଓ

From the *Aṣṭasāhasrikāprajñāpāramitā*:

> The Blessed One said: "Subhūti, since bodhisattva-mahāsattvas desire to renounce saṃsāra in order to reach unsurpassed perfect enlightenment, they abide in equanimity toward all living beings. Produce this mind of equanimity toward everyone: consider all beings with a mind that is without non-equanimity, with a loving mind, with a helpful mind, with a virtuous mind, with a mind without pride, with a mind without anger, with a mind without thought to harm, with a mind without reproach.
>
> Consider them impartially, conceiving all living beings as your mother, as your father, as your son, and as your daughter. Subhūti, as bodhisattva-mahāsattvas desire to become buddhas, to manifest enlightenment that is perfect and unsurpassed, you should abide in equanimity toward all living beings. Learn to do this and become the protector of all beings."

ଓଡ଼ୃଓ

The second part of mind-practice for the higher being is to learn the bodhisattva's deeds. This has two parts: the first is the way of learning the Mahāyāna, which includes the general way of learning the bodhisattva's deeds and the particular way of learning the last two transcendences. The second is the particular way of learning the Vajrayāna. About the general way of learning the bodhisattva's deeds, the root text says:

> *Bodhi-mind alone, without cultivation*
> *Of the three moral practices, does not lead to enlightenment.*

Having realized this, may I practice
With intense effort the bodhisattva vow.

Bodhi-mind alone, without cultivation
Of the three moral practices, does not lead to enlightenment:

There are great benefits in producing even the aspiration for enlightenment, but you will not accomplish unsurpassed and perfect enlightenment if you do not repeatedly cultivate the moral practices of vows, of accumulating virtuous actions, and of working for the benefit of all living beings. These three moral practices, together, are the key to all the bodhisattva's deeds.

Having realized this, may I practice
With intense effort the bodhisattva vow:

Since obtaining enlightenment depends on accomplishing the essence of the Mahāyāna path, take up the bodhisattva vow and do not give it up though it cost your life. Through all stages of learning, guard your vow from contamination by the eighteen major and forty-six minor failings. Apply yourself, respectfully and with great effort, to the wonderful deeds of the bodhisattvas, which conjoin both method and wisdom, perfecting yourself through the six transcendences and perfecting others through the four ways of assembling.

❧

From the *Dharmasaṃgītisūtra:*

> When asked, "What do bodhisattvas accomplish?" the Blessed One said, "Any action of body, any action of speech, any action of mind of a bodhisattva is done with an eye to all living beings. All his actions are preceded by great compassion and empowered by great compassion. All his actions benefit all living beings, arising as they do from the high resolve to provide happiness and benefit to everyone. In this

way bodhisattvas decide: 'Whatever brings benefit and joy to all living beings, that I will accomplish.'

"If you ask, 'What are the powers that bodhisattvas accomplish?' they are ten: the power of accomplishing giving, of accomplishing moral practice, of accomplishing patience, of accomplishing effort, of accomplishing meditation, of accomplishing wisdom, of accomplishing method, of accomplishing prayer, of accomplishing power, and of accomplishing sublime wisdom. These are the ten accomplishments of a bodhisattva. All a bodhisattva's transcendent accomplishments are included within these ten.

"If you ask, 'What is a bodhisattva's accomplishment of giving?' there is nothing a bodhisattva does not give to living beings, except that which would be harmful to them. It is not easy to believe, much less to understand, this beneficent mind of a bodhisattva unless one is a tathāgata or a bodhi-sattva who has obtained patience.

"By giving, you obtain great enjoyment. By moral practice, you can obtain rebirth as a human or god. By patience, everything around you will be beautiful. By effort, you can quickly obtain clairvoyance. By meditation, you can obtain a mind suitable for anything. By wisdom, you become exalted among the worldly. By method you can become able to do anything. By prayer, anything can be done without difficulty. By power, you will be indestructible. By sublime wisdom, you will be able to teach the whole world."

The next step is to understand the last two transcendences. Learn that abiding tranquility is included within the transcendence of meditation, and intense insight is included within the transcendence of wisdom. Concerning this, the root text says:

By quieting attraction to objects that are false
And analyzing the meaning of reality,
May I quickly produce within myself
The path that unifies tranquility and insight.

Consider the benefits of cultivating abiding tranquility and intense insight, and stay in a place that has the five necessary qualifications (that it is easy to find: food, clothing, and so forth). Have few desires, be content, give up many activities, abandon desirous feeling, and achieve pure moral practice. Depend on a holy being who has done all these things. By listening to the profound Dharma and contemplating its meaning, one can produce the view that realizes "just-thatness" (voidness). Depend on the various causes of quickly achieving abiding tranquility and intense insight.

By quieting attraction to objects that are false:

When the six sense objects (form, sound, smell, taste, touch, and other phenomena), which are false in that their way of appearance and way of existence do not accord,[55] make contact with the six sense organs (eyes, ears, nose, tongue, body, and mind), six corresponding consciousnesses are produced. These consciousnesses then produce the feelings of desire for pleasing sense objects, aversion for those that are displeasing, and delusion, which is attached to the idea that the objects of the senses truly exist. Seeking to achieve pleasure and prevent displeasure, you have accumulated and will accumulate many aspects of karma through body, speech, and mind.

By the bonds of various attractions—of karma and fettering passions—grasping inner or outer objects in this way, we have been bound up in the prison of saṃsāra from beginningless time and have been tortured ceaselessly by unsought and unbearable misery.

Understanding this, be motivated from the first by aversion for the high states of humans and gods, seeing that they are like islands of cannibals. With this motivation, begin to meditate.

Sit in the meditation posture,[56] and take as your object of focus either Buddha or voidness.

There are five failings in meditation: laziness, lack of inclination to achieve samādhi; forgetfulness of the object of focus; failure to identify listlessness and excitement; after identifying them, failure to apply their countermeasures; and continuing to apply the countermeasures after you are free from listlessness and excitement.

There are eight activities that remedy these five failings. The first four are antidotes to laziness. These are faith in the excellence of samādhi; intense desire for samādhi; effort that strives for samādhi; and the well-practiced mind and body that are the effect of that effort. The remedy for forgetting your object of focus is remembrance. The remedy for not identifying listlessness and excitement is discernment. The remedy for failure to apply the countermeasures to listlessness and excitement is the mind of activation; and the remedy for excessive application of the countermeasures is the balanced equanimity that knows when to cease such application.

There are also five obstacles, five defilements, and five distractions that impede progress toward abiding tranquility and intense insight. The five obstacles are: concern for the body, concern for enjoyments, not doing as the āryas instruct, mingling too much with others, and being content with superficial study. The five defilements are: excitement and regret, depression and sleepiness, doubt, desire for desirable objects, and harmful mind. The five distractions are: mental distraction, outer distraction, inner distraction, symbolic distraction, and the distraction of wrong tendencies. Abandon all these, and meditate properly.

There are six powers: listening, thinking, remembrance, discernment, effort, and thorough knowledge of the subject matter. Through these one gradually accomplishes the nine states of mind: directing the mind, directing the mind continuously, redirecting the mind, directing the mind completely, subduing the mind, calming the mind, completely calming the mind, directing the mind one-pointedly, and directing the mind in equanimity. When, by the power of gradually developing these nine states, you attain the special bliss of well-practiced mind and body, you will have achieved abiding tranquility.

And analyzing the meaning of reality (voidness):

At the time we perceive an ego in ourselves, it does not appear to be merely an imputed name or sign; it appears to exist independently, from the beginning. We feel that this object of the egoistic mind, the ego, truly exists as it appears to us. But the ego held in this way is the very object to be negated. If the ego, the imputed phenomenon,[57] were actually to exist independently from the beginning, it would have to be either the same as or different from its basis of imputation,[58] the five aggregates, mind and body. There is no third way for it to exist. If that ego, 'I,' and the aggregates were truly the same, as the ego is an indivisible entity, the five aggregates would either be one, or there would be five egos. As this cannot be, the ego is not the same as the five aggregates.

If the ego were to exist separately from the five aggregates, since to be truly separate is to be completely without connection, it logically follows that the ego would be uncompounded like a flower of the sky (and thus nonexistent).[59] The ego would then be pictured as a completely different entity from the aggregates, and as it is not pictured like this, be certain that the ego does not exist separately.

In the same way, analyze the environment of the ego (that which is 'mine') and all other phenomena, with the wisdom that investigates the meaning of voidness.

May I quickly produce within myself
The path that unifies tranquility and insight:

At the completion of analysis, when you enter into one-pointed equipoise through successive development of the four mental activities (entering heedfully, entering ceasingly, entering ceaselessly, and entering effortlessly), you then obtain intense insight and the well-practiced mind and body developed by the power of analyzing. Entering thus into unified abiding tranquility and intense insight, learn the good path of the Conqueror, which unifies appearance and voidness, perceiving that, from the perspective of realization, all is void of self-nature, and from the perspective of appearance, all is like a magician's illusion.

ᐉᐊᐉ

From the *Saṃdhinirmocanasūtra:*

> "Of the five obstacles pointed out by the Blessed One, how many are obstacles to abiding tranquility, how many to intense insight, and how many to both?"
>
> "Maitreya, concern for enjoyment and concern for body are obstacles to abiding tranquility. Not doing as the āryas instruct is an obstacle to intense insight. Mingling too much with others and being content with superficial study are obstacles to both, for by the former, you cannot apply yourself in meditation, and by the latter, even if you apply yourself, there can be no final accomplishment."
>
> "Lord, of the five defilements, how many are defilements of abiding tranquility, how many are defilements of intense insight, and how many are defilements of both?"
>
> "Maitreya, excitement and regret are defilements of abiding tranquility. Depression and sleepiness are defilements of intense insight; doubt is also a defilement of intense insight. Desire for pleasurable objects and harmful mind are obstacles to both."
>
> "Lord, how can one obtain the path of completely pure abiding tranquility?"
>
> "Maitreya, at a time when you have completely destroyed sleepiness and depression."
>
> "Lord, how can one obtain the path of completely pure

intense insight?"

"Maitreya, at a time when you have completely destroyed excitement and regret."

"Lord, as bodhisattvas are entering into abiding tranquility and intense insight, how many kinds of distraction are there?"

"Maitreya, there are five kinds of distraction. There are mental distraction, outer distraction, inner distraction, symbolic distraction, and the distraction of wrong tendencies. If a bodhisattva gives up the mental activities of the Mahāyāna and falls into the mental activities of the śrāvaka or pratyekabuddha, this is mental distraction. If your mind is attracted to the five kinds of external desire objects, to activity, to designations, to habitual thoughts, to related passions,[60] or if you project your mind to any outside image, that is outer distraction. If, depressed and sleepy, you are lethargic or relish contemplative equipoise too much or are prevented by any passion from entering the state of contemplative equipoise, that is inner distraction. If you depend on outer signs and make these signs the object of your inner meditation, this is symbolic distraction. If you depend on inner mental concepts and produce the proud mind that thinks, 'I,' 'I,' this is the distraction of wrong tendencies."

Having identified these distractions, rely on their countermeasures.

Many objects of focus have been taught for the meditation of abiding tranquility and intense insight, but it is best to hold in your mind the form of the Buddha. This is important for many reasons but particularly for sustaining remembrance of Buddha, practicing accumulation and purification, and practicing the yoga of the divine mantras.

You should also focus on the meaning of voidness, for having focused on that, one can accomplish abiding tranquility through the nine stages. Also, producing the wisdom that realizes voidness is most important in the way of practice and the causes of intense insight, which have been previously explained. Therefore, contemplate the benefits of the realization of voidness and the troubles that arise from not realizing it. Then, having become convinced of the egolessness of persons and phenomena, meditate on that egolessness and perceive that everything is like a magician's illusion.

From the *Samādhirājasūtra:*

> Illusory, like a city of celestial musicians,
> Like a mirage, like a dream—
> Meditate that designations are empty in nature;
> Understand all existence in this way.

After this, one can learn the Vajrayāna. This has five aspects: to receive the initiations that make you a suitable vessel; having become a vessel, to keep pure vows and obligations; having maintained your vows, to accomplish the profound path of secret mantras; to make supplication that obstacles to achieving this good path of sutra and mantra be surmounted; and to pray to obtain quickly the high position of the three kāyas (nirmāṇakāya, saṃbhogakāya, and dharmakāya).

Concerning the first of these, the root text says:

> *When, by this practice, I become a vessel of the general path,*
> *May I soon enter*
> *The great gateway of the fortunate ones:*
> *The Vajrayāna, supreme of yānas.*

When, through gradual practice of the general path of Sūtrayāna and Mantrayāna (which includes the three lower tantras), one becomes a fit vessel, one can enter the Vajrayāna. It is superior to all other yānas, the Śrāvakayāna, the Pratyekabuddhayāna, and even the Mahāyāna Pāramitāyāna, as it creates as the path the fruits of buddhahood—a buddha's place, body, enjoyments, and deeds. It quickly completes the accumulation of merit and wisdom by many methods more rare and wonderful than those found in any other teaching. It is the profound short path through which one can quickly gain the high state of Vajradhara.

May I soon enter
The great gateway of the fortunate ones:

In the Vajrayāna is found the extraordinary indivisibility of method and wisdom; it is the great gateway for spiritual beings of good fortune, disciples who are like wish-fulfilling jewels. Such disciples, moved to great faith by their compassion, have great capacity to deliver all living beings, their kind mothers from the ocean of saṃsāric misery. Exerting themselves to the fullest, such beings will enter the Vajrayāna free from doubt.

The door of entrance is the pure initiation of water, diadem, and so forth, as explained in the precious tantras. The initiate will quickly enter the Vajrayāna path by receiving a sacred initiation from a qualified Vajrayāna teacher whom he has pleased in the three ways. This initiation ripens him, empowering him to hear the explanation of the path of secret mantras and to meditate on the three kāyas of an enlightened being.

You must obtain initiation in order to hear and meditate on the path of mantra. The *Mahāmudrātilakatantra* says:

> Just as butter is not churned from sand,
> Without initiation, there is no siddhi.

It is also very important for teacher and disciple to carefully consider each other. It says in the sutras that the best teacher is a monk, the next best a novice *(śrāmaṇera),* and then a householder. Rely on the most excellent.

It says in the *Vajradāka Tantra:*

One who is angry and deceitful,
Extremely harsh in speech,
Complacent in his knowledge—
Such a one should not be relied on as a lama.

One who takes pleasure in meditation and virtuous work,
Who always respects the lama,
Who always gives offerings to the deities—
One who has such qualifications is a disciple.

The second of the five aspects of Vajrayāna is to keep pure vows and obligations once you have become a vessel. The root text says:

The basis of achieving the two siddhis
Is the pure vow one takes on entering this path.
Having found real understanding of it,
May I keep this vow though it cost my life.

The basis of achieving the two siddhis
Is the pure vow one takes on entering this path:

Keeping the pure vows and obligations taken with the lamas and deities as witness at the time of receiving sacred initiation is the indispensable foundation of producing within yourself the profound path of mantra and of accomplishing both siddhis—the ordinary and the superior. This is repeatedly stated in the tantras.

Having found real understanding of it,
May I keep this vow though it cost my life:

Having come to real certainty of this and not merely the formulated understanding derived from the assurance of others, you must guard your vows and obligations more dearly than your life, abandoning the fourteen major transgressions and the eight gross infractions. The gravest fault is to despise your Vajrayāna teacher.

ര്യ

From the *Kṛṣṇayamāritantra:*

Do not despise your teacher.
Do not stray from the Sugata's teaching.
Do not criticize or feel anger
Toward your brothers.
Do not give up the bodhi-mind.
Do not despise your own or others' religion.
Show pure loving-kindness toward all living beings,
Never abandoning them.
Do not show secret teachings
To beings who are not completely ripened.
Do not abuse the aggregates of yourself or others.
Do not trouble the existence of worldly people.

Always give love, even to the worst.
Do not discriminate between the teachings.
Do not deceive the faithful.
Always keep your vows.
It is also wrong to despise
The wisdom nature of women.
Do not feel that yogis are beggars,
And always respect them.

Always repeat the secret mantras,
And always keep your vows.
Yet, if through carelessness
You should break your vow to the lama,
Draw the sacred maṇḍala

And confess your failure before the sugatas.
Without doubt, with compassion,
And with faithful mind, guard your vow to the lama.

❧

The third aspect of the Vajrayāna is to complete the profound path of secret mantra. The root text says:

Having realized the significance of the two stages,
Which are the essence of the Vajrayāna,
By unswerving effort in the four sessions of yoga,
May I achieve what the holy lama has taught.

Having realized the significance of the two stages,
Which are the essence of the Vajrayāna:

Guard the pure vow. Then realize that your teacher is the perfect teacher—the great Vajradhara; your surroundings, the perfect surroundings; your attendants, the perfect companions; the teachings, the perfect teaching—the glorious *Guhyasamāja Tantra,* king of all tantras. Realize the key meanings of symbolic and non-symbolic yoga in the three lower tantras, and realize the two stages—development and fulfillment—in anuttarayoga tantra. These include the essence of all the teachings of the four precious tantras.

By unswerving effort in the four sessions of yoga
May I achieve what the holy lama has taught:

Having realized by hearing and contemplation the key meanings of the tantras, make strong continuous effort in this profound path, not wavering even for an instant. Practice yogic meditation in four sessions—early dawn, morning, afternoon, and evening. Without regard for life and body, accomplish what is taught in the *Caryāmelakapradīpa,* the *Pañcakrama,* and others. Our holy forebears mercifully taught to fortunate disciples these special precepts, which they themselves realized intuitively after they had understood the significance of the root tantras from the explanatory tantras and had thus reached exalted states and obtained siddhis and wisdom.

❧

The fourth aspect of the Vajrayāna is to make supplication for help in surmounting all obstacles to this good path of sutra and tantra. The root text says:

> *May the spiritual teacher who has shown me the good path*
> *And all my spiritual friends who practice it have long life.*
> *May I at last completely surmount*
> *All inner and outer obstacles.*

May the spiritual teacher who has shown me the good path
And all my spiritual friends who practice it have long life:

All the conquerors and their offspring in the three times have gone and will go to buddhahood by the good path of sutra and tantra that has been explained above. Our spiritual teacher accomplishes the deeds of the Conqueror, for he teaches us this good path that is without error in its nature, without mistake in its stages, and that omits nothing, yet is not excessive in its enumerations. May the spiritual teacher and the holy Dharma friends who hear, think, and meditate on this path with us walk with a firm step of their lotus feet, and may their lives be long and of adamantine nature.

May I at last completely surmount
All inner and outer obstacles:

May I increase all helpful qualities—faith, effort, strength of heart, and wisdom. By the power of the lamas, deities, and the Three Jewels, may none of the inner and outer obstacles that hinder accomplishing this good path arise for even a moment—the outer obstacles of harmful sentient beings, demons, and so forth, and the inner obstacles of ills arising from imbalance of the four elements within the body and from a penchant for the three poisons. If, by the power of bad karma, any of these obstacles should arise, may I subdue it immediately.

You must earnestly seek blessings and from the depths of your heart make supplication to the lamas, deities, guardians, and Three Jewels, that you may quickly achieve all the realizations of the path. Pray that you may reach the final goal without hindrance. If you do so, their blessings will quickly enter into you and you, will certainly accomplish all you desire.

✤

The fifth aspect of the Vajrayāna is to make wishing-prayers and to dedicate one's virtue in order to obtain the higher state of Vajradhara as quickly as possible. The root text says:

May I in all births enjoy the glorious Dharma,
Inseparable from the perfect lama;
Having completed the stages and paths,
May I quickly obtain the high state of Vajradhara.

✤

Closing Dedication

As Śāntideva said at the beginning of the *Bodhicaryāvatāra:*

> I do not express here anything previously unsaid,
> Nor have I any skill in composition.
> I do not expect to be of great help to others,
> But I write this in order to train my own mind.

All the selections in this volume express the teachings of Buddha Śākyamuni and his commentators, the renowned scholars of India and Tibet, Nāgārjuna, Asaṅga, Atīśa, Tsongkhapa, and the other great Tibetan lamas.

By the kindness of my lamas, His Holiness the Dalai Lama and his two teachers, His Holiness Ganden Tripa Ling Rinpoche and His Holiness Trijang Rinpoche, and by the kindness of my former lamas in giving me the opportunity to undertake this work, I have been able to translate these selections to the best of my knowledge. Any errors I may have made, I present to the omniscient eyes of the great scholars for their discerning judgment.

I pray that the teaching of Buddha Śākyamuni, the source of happiness and peace, extend and flourish in the world. May its benefits rain on the field of honest and fortunate listeners who have the earnest intention to learn the doctrine of Buddha. May it extend its rays like sunshine and long remain in the world, upheld by holy teachers. By this may the blessings of the Three Jewels extend to all. According to the good wishes of the buddhas and bodhisattvas, may living beings turn from wrongdoing to virtue, and may their sorrow be turned into joy. I dedicate the merit of my small effort in the manner of the supplications of the buddhas and bodhisattvas of the past, present, and future, that all living beings might attain, temporarily, prosperity of life, and finally, the perfect enlightenment of buddhahood.

Notes

1. For more on Dorzhiev and this interesting period of Russian and Asian history, see J. Snelling, *Buddhism in Russia: The Story of Agvan Dorzhiev, Lhasa's Emissary to the Tsar* (Rockport: Element Books, 1993).

2. *Tripiṭaka*, or Three Baskets; the three sections of Buddha's teaching: sutra, abhidharma, and vinaya.

3. From *Precious Garland of Tenets (Grub pa'i mtha'i rnam bzhag rin po che'i phreng ba)* by Könchog Jigme Wangpo (*dKon mchog Jigs med dbang po*, 1728–1781), translated into English by Jeffrey Hopkins in *The Buddhism of Tibet*, Ithaca: Snow Lion, 1987.

4. See Glossary: arhatship; four stages of perfection.

5. The story of the seven successors was adapted and translated from Tāranātha's *History of Buddhism in India (dam pa'i chos rin po che'i phags pa'i yul du ji ltar dar ba'i tshul gsal bar ston pa dgos 'dod kun 'byung)*, written in 1608. Trans. Lama Chimpa and Alaka Chattopadhyaya (Calcutta: Bagchi, 1980).

6. E. Obermiller, *History of Buddhism by Bu ston,* Suzuki Reprint Series, 1931. Vol. II, p. 127.

7. *Byams pa'i chos lnga.* See Glossary: Asaṅga.

8. The preceding histories of the great Indian pandits can be found in Bu tön's (Bu ston) *History of Buddhism in India and Tibet* (written between 1290 and 1364), and in Tāranathā's *History of Buddhism in India* (written c. 1608). See notes 5 and 6 above.

9. Bhṛkuti is an emanation of Tārā.

10. The ten transcendences are also known as the ten *pāramitās* (perfections). These are giving, moral practice, patience, effort, meditation, wisdom, method, prayer, power, and sublime wisdom. See chapter 3.

11. This history of Avalokiteśvara was taken from *History of the Tibetan Kings (rgyal rabs rnams kyi byung tshul gsal ba'i me long chos 'byung)* written by Sakyapa Sonam Gyaltsen (*Sa skya pa bSod nams rgyal mtshan*) in the fifteenth or sixteenth century.

12. *Byang chub lam gyi sgron ma;* Skt. *Bodhipathapradīpa.* Translated into English with commentary in *A Lamp of the Path,* trans. Richard Sherburne, London: RKP, 1978.

13. For example, the three aspects of giving are: the act of giving, the giver of the gift, and the recipient of the gift.

14. Skt. *prapañca;* Tib. *spros pa.*

15. This refers to one who has entered the bodhisattva yāna but has not yet reached the second of the five bodhisattva paths, the application path (Skt. *prayogamārga).*

16. This refers to one who has reached the third of the bodhisattva paths, the insight path (Skt. *darśanamārga).*

17. This precept was given to monks; nuns would substitute 'father' for 'mother,' 'man' for 'woman,' and so on.

18. *'thub pa'i dbang po'i 'bstod pa legs 'bshed sñing po.* Munīndra is an epithet of Śākyamuni Buddha, meaning chief of the sages.

19. These first eight lines are the beginning of Nāgārjuna's *Mūlamadhyamakakārikā* and indicate the eight aspects of voidness.

20. Tib. *blo dang ldan pa;* Skt. *Matimāt.* An epithet of bodhisattvas.

21. Who hold on to the view of dependent origination.

22. A phenomenon not dependent upon its basis of imputation does not exist, just as a flower of the sky does not exist.

23. Nirvāṇa.

24. These two verses refer to the Cittamātrins and Svātantrika-Mādhyamikas, who accept that phenomena exist by self-nature, using as proof dependent origination, i.e., that things come out depending on their source. In the Prāsaṅgika-Madhyamaka system dependent origination is used as the proof that phenomena have no self-nature.

25. By Nāgārjuna and others.

26. Between following and not following the teaching of Buddha.

27. Attainment of the high positions of humans and gods, and attainment of perfect enlightenment.

28. The thirty-two signs and the eighty distinguishing marks of a buddha.

29. Prajñāpāramitā.

30. This is a play on the name of Candrakīrti (Moon-Famed). Candrakīrti wrote many commentaries on the works of Nāgārjuna, and it was through study of these works that Tsongkhapa attained great realization. The lotus garden of Nāgārjuna's commentaries refers to the *guṇḍa* lotus, which blooms in the light of the moon.

31. Of existence or non-existence.

32. There are six aspects of preparation: (1) clean the room where you are practicing, placing any religious objects of meditation in front of you; (2) make pure offerings; (3) sit in the Buddha's meditation position and repeat the refuge, and so on; (4) imagine the field of assembly in front of you; (5) offer the maṇḍala and perform the seven acts of purification and accumulation; and (6) make prayers to realize the purpose of your meditation.

33. The seven acts of worship are: bowing down, making offerings, confessing sins, welcoming all virtuous activities, requesting the buddhas to turn the wheel of Dharma, praying to the teachers to remain in the world, and dedicating merit.

34. The three vows are the vow of individual liberation, the vow of the bodhisattva, and the tantric vow. They precede renunciation, bodhi-mind, and right view.

35. There is a difference in the effect of an action, depending on how it is done in relationship to these four. Helping or harming a bodhisattva has greater effect than helping or harming an ordinary person (field). Actions done with the motivation of helping others have greater effect than action done with the motivation of helping oneself (motivation). A fine gift is better than a poor gift (substance). Actions done in conjunction with a vow have greater effect than actions done without a vow (context).

36. Tib. *nyer len gyi phung po;* Skt. *upādānaskandha.* An embodiment taken compulsively by the power of karma and fettering passions.

37. The five portents of death that eventually come to a god of the desire realm are: dust gathering around the body, sweat coming from the armpits, fading of the garlands of flowers, the body smelling bad, and dissatisfaction with the surroundings.

38. Conditioned embodiment (Tib. *'du byed gyi phung po*; Skt. *saṃskāraskanda*) indicates the third of the three miseries, the pervasive misery of conditioned activity.

39. As it is essential that bodhisattvas learn this, this sutra taught to Prasenajit was specifically quoted by Śāntideva in the *Śikṣāsamuccaya.*

40. The body and mind are made up of five aggregates (Skt. *skandha,* Tib. *phung po*): form, feeling, perception, conditioned

activities, and consciousness.

41. All compounded things are impermanent. Non-compounded things, such as sky and voidness, are permanent.

42. These are: living in a place where the necessities for practicing the Mahāyāna are easily found; relying on a holy being who practices and teaches the Mahāyāna; having great aspiration for the practice of the Mahāyāna; and having produced great merit in the past.

43. The *One Hundred Thousand Verse Prajñāpāramitā Sūtra.*

44. Atīśa. He received the teachings of the two great lineages: the lineage of extensive deeds (compassion), given by Buddha to Maitreya and descended through Asaṅga; and the lineage of profound view (wisdom), given by Buddha to Mañjuśrī and handed down through Nāgārjuna. Thus, Nāgārjuna and Asaṅga are the two great vehicles mentioned here.

45. The four powers are the power of the objects of refuge (lama, Buddha, Dharma, and Saṅgha), the power of doing virtuous actions as countermeasures, the power of removing wrongdoing, and the power of turning away from wrong.

46. Bodhisattvas.

47. The ten bodhisattva stages are: the joyful; the undefiled; the illuminating; the radiant; the difficult to practice; the manifest; the far-reaching; the unwavering; the perfectly intelligent; and the cloud of Dharma. At the final stage, one enters buddhahood.

48. The five paths are the paths of accumulation, application, insight, cultivation, and no-more-learning. When one reaches the bodhisattva's path of insight, one begins the first of the bodhisattva stages (Skt. *bhumis*).

49. The three ways of pleasing a teacher. See "The Three Principles of the Path: Instructions for Meditation" in chapter 6, p. 155.

50. See "The Three Principles of the Path: Instructions for Meditation," chapter 6, pp. 166–7, and the Glossary.

51. Causing, respectively, birth in the lower states of being, in the realms of humans and gods, or in the form or formless realms.

52. The vow of individual liberation (Tib. *so sor thar pa*; Skt. *pratimokṣa*).

53. See chapter 4, p. 105. For a fuller explanation see *Opening the Eye of New Awareness,* by His Holiness Tenzin Gyatso, the Fourteenth Dalai Lama of Tibet (Wisdom, 1985), specifically, the three chapters entitled "Training in Special Ethics," "Training in Special Meditative Stabilization," and "Training in Special Wisdom."

54. The three great purposes are great mind, great abandonment, and great realization.

55. The way of appearance and way of existence (Tib. *snang tshul, gnas tshul)* of sense objects do not accord, for sense objects appear to truly exist but, in reality, are empty of true existence.

56. This has eight aspects: sit on a soft cushion in the lotus position; rest your hands on your heels, palms upturned, left hand underneath and thumbs touching; keep the body straight; keep the teeth and lips as usual, tongue touching the upper teeth; keep the head in a straight line from the nose to the navel; keep the eyes half-open, gently focused on the point of the nose; set the shoulders evenly; and breathe quietly and gently, with in- and out-breaths of the same length.

57. Tib. *btags chos.*

58. Tib. *gdags gzhi.*

59. Anything that is uncompounded has not come into being as the effect of causes and conditions and cannot itself act as a cause or condition giving rise to other effects. A truly existent

ego must logically be uncompounded and, as such, would have no cause-and-effect relationship with anything else. This is the case with the concept of the flower of the sky, and thus, like the flower of the sky, the uncompounded ego is completely non-existent. For fuller development of the refutation of true existence, see chapter 6, pp. 171–3.

60. Those passions that arise through the fettering passions of desire, hatred, and ignorance. (Skt. *upakleśa;* Tib. *nye ba'i nyon mongs*).

Glossary

A

abhidharma (Tib. *chos mngon pa*). The third Basket of the *Tripiṭaka*; the systematized philosophical and psychological analysis of existence that is the basis for the Buddhist systems of tenets and of mind-training.

abiding tranquility (Tib. *zhi gnas;* Skt. *śamatha*). A high level of meditative concentration or mental one-pointedness; a necessary foundation for intense insight. *See* intense insight.

ācārya. Sanskrit title meaning teacher.

adamantine body (Tib. *rdo rje'i sku*). The indestructible body of a buddha. *See* vajra.

aggregates (Tib. *phung po;* Skt. *skandha*). The body and mind are made up of the five aggregates: form, feeling, perceptions, conditioned activities, and consciousness.

Amitābha (Tib. *'Od dpag med* or *sNang ba mtha' yas*). The Buddha of Infinite Light, who presides over the western paradise, Sukhāvatī. He is associated with infinite compassion and is the teacher of Ārya Avalokiteśvara. The Panchen Lamas of Tibet are incarnations of Amitābha.

anuttarayoga tantra (Tib. *rnal 'byor bla na med pa'i rgyud*). The highest of the four tantras. *See* tantra.

arhat (Tib. *dgra bcom pa*). One who has obtained arhatship. One who has conquered the inner defilements. *See* arhatship.

arhatship. In the Hīnayāna systems, arhatship is the highest attainment, the culmination of the four stages of perfection when an arhat attains nirvāṇa. According to the Mahāyāna system, śrāvakas and pratyekabuddhas attain arhatship when they reach the fifth of the five paths, the path of no-more-learning (Tib. *mi lob lam*; Skt. *aśaikṣamārga*). *See* five paths; four stages of perfection; nirvāṇa; pratyekabuddha; śrāvaka.

ārya (Tib. *'phags pa*). A title meaning exalted or noble. It indicates one who has attained the third of the five paths, the path of insight (Tib. *mthong lam;* Skt. *darśanamārga*).

Asaṅga (Tib. *Thogs med*). Propounder of the Cittamātra or "Mind Only" school of tenets. He brought back from Tuṣita heaven the five treatises of Maitreya: the *Mahāyānasūtrālaṃkāra* (Tib. *mDo sde rgyan*), the *Mahāyānottaratantraśāstra* (Tib. *Theg pa chen po rgyud bla ma'i bstan bcos*); the *Madhyāntavibhāga* (Tib. *dBus dang mtha' rnam 'byed*); the *Dharmadharmatāvibhāgakārikā* (Tib. *Chos dang chos nyid rnam par 'byed pa'i tshig leur byas pa*); and the *Abhisamayālaṃkāra* (Tib. *mNgon par rtogs pa'i rgyan*).

attainments. See siddhi.

Avalokiteśvara (Tib. *sPyan ras gzigs*). The great bodhisattva of compassion, the chief disciple of Amitābha. The Dalai Lamas of Tibet are incarnations of Avalokiteśvara.

B

Bamboo Grove (Tib. *'od ma tshal*). A famous place of retreat near Rājagṛha, given to the Buddha by King Bimbisāra.

bardo. The intermediate state between death and rebirth. One remains in that state anywhere from a moment to forty-nine days. During the process of transmigration, everyone passes through this state.

bhikṣu (Tib. *dge slong*). A fully ordained Buddhist monk; an actual member of the Saṅgha.

Bodhgayā (Tib. *rdo rje gdan*). The place in northern India (modern Bihar state) where Śākyamuni Buddha manifested enlightenment in the early sixth century B.C.

bodhi (Tib. *byang chub*). Enlightenment.

bodhi-mind (Tib. byang chub sems; Skt. *bodhicitta*). A mind that is directed toward enlightenment, the attainment of buddhahood, for the sake of all living beings. There are seven cause-and-effect precepts for the generation of bodhi-mind; once one has generated bodhi-mind, one enters the first of the bodhisattva paths, the path of accumulation (Tib. *tshogs lam;* Skt. *saṃbhāramārga*).

bodhisattva (Tib. *byang chub sems dpa'*). Also called 'offspring of the Conqueror' (Tib. *rgyal sras*), one who has vowed to attain enlightenment for the sake of all living beings. The term bodhisattva refers to those at many levels, from those who have generated the aspiration to enlightenment for the first time through those who have actually entered the bodhisattva path, which is developed through the ten stages and culminates in enlightenment, the attainment of buddhahood.

bodhi tree. The tree under which Buddha manifested enlightenment at Bodhgayā, popularly called the *pipal* tree. An offshoot of that same tree is still in existence in Bodhgayā.

Brahma (Tib. *Tshangs pa*). A king of the gods who dwells in the form realm.

Brahmin. A person of the highest caste of Hindu society.

Buddha (Tib. *sangs rgyas*). A being who has completely purified (*sangs*) all the defilements and completely extended (*rgyas*)—that is, perfected—his understanding. He is a fully enlightened being, perfect in omniscience and compassion. Every being has the potential to become a completely enlightened buddha. There are countless buddhas; Śākyamuni Buddha is the fourth buddha in this golden age, which is to have one thousand buddhas.

buddha-field. The realm of existence of a buddha.

C

Cittamātra (Tib. *sems tsam pa*). The 'Mind Only' school of tenets, also known as Yogācāra or Vijñānavāda, developed by Asaṅga and his brother Vasubandhu. This Mahāyāna system of tenets accepts as literal the teachings of the third turning of the wheel of Dharma, particularly those of the *Saṃdhinirmocanasūtra.*

contemplative equipoise (Tib. *mnyam par gzhag pa;* Skt. *samāhita*). The state of "equal placement" of mind; concentration.

D

ḍākinī (Tib. *mkha' 'gro ma*). In the tantras, the class of female deities embodying wisdom.

Dalai Lama (Tib. *yid bzhin nor bu*). An incarnation of Avalokiteśvara and the spiritual and temporal head of the Tibetan people. The present Dalai Lama, the fourteenth, is His Holiness Tenzin Gyatso.

degenerate age. That period when the traditions of Buddha's teachings are no longer pure and the world situation makes it difficult to practice the Dharma properly. *See* kaliyuga.

dependent origination (Tib. *rten cing 'brel bar 'byung ba;* Skt. *pratītya-samutpāda*). The dependent nature of all phenomena. In the highest sense, the proof of the self-naturelessness or voidness of all things. In general, the twelve nidānas, or links, that condition the cycle of the arising and subsiding of all saṃsāric existence.

desire realm (Tib. *'dod khams;* Skt. *kāmadhātu*). One of the three realms of saṃsāra. In this realm, which includes the spheres of hell beings, hungry ghosts, animals, humans, demigods, and the six lower classes of gods, consciousness is preoccupied with desire for objects of the six senses.

Devadatta. A cousin of Buddha Śākyamuni who was his persistent antagonist throughout all his lifetimes.

Dharma (Tib. *chos*). The doctrine of the Buddha; it has the two aspects of instruction and understanding, the former being what one learns and the latter, one's internal realization.

dharmakāya (Tib. *chos kyi sku*). The dharma-body. It is the effect of the assembling of wisdom. When one attains buddhahood, one attains the dharmakāya. This has two parts: the *svabhāvakāya* (Tib. *ngo bo nyid kyi sku*), which is the buddha-nature; and the *jñānakāya* (Tib. *ye shes kyi sku*), which is the omniscient wisdom of a buddha. *See* trikāya.

dharmarāja. Any Buddhist king who greatly helped to further the Dharma. Aśoka, an Indian king of the third century B.C., was considered a great dharmarāja, as were the Buddhist kings of early Tibet.

discernment (Tib. *shes bzhin*; Skt. *samprajanya*). Comprehension; clear distinguishing between what is right and what is not, accompanied by the understanding of how to direct one's activities of body, speech, and mind to the right path.

E

effort (Tib. *brtson 'grus;* Skt. *vīrya*). The fourth of the six transcendences. It has three aspects: armor-like effort—working with pleasure and without regret in order to achieve the qualities of a buddha and staying in the world as long as necessary to help a single living being; the effort of gathering virtue—accomplishing the six transcendences, and so on; and the effort of working for the benefit of living beings.

ego (Tib. *nga* or *bdag;* Skt. *ātman*). Buddhism does not accept the existence of an independent, self-existent, unchanging ego, because if such were to exist, a person would be unchanging and thus unable to purify himself of fettering passions and attain buddhahood. There is acceptance of a relative, impermanent, changeable, conscious entity, which is the continuation of life, linking one's former life to this life and this life to future lives.

egolessness (Tib. *bdag med;* Skt. *anātman*). The absence of a truly existing self-nature, both in persons and in phenomena.

ego-reflection (Tib. *spros pa;* Skt. *prapañca*). Reflective thought-flow on external or internal objects; it is incited by ego-illusion and functions to reinforce it.

eight aspects of leisure (Tib. *dal ba brgyad;* Skt. *aṣṭakṣaṇa*). These are eight qualities of a human life that is free from eight states that prevent study of the Dharma. These eight are: (1) being born in one of the hells; (2) being born as a hungry ghost; (3) being born as an animal; (4) being born as a barbarian (whose harmful activities are incorporated within one's religious beliefs, and where even the taking of life is called a virtuous deed); (5) being born as a long-lived god; (6) being born with wrong views (so that one has no desire to do virtuous work); (7) being born in a dark age when no buddha has appeared and the highest teachings have not been extended; and (8) being born without the faculties to apprehend the Dharma.

eight worldly concerns. These are concern for gain and loss, fame and disgrace, praise and blame, pleasure and pain.

eightfold path. The path indicated by the fourth Noble Truth: right view, right thought, right speech, right conduct, right livelihood, right effort, right mindfulness, and right meditation.

enlightenment (Tib. *byang chub;* Skt. *bodhi*). The final goal of the path. This consists in the purification *(byang)* of the defilements and the correct understanding *(chub)* of all existence.

eon (Skt. *kalpa*). The period of time that it takes a dove to exhaust a mountain of grain the size of Mount Everest by removing one grain every thousand years.

eternalism (Tib. *rtag lta*). Belief in an unchanging ego or self-nature in either persons or phenomena. One of the two extreme views and the opposite of nihilism.

extremes (Tib. *mtha';* Skt. *anta*). Incorrect nihilistic or eternalistic views.

F

fettering passions (Tib. *nyon mongs;* Skt. *kleśa*). Defilements or afflictions. The principal ones are desire, hatred, and ignorance, which are called the three mental poisons. Ignorance is the root cause of wandering in saṃsāra.

five aggregates. See aggregates.

five paths. To attain either nirvāṇa or buddhahood, one must progress through five graded paths of realization. These are: the path of accumulation (Tib. *tshogs lam;* Skt. *saṃbhāramārga*); the path of application (Tib. *sbyor lam;* Skt. *prayogamārga*); the path of insight (Tib. *mthong lam;* Skt. *darśanamārga*); the path of cultivation (Tib. *sgom lam;* Skt. *bhāvanāmārga*); and the path of no-more-learning (Tib. *mi slob lam;* Skt. *aśaikṣamārga*). One can pass through these five paths either as a śrāvaka or a pratyekabuddha to attain the final goal of arhatship, or as a bodhisattva seeking the final attainment of buddhahood.

five treatises of Maitreya. See Asaṅga.

form realm (Tib. *gzugs kyi khams*; Skt. *rūpadhātu*). The second of saṃsāra's three realms, in which consciousness is involved in meditations with form. Seventeen classes of gods abide in this realm; they are still under the influence of fettering passions.

formless realm (Tib. *gzugs med kyi khams;* Skt. *ārūpyadhātu*). The highest of saṃsāra's three realms, in which consciousness is involved in formless meditations. The four highest classes of gods abide in this realm.

four immeasurables (Tib. *tshad ma med pa'i bzhi;* Skt. *apramāṇa*). These are: equanimity, love, compassion, and joy. They are called immeasurable because they are measureless equanimity, love, compassion, and joy toward all living beings.

Four Noble Truths. These are: suffering is inherent in existence; there is a cause of this suffering; this suffering can be stopped; and the way to stop this suffering is the truth of the superior path. This is the teaching of the first wheel of Dharma.

four powers. These are the four countermeasures by which one purifies oneself from sins. They are: the power of the objects of refuge, the power of doing virtuous actions, the power of removing wrongdoing, and the power of turning away from wrong.

four stages of perfection. These are the fruits of practice attained by followers of the Hīnayāna schools of Buddhism and are stream-winning, once-returning, non-returning, and arhatship. Arhatship is the highest attainment of śrāvakas and pratyekabuddhas.

full lotus (*padmāsāna* or *vajraparyaka*). The most familiar and classic position for meditation: cross-legged with the feet crossed and locked, soles upward and resting upon the opposite thighs.

G

garuḍa. A large mythical bird, like an eagle, which is the enemy of the snake of hatred.

Gautama. Family name of Śākyamuni Buddha.

geshe (Tib. *dge bshes*; Skt. *kalyānamitra*). "Spiritual friend." Title given to a spiritual teacher.

ghee. Clarified butter.

giving (Tib. *sbyin pa;* Skt. *dāna*). The first of the six transcendences. As practiced by the bodhisattvas, it has three aspects: the giving of things—giving necessities without hope of return or reward; the giving of protection—rescuing living beings from harm; and the giving of Dharma—teaching the Dharma according to the ability of the disciple, not looking for gain or respect.

golden age (Tib. *bskal pa bzang po*). According to the Mahāyāna tradition, this is the golden age in which one thousand buddhas will appear. Śākyamuni Buddha is the fourth; the next buddha will be Maitreya.

Guhyasamāja Tantra (Tib. *gsang ba dus pa*). One of the tantras of anuttarayoga tantra, the fourth and highest class of tantra.

guru (Tib. *bla ma*). Spiritual teacher, lama.

H

Hīnayāna (Tib. *theg dman*). "Lesser Vehicle." *See* Theravāda.

hungry ghost (Tib. *yi dvags*; Skt. *preta*). Inhabitant of one of the three lower states of being. Those born there suffer continual insatiable hunger and thirst.

I

ignorance (Tib, *ma rig pa;* Skt. *avidyā*). The root cause of suffering. The first link in the causal chain of dependent origination; also, the primary element of the three mental poisons. *See also* fettering passions.

Indra (Tib. *lha yid bang po* or *brgya byin*). Lord of the thirty-three gods of the desire realm. Also called Śakra.

indranīla. Sapphire.

initiation (Tib. *dbang;* Skt. *abhiṣeka*). Ritual empowerment conferred by a lama on his disciple. Initiation is required before certain levels of practice in the Mantrayāna path may be undertaken.

intense insight (Tib. *lhag mthong;* Skt. *vipaśyanā*). Fine investigation of the nature of phenomena leading ultimately to the realization of voidness. When a practitioner accomplishes the direct experience of voidness together with stability based on abiding tranquility, he or she becomes an ārya and has achieved the third of the five paths, the path of insight (Tib. *mthong lam;* Skt. *darśanamārga*).

J

Jambudvīpa (Tib. *'dzam bu gling*). According to Buddhist cosmology as found in the abhidharma texts, this is the southern continent of the four continents that surround Mount Meru. Historically, the Indian subcontinent.

Jātakas (Tib. *skyes rabs*). Descriptions of the Buddha's previous lives.

K

kaliyuga. An age characterized by turmoil, upheaval, and destruction.

kalpa. *See* eon.

Kangyur (Tib. *bka' 'gyur*). The Tibetan collection of the *Tripiṭaka*: the sutras, the vinaya, and the abhidharma— in one hundred and eight volumes; the Buddha's recorded speech.

karma (Tib. *las*). Action and its consequences; the totality of an individual's deeds and their consequences. By the infallible ripening of karma (like the ripening of seeds), beings experience misery, happiness, and so on.

L

lama (Tib. *bla ma;* Skt. *guru*). The spiritual teacher. Literally, it means the one without superior, the highest.

Lhasa. The capital city of Tibet, located in the central region.

M

Madhyamaka (Tib. *dbu ma pa*). The Mahāyāna system of tenets based on the prajñāpāramitā sutras. It has two divisions: Svātantrika and Prāsaṅgika. This school accepts as literal the teachings of the second turning of the wheel of Dharma.

Mahākāla (Tib. *Legs ldan nag po* or *Mgon po phyag drug*). Six-armed protector of the Dharma.

mahāsattva (Tib. *sems pa chen po*). "Great being." A high bodhisattva.

Mahāyāna (Tib. *theg chen*). "The Great Vehicle." The vehicle of the bodhisattvas leading to the attainment of buddhahood.

Maheśvāra (Tib. *dBang phyug chen po*). "Great god," or "great lord." One of the non-Buddhist deities.

Maitreya (Tib. *Byams pa*). The bodhisattva of love. Predicted by Buddha Śākyamuni to be the next buddha, he presently presides over Tuṣita heaven, having received this position from Śākyamuni before the latter manifested himself in Jambudvīpa. Maitreya received from Buddha Śākyamuni the teachings of compassion, the lineage of extensive deeds. He transmitted this lineage to Asaṅga. *See* Asaṅga; Jambudvīpa; Tuṣita.

maṇḍala (Tib. *dkyil 'khor*). As part of the seven branches of practice, the maṇḍala offering is symbolic of offering the entire universe to the buddhas and to your lama. More generally, a symbolic representation of a deity's realm of existence.

Mañjuśrī (Tib. *Jam dpal*). The bodhisattva of wisdom. He received from Śākyamuni the teachings of wisdom, the lineage of the profound view of voidness, which he handed down to Nāgārjuna.

Mañjughoṣa (Tib. *Jam pa'i dbyangs*). Another name for Mañjuśrī.

mantra (Tib. *sngags*). A set of words or syllables whose recitation has special effects based on the power of sound.

Mantrayāna (Tib. *sngags kyi theg pa*). The vehicle of mantra, it includes all four levels of tantra.

Māra. Personification of the evil principle. The tempter, or king of demons.

Marpa. A great Tibetan yogi of the eleventh and twelfth centuries, disciple of Nāropa, and teacher of Milarepa.

meditation (Tib. *sgom;* Skt. *dhyāna*). The fifth of the six transcendences. Meditation can be seen from three viewpoints. From the viewpoint of location, meditation is within or beyond saṃsāra. From the viewpoint of direction, there are abiding tranquility, intense insight, and the unification of these two. And from the viewpoint of activity, there are (a) the meditation of happiness of mind and body, (b) the meditation of creating the basis of excellence, and (c) the meditation of working for the benefit of all living beings.

Milarepa. A Tibetan yogi who achieved buddhahood in one lifetime; he was the disciple of Marpa. Milarepa's biography is a favorite example of hardship undertaken in order to attain enlightenment.

moral practice (Tib. *tshul khrims;* Skt. *śīla*). Second of the six transcendences, it has three aspects: the moral practice of vows, the moral practice of gathering virtuous actions, and the moral practice of working for the benefit of other living beings.

Mount Meru. Sacred mountain in the Himalayas. In the Buddhist and Hindu traditions, the center of the cosmos.

mudrā (Tib. *phyag rgya*). Symbolic ritual gesture. Literally, 'seal.'

Munīndra. Epithet of Śākyamuni Buddha.

N

nāga (Tib. *glu*). Dragon-like beings who inhabit and have influence over the waters of the world. In Buddha's time, they listened to his teachings and took them to their own land.

Nālandā. One of the famous Buddhist universities in India; during the time that Buddhism flourished there, many thousands of monks lived and studied at Nālandā.

namo. A salutatory form used at the beginning of texts meaning "praise," or "glory."

Nāropa. Indian scholar-yogi who, after serving as an abbot of the northern gate at Nālandā, obtained the highest teachings from Tilopa. His disciple was Marpa, who took these teachings to Tibet.

natural existence (Tib. *rang bzhin;* Skt. *svabhāva*). Another term for true existence, which we erroneously attribute to persons and phenomena.

nihilism (Tib. *chad lta*). Belief that phenomena are completely non-existent. One of the extremes to be avoided; the opposite of eternalism.

nirmāṇakāya (Tib. *sprul sku*). One of the three bodies, or trikāya, of a buddha. A magically created body, like that of Śākyamuni Buddha which manifested in India in the sixth century B.C. Together with the saṃbhogakāya, it makes up an enlightened being's rūpakāya, or form body.

nirvāṇa (Tib. *mya ngan las das pa*). Literally means "passed from suffering," the state of ceaseless bliss and extinction of all fettering passions.

non-returning. See arhatship; four stages of perfection.

O

omniscience, six kinds of. See six kinds of omniscience.

once-returning. See four stages of perfection.

P

Padmasambhava or *Guru Rinpoche.* The great Indian ācārya who brought tantric teachings to Tibet in the eighth century. He founded the tantric lineage of the Nyingma sect.

Panchen Lama. Lineage representing incarnations of Amitābha Buddha. The Panchen Lama and the Dalai Lama are the two highest spiritual leaders of Tibet.

pandit (Skt. *paṇḍita*). Scholar-teacher.

pāramitā (Tib. *pha rol tu phyin pa*). *See* transcendences.

parinirvāṇa. Final nirvāṇa. Mahāparinirvāṇa refers to the historical passing of Śākyamuni.

path (Skt. *mārga*). *See* five paths; eightfold path.

patience (Tib. *bzod pa*; Skt. *kṣānti*). The third of the six transcendences. It has three aspects: the patience of not reacting negatively when harmed; the patience of purposely taking the misery of others on oneself; and the patience of having confidence in the Dharma.

prajñāpāramitā (Tib. *shes rab kyi pha rol tu phyin pa*). 'Perfection of wisdom.' The prajñāpāramitā sutras of eight thousand, twenty-five thousand, and one hundred thousand verses are Buddha Śākyamuni's discourses from the viewpoint of the second wheel of Dharma, teaching that phenomena lack true or natural existence.

pratyekabuddha (Tib. *rang rgyal*). One whose aim is his or her own liberation from saṃsāra. To attain nirvāṇa, such a practitioner does not wish to depend on a teacher, even Buddha.

Prāsaṅgika-Madhyamaka (Tib. *dbu ma thal 'gyur pa*). System of Madhyamaka tenets following Candrakīrti's clarification of Nāgārjuna's work. This school accepts that entities lack true existence by their own nature.

R

rakṣa. Cannibal demon.

ratna (Tib. *nor bu*). Rare and precious; precious jewel.

remembrance (Tib. *dren pa;* Skt. *smṛti*). Remembrance and mindfulness of what has been taught.

right view (Tib. *yang dag pa'i lta ba*). Wisdom; the view that realizes voidness as the nature of all persons and phenomena.

rishi. A great sage.

rūpakāya (Tib. *gzugs kyi sku*). The form body of a buddha, including both the magically created body, like that which appeared in India in the sixth century B.C. (nirmāṇakāya), and the body of perfect enjoyment (saṃbhogakāya). It is the effect of the assembling of merit.

S

Śākya. Clan name of the historical Buddha who was born around 560 B.C.

Śākyamuni Buddha. Name of the historical Buddha who appeared in the sixth century B.C. Literally, "the Buddha who is the sage of the Śākya clan." He is the fourth of the thousand buddhas of this golden age.

samādhi (Tib. *ting nge 'dzin*). One-pointed concentration.

Samantabhadra (Tib. *kun tu bzang po*). A bodhisattva known for his heroic aspiration and offerings.

saṃbhogakāya (Tib. *longs spyod sku*). The body of a buddha that resides in the buddha-fields and upper realms; the fully adorned body of a buddha, complete with all the extraordinary signs, which is continually teaching the Mahāyāna path to a circle of bodhisattva āryas. This, together with the nirmāṇakāya, makes up the rūpakāya of a buddha.

saṃsāra (Tib. *'khor ba* or *srid pa*). The cycle of existence in the three realms—the desire realm, the form realm, and the formless realm.

Saṅgha. The third of the Three Jewels; the assembly of monks or bhikṣus, and nuns. *See* Buddha; Dharma; Three Jewels.

Sarasvatī (Tib. *dbyangs can ma* or *tshangs dbyangs*). The goddess of learning and eloquence for both Hindus and Buddhists. The embodiment of beauty and clarity of speech.

Śāriputra. An arhat; one of the Buddha's two chief disciples, the other being Maudgalyayāna.

seven acts of worship (Tib. *yan lak 'dun*). *See* note 33.

seven cause-and-effect precepts of generating bodhi-mind. These are: to understand that all living beings have been your mother; to contemplate their great kindness; to determine to repay their kindness; to generate love toward all living beings; to generate compassion toward all living beings; to generate high resolve; and to generate bodhi-mind. The first six are the casual precepts; the seventh precept is the result. When one attains the seventh of these, one enters the first path, the path of accumulation (Tib. *tshogs lam;* Skt. *saṃbhāramārga*) of the bodhisattva vehicle.

siddha (Tib. *grub thob*). One who has attained siddhis.

siddhi (Tib. *dngos grub*). Attainment. There are eight ordinary siddhis and one superior siddhi. The eight ordinary siddhis are: magical sword, magical pills, magical eye medicine giving magical vision, the power of walking miraculously, the magical elixir of youth, the practice of miraculously changing the body into the state of the gods, the power of miraculously disappearing, and the power of passing through a wall, mountain, or earthly barrier without any difficulty. The superior siddhi is buddhahood.

Śīva. A very powerful Hindu deity, Maheśvara.

six kinds of omniscience (Tib. *mngon shes;* Skt. *abhijñā*). The six clairvoyances: divine eye, divine ear, knowledge of others' minds, remembrance of former lives, miraculous power, and knowledge of the removal of defilements.

six aspects of preparation. See note 32.

six transcendences. These are the six perfections, which include all the deeds of the bodhisattvas. They are transcendent giving, moral practice, patience, effort, meditation, and wisdom. A bodhisattva's practice of these transcends that of ordinary beings. *See entries under each transcendence*; ten transcendences; transcendences.

six worlds. The desire realm is made up of six realms or worlds: those of hell-beings, hungry ghosts, animals, humans, demigods, and the first six classes of gods.

śrāvaka (Tib. *nyan thos*). One who follows the Hīnayāna teachings and works for his or her own liberation by listening to and studying the teachings of the Buddha.

stream-winning. See arhatship; four stages of perfection.

stūpa (Tib. *mchod rten*). A monument containing relics.

Subhūti. One of Śākyamuni Buddha's chief disciples.

sugata (Tib. *bde bar gshegs pa*). An epithet for a buddha, and for Śākyamuni Buddha in particular, meaning 'blissfully gone.'

Sukhāvatī (Tib. *bde ba can*). The heaven of Amitābha, the Buddha of Infinite Light.

sutra (Skt. *sūtra*; Tib. *mdo*). The discourses of the Buddha.

Sūtrayāna. The vehicle or path taught by the Hīnayāna and Mahāyāna sutras.

Svātantrika-Madhyamaka (Tib. *dbu ma rang rgyud pa*). System of Madhyamaka tenets following Bhāvaviveka's interpretation of Nāgārjuna's work. This school accepts an existence by self-nature.

T

tantras (Tib. *rgyud*). The canon of the Mantrayāna. There are four classes of tantras: kriya tantra (Tib. *bya ba'i rgyud*); carya tantra (Tib. *spyad pai rgyud*); yoga tantra (Tib. *rnal 'byor ba'i rgyud*); and anuttarayoga tantra (Tib. *rnal 'byor bla na med pa'i rgyud*). The fourth is the highest.

Tārā (Tib. *sgrol ma*). Compassionate savior goddess. She was born from a tear of Avalokiteśvara and vowed to help him to liberate all living beings from saṃsāra.

tathāgata (Tib. *de bzhin gshegs pa*). An epithet of a buddha, meaning "one who is thus-gone."

ten aspects of opportunity (Tib. *'byor bcu*). There are five "inner" conditions of opportunity: being born as a human being, being born in a civilized land, possessing sound sense faculties, being without non-reversible negative karma, and having faith in the *Tripiṭaka*; and five "external" conditions of opportunity: that the Buddha visited the world, that he taught the holy Dharma; that his teaching remains to the present; that there are still followers of the teaching; that the people of one's environment have love and mercy for others.

ten bodhisattva stages. See note 47.

ten non-virtues, or *non-virtuous activities.* These are killing, stealing, sexual misconduct, lying, slandering, speaking harshly, speaking senselessly, coveting, bearing ill will, and holding wrong views.

ten transcendences, or *perfections.* The six transcendences plus method, prayer, power, and sublime wisdom. *See* six transcendences; transcendences.

ten virtues, or *virtuous activities.* These are the opposites of the ten non-virtuous activities. *See* ten non-virtues *above.*

Theravāda. "Vehicle of the Elders" (Skt. *sthavīravāda*) tradition of Buddhism, currently practiced in Sri Lanka, Burma, and Thailand; the modern form of one of the eighteen Vaibhāṣika schools, which, together with the Sautrāntika, make up the Hīnayāna. Its final goal is arhatship.

thirty-two major extraordinary signs of a buddha. Unique physical characteristics of a buddha.

three aspects of action (Tib. *'khor gsum*). Every action has three aspects: the actor, the action, and the recipient of the action. *See* note 13.

Three Baskets. See Tripiṭaka.

Three Jewels (Tib. *dkon mchog gsum*; Skt. *triratna*). The Buddha, his teaching (Dharma), and his followers (Saṅgha).

three kāyas, or *bodies. See* trikāya.

three mental poisons. See fettering passions.

three miseries. All saṃsāra is pervaded by misery: suffering itself is the *misery of misery*; worldly happiness is the *misery of change*; and all else is the pervasive *misery of conditioned activities.*

three precepts. Exceptional moral practice, exceptional meditation, and exceptional wisdom. These three precepts comprise the instruction aspect of the Dharma.

three realms. Desire realm, form realm, and formless realm.

three times. Past, present, and future.

transcendences (Skt. *pāramitā*; Tib. *pha rol tu phyin pa*). Sometimes known as 'perfections.' The complex of practices that are the basis of Mahāyāna practice. For this reason the Mahāyāna is also referred to as the Pāramitāyāna, or Vehicle of the Transcendences. They form an integrated system of behavioral and mental techniques for initiating, developing, and focusing energy and activity from the beginning of Dharma practice until buddhahood. *See* six transcendences; ten transcendences.

trikāya. The three bodies of a buddha: dharmakāya, saṃbhogakāya, and nirmāṇakāya. *See entries under each.*

Tripiṭaka (Tib. *sde snod gsum*). The three sections of the Buddhist canon: sutra, vinaya, and abhidharma.

triratna. See Three Jewels.

Tsongkhapa. The great fourteenth-century scholar and teacher who reformed the Kadampa tradition, thus founding the Gelugpa sect. His many treatises finalized the work begun by Atīśa of clarification and synthesis of the vast body of Indian scriptures and schools of practice into a unified exposition of Sūtrayāna and Tantrayāna paths.

Tuṣita (Tib. *dga' ldan*). The heaven presided over by the future buddha, Maitreya.

two stages of Vajrayāna. These are the two stages of the highest tantra, the anuttarayoga tantra. They are the development stage and the completion stage.

two truths. All objects of cognition have two modes of existence, called "truths": the truth of appearance, or relative truth (Skt. *samvṛtisatya*), is the aspect of existence according to worldly convention and expression; absolute truth (Skt. *paramārthasatya*) is the voidness of all phenomena, the reality of existence.

U

upāsaka (Tib. *dge bsnyen*). A male lay Buddhist who has vowed to uphold any or all of the five vows: not to kill, steal, lie, commit sexual misconduct, or take intoxicants.

upāsikā (Tib. *dge bsnyen ma*). Female lay Buddhist. *See above.*

V

vajra (Tib. *rdo rje*). Diamond; thunderbolt; scepter. That which is indivisible and indestructible. Often-used metaphor for the abiding quality of buddhahood.

Vajradhara (Tib. *rdo rje 'chang*). Tantric manifestation of Buddha Śākyamuni.

Vajrapāṇi (Tib. *phyag na rdo rje*). The bodhisattva who received from Buddha Śākyamuni the teachings of the Mantrayāna.

Vajrayāna (Tib. *rdo rje theg pa*). "Diamond Vehicle." The vehicle of anuttarayoga tantra, highest of the four tantras.

vajra throne (Tib. *rdo rje gdan*). The place in Bodhgayā where Śākyamuni manifested complete, perfect enlightenment.

Vikramaśīla. One of the famous Buddhist universities in India. Atīśa headed this monastery before going to Tibet.

vinaya (Tib. *'dul ba*). The first of the three major divisions, or baskets, of the Buddhist canon, the *Tripiṭaka.* It also refers to the code of behavior contained in this vinaya basket, followed by those who have taken the vows of the Buddhist order.

virtues. See ten virtues.

voidness (Tib. *stong pa nyid*; Skt. *śūnyatā*). The ultimate nature of existence, or absolute aspect, of all cognizable things. Extensively and variously discussed by the different schools.

W

wheel of the Dharma (Tib. *chos kyi khor lo;* Skt. *dharmacakra*). The expression "turning the wheel of the Dharma" means Buddha's acts of teaching. There are three basic viewpoints. In general, the Mahāyāna schools hold that the first wheel expounds the Four Noble Truths, the principal objects of realization for those who accept the true existence of eternal objects. The second wheel expounds the absence of true existence of internal and external objects. The third wheel explains the absence of real contradiction between the first and second wheels. The first wheel is the basis of the Hīnayāna schools, the second, of the Madhyamaka school, and the third, of the Cittamātra, or Mind-Only, school.

wisdom (Tib. *shes rab;* Skt. *prajñā*). The sixth of the six transcendences. It has three aspects: the wisdom that realizes absolute truth, or voidness; the wisdom that realizes the relative, or apparent, truth and the five branches of knowledge; and the wisdom that understands perfectly the way to achieve the two purposes of living beings.

Y

yakṣa (Tib. *gnod spyin*). A harmful or mischievous deity.

Yama (Tib. *bshin rje*). The Lord of Death.

yāna (Tib. *theg pa*). Vehicle; means of traveling across the ocean of saṃsāra to the door of liberation. The usual division of the Dharma is into the three yānas—Śrāvakayāna, Pratyekabuddhayāna, and Mahā- or Bodhisattvayāna. The Mahāyāna can also be further divided into the Pāramitāyāna and the Mantrayāna.

yidam (Skt. *iṣṭadevatā*). Any of those deities, often in fierce aspect, associated with teachings of the Mantrayāna. A tantric yogi chooses or recognizes one yidam, a so-called tutelary deity, as having a special relationship to him- or herself, though he or she may in the course of practice associate with other deities, invoke them, and identify with them in meditation.

yogi (Tib. *rnal 'byor pa*). One who is especially devoted to and particularly accomplished in meditation; fem., *yoginī*.

Index

abhidharma 16, 21, 33, 43, 223, 234
-*piṭaka* 15, 21, 41, 215, 234, 246. *See* sutra; Tripiṭaka; vinaya
Abhisamayālaṃkāra 224
abhiṣeka 233. *See* initiation
abiding tranquility 95, 179–180, 184, 200–205, 223, 233, 236. *See also* contemplative equipoise; samādhi
benefits of 201
ācārya 223, 238
accumulation
of karma xviii, 68, 104, 106, 109, 119, 145, 189–190, 199, 201.*See also* actions; karma; non-virtuous actions; virtuous actions.
of merit and wisdom 11, 19, 46, 49, 86, 94–95, 98, 101, 108–109, 117, 119, 142, 151, 163, 177, 205, 207, 217; three branch methods 95. *See also* wisdom.
acinta 32
actions 234. *See also* deeds; karma.
motivation for 199, 218
of buddhas 40, 47, 141
three aspects of 85, 98, 107, 216, 245
after-attainment 167–169, 180
aging 193–194
Ajātaśatru 21–23
Akaniṣṭha ('Og min) 4
Amdo 42
Amitābha 34–35, 37–39, 223–224, 238, 243
analysis 137, 165–167, 169, 179–180, 184, 201, 203–204, 223. *See also* four keys.
Ānanda 20–23, 65, 77, 80
Anāthapiṇḍika 48, 57, 77, 80
anātman 229
animal realm 37, 189, 227, 229, 242
rebirth in 190. *See also* six realms; lower realms
Antīvāhana, King 25
anuttarayoga tantra 210, 223, 232, 243, 246–247. *See also* tantra
appearance 84, 96, 117–118, 203, 246
and voidness 111, 117, 137, 169–170, 204. *See also* voidness
way of 128, 167–168, 201, 203–204, 220. *See also* magician's illusion; illusion; illusory.
apramāṇa 231
ardzaka plant 38
arhat xix, 20–23, 65, 77, 224, 241
arhatship 9, 19–23, 54–58, 81–82, 215, 224, 230–231, 244. *See also* Hinayāna; nirvāṇa.
ārūpyadhātu 231
ārya 10, 35, 128, 202, 204, 224, 233, 241
four qualities of 101–102
stages of 97
Āryadeva 4–5, 26–29, 85, 123, 148
debate with Mātṛceta 28–29
miraculous birth of 26
training by Nāgārjuna 27–28
aśaikṣamārga 224, 230. *See also* five paths
Asaṅga 3, 5, 14, 41–43, 174, 213, 219, 224, 226, 235
and Maitreya 31–32
birth of 31
Aśoka 228

Aṣṭasāhasrikāprajñāpāramitā 198
Aśvaghoṣa 4, 26
Atīśa xxix, 3, 5, 13, 40–42, 83–84, 86–87, 90, 93–94, 99, 122–123, 173–174, 213, 219, 246–247
  as lineage holder 13–14
  his teachings of the stages of the path 14–15, 42, 173
  journey to Tibet 41–42
ātman 228
attachment 85, 88, 91, 102, 105, 115, 118, 154, 157, 192, 195. *See* desire
  abandonment of 84, 113, 157–158. *See also* non-attachment
  faults of 78, 114, 193
Avalokiteśvara 4, 12, 33–39, 43, 216, 223–224, 227, 243
  vow of 12, 33, 37
avidyā 233
Bamboo Grove 33, 46, 50, 225
bardo 86, 225
Beijing xi, xxv
Bell, Sir Charles xxv
Benjagpa ('Ban 'jag pa), Geshe 113
Bharadvājā 21–22
bhāvanāmārga 230. *See also* five paths
Bhāvaviveka 30–31, 123, 243
bhikṣu 20–23, 28, 50, 56, 90, 132, 225, 241. *See also* Saṅgha
  benefits of becoming xiv, xviii, 195
  proper activities of xv, xxiv, 90–91, 93, 191
  training of xii
Bhṛkuti 38, 216
bhumi 219
Bimbisāra, King 21, 49–53, 58, 60–61, 63, 65, 225
birthlessness 6, 94, 114
Black Conqueror 26
Bodhgayā 19, 225–226, 247
bodhi 225, 229. *See also* buddhahood; omniscience
bodhi tree 24, 226. *See also* vajra throne
bodhi-mind 6, 9, 35–36, 38, 41–42, 46, 51–52, 55–58, 65, 86, 91–92, 94–95, 98–101, 117, 119, 135–137, 141, 143, 151, 156, 162–165, 171, 177, 184, 197–199, 209, 218, 225
  absolute 94–96. *See also* bodhisattva
  as motivation 11, 162, 164
  gateway to the Mahāyāna 12, 195, 197
  generation of 6, 11, 19, 55, 90, 94–95, 112, 139–140, 156, 162–165, 177, 188, 195–197, 225, 241; three root methods 94
  meditation on 152
  obstacles to 157
  relative 94–96
  seven causal precepts 55, 156, 158, 225, 241
  two aspects of 94–97, 109
bodhi-path 14, 117. *See also* path
  stages of 174
Bodhicaryāvatāra 99, 106–108, 213
Bodhipathapradīpa 14, 173, 216
bodhisattva 3–5, 12, 26, 31, 37, 93, 104, 108, 114, 122, 142–143, 149, 162, 193–194, 200, 213, 216, 218–219, 225, 230, 240, 247
  definition of 11
  of compassion 4, 12, 33, 35–36, 38–39, 224. *See also* Avalokiteśvara
  of love 31
  of wisdom 15, 31, 40, 235. *See also* Mañjuśrī
  offspring of the buddhas 11, 135, 148, 151, 177, 211, 225
  practices of 9, 136, 156, 162–163, 165, 171, 177–178, 180, 189, 196–200, 205, 232, 242, 245
  stages of 9, 145, 185, 219, 225, 244
  vows of 84, 114, 184, 199, 218, 225
bodhisattva-mahāsattva 198, 235
bodhisattva-monkey 12, 36–37
Bolshevik
  government xix

revolution xvi, xx
Borisov, Sergey Stepanovich xix–xxiv
Brahma 48, 56–57, 67, 133, 226
Brahmadatta, King 47, 53, 55
Brahmarāja, King 57
Buddha. *See also* refuge; Three Jewels
actual 10
as doctor 10, 58
as object of refuge 4, 10–11, 13
relative 10
teachings of 24
Buddha Śākyamuni xviii, 3, 5, 9, 12–15, 17, 19, 24, 33, 45–46, 50, 99, 123–124, 131, 133, 141, 149–150, 213, 216, 225–227, 232, 235, 237–240, 243, 247. *See also* Gautama Buddha; Siddhārtha
parinirvāṇa of 19–20, 31
teachings of 4–6, 20, 25, 37, 248
buddha-essence 195–196. *See also* tathāgatagarbha
buddha-field 4, 141, 146–147, 226, 240
buddha-nature 45. *See also* tathāgatagarbha
buddha-to-come 31. *See also* Maitreya
buddhahood 6, 9–12, 14, 45–46, 49, 55, 77, 86, 94, 98–99, 102, 104, 116, 119, 139, 150, 152–153, 162–165, 172, 195–196, 198, 207, 211, 213, 219, 226, 228, 230, 235–236, 242, 246–247. *See also* bodhi; liberation; omniscience
Buddhapālita 123
cakravartin 56. *See also* world sovereign
Candrakīrti 31, 43, 123, 217, 239
carya tantra 243. *See also* tantra
Caryāmelakapradīpa 210
Ch'an 40
Changtang (Byang thang) xvii
Chayulpa, Geshe 117
Chen-ngawa, Geshe 94, 105, 108, 110
Chenrezig 12. *See also* Avalokiteśvara
Chimbupa, Geshe 118
Chö-nyen xxi, xxiii
Cittamātra 7, 217, 224, 226, 248. *See also* tenets
commentaries
definition of xxix
compassion 3, 6, 9, 14, 30–32, 35–36, 38, 45, 55, 57, 67, 80, 86, 93–96, 98–101, 106–107, 113–114, 118, 139, 142–143, 146–148, 150–151, 163, 174, 199, 207, 210, 219, 223, 226, 231. *See also* bodhi-mind; love
and voidness 84. *See also* voidness
cultivation of 88, 103, 106–107, 112, 161, 241
meditation of 24, 95
compulsive embodiment 155–156. *See also* rebirth
Concise Meaning of the Stages of the Path, The 42, 172–173
conditioned embodiment 218. *See also* rebirth
confession 65, 116, 144–145, 190, 218
Confessions of Sins 144
contemplative equipoise 169, 203, 205, 226. *See also* abiding tranquility; samādhi
like space 167–169, 180
ḍākinī 28, 142, 227
Dalai Lama 213, 224, 227, 238
fifth xiii
first 43
fourteenth xiii, xxvii, 3, 12, 43, 227
from Mongolian language xiii
manifestation of Avalokiteśvara 12
thirteenth xix–xx
Damamūrkhanāmasūtra 45
Daṇḍin 5
darśanamārga 216, 224, 230, 233
death 7, 19, 46, 78, 86, 89, 92–93, 110–111, 115–116, 120, 130, 155–156, 161, 176, 184, 188–189, 191, 193–194, 225, 248

certainty of 103
five portents of 155, 218
imminence of 90, 98, 101–102, 111, 116, 148, 152, 184, 188–189
meditation on 101
of Ajātaśatru 23
of King Bimbisāra 21
of Ānanda 22
debate xx, xxiv, 4–5, 26–27, 29–30, 40, 122
dedication of merit 64, 81, 84, 86–87, 98, 113, 122, 132, 135, 139, 145, 148, 170, 181, 212–213, 218
deeds 3, 43, 58, 64, 96–97, 101, 114. *See also* actions; karma; non-virtuous actions; virtuous actions
definition of 86
miraculous 4, 21–22, 45–50, 52–54, 60, 63–64, 81
of bodhisattvas 9, 11–12, 82, 139, 145, 162–163, 177, 180, 189, 197–199, 242
of the buddhas 4, 141, 150, 171, 174, 211
of the Mahāyāna 117
defilements 9, 11, 56, 82, 85, 89, 109, 138, 140, 142, 164, 170, 176, 178, 196, 202, 204, 224, 226, 229–230, 242. *See also* fettering passions; five defilements; karma
degenerate age 149, 152, 172, 227
deity 30, 142, 152
dependent origination 15, 123–130, 133, 137, 148, 169, 175, 193, 216–217, 227
twelve links of 15, 193–194, 227, 233
derived meaning 6
desire 13, 56, 113, 115, 119–121, 161, 191, 195, 202, 204–205, 221, 230
abandoning 105, 112, 118–119, 157, 201. *See also* attachment
as cause of fettering passions 104
desire realm 155, 189, 218, 227, 233, 241–242, 245. *See also* three realms
Devadatta 13, 21, 65, 77, 227
Dharma. *See also* refuge; Three Jewels
actual 10
and non-Dharma, differences 100–101, 120
as medicine 10
as object of refuge 10, 13
as opposite of worldly concerns 100
as opposition to fettering passions 100
instruction aspect 16, 171
relative 10
three stages of practice 114
understanding aspect 16, 171
Dharma-eye of great omniscience 90
dharmakāya 10, 24, 94, 96, 151, 206, 228, 246. *See also* trikāya
Dharmakīrti, Ācārya 41
dharmarāja 12, 34, 39–40, 228
Dharmasaṃgītisūtra 199
Dhītika, Ārya 24
Dikdun, Prince 66, 70–77
Dīpaṃkara Śrījñāna 14, 41. *See also* Atīśa
direct meaning 6
discernment 115, 184, 191, 194–195, 202, 228
disciple
qualities of 208. *See also* spiritual teacher
Dongdum, Prince 61–63, 65
door of liberation 4, 6, 14, 16, 165, 249
Dorzhiev, Lama Agvan xv–xxiii, 215
Dragyaba, Geshe 115
Drepung Monastery xi, xx, xxiv
Dromtönpa, Geshe 42, 83–84, 94, 96–100
as disciple of Atīśa 98
earth-touching mudrā 56
effort 5, 9, 20, 38, 81, 84–86, 89–90, 93–94, 101, 103, 109, 113–114, 116–117, 131–133, 137, 139, 147, 162–163, 171–172, 175, 178–180, 183–186, 191, 199–200, 202,

210–211, 213, 216, 228–229. *See also* transcendences
ego 110, , 122, 146, 165, 167, 169, 203, 221, 228, 230. *See also* self; self-nature
ego-reflection 95, 124–125, 127, 229
egolessness 84, 110, 112, 146, 166, 206, 229. *See also* empty of true existence; voidness
meditation on 95
of person 98, 165–167
of phenomena 98, 165, 168
eight aspects of leisure 187, 229. *See also* leisure and opportunity
eight worldly concerns 84, 100, 118, 121, 188, 229. *See also* worldly concerns
eightfold path 55, 229
empty of true existence 95, 111, 167, 220, 239. *See also* egolessness; voidness
equanimity 10, 139–140, 156–158, 197–198, 202–203, 231
Essence of Good Explanation: Praise of Munīndra, The 15, 123–124
eternalism 96, 124, 230, 238. *See also* two extremes
extremes, two 25, 96, 124–125, 127, 132, 137, 146, 148, 170, 179, 230, 238. *See also* eternalism; nihilism
faith xviii, xxi, 5, 11, 13, 47, 52, 56–58, 64, 81, 92, 101, 110, 114, 117–118, 120, 125, 130, 144, 147, 149, 154, 186, 190, 202, 207, 209–211, 244
fettering passions 13, 17, 57, 102, 109, 121, 161, 191–192, 218, 221, 228, 230. *See also* attachment; defilements; desire; ignorance
and buddha-essence 196
and self-grasping 108
as a poisonous snake 113
as cause of misery 108
as cause of saṃsāra 193, 197, 201
causes of 105
decrease of 91
demons of 92, 160
extinction of 104, 179, 197, 238
increase of 87, 92, 110
influence of 106–107, 115, 154, 156, 187, 231
opposition to 98, 100, 102, 104, 118, 178
remedy for 85, 92–93, 104, 164, 178; exceptional wisdom as 104
roots of 104, 117
field of assembly 141–142, 146, 149, 153–154, 170
five aggregates 118, 166–167, 203, 209, 218, 223
five areas of study xxiv
five defilements 202, 204. *See also* defilements
five distractions 202, 205. *See also* meditation
five failings in meditation 202. *See also* meditation
five obstacles 202, 204. *See also* meditation
five paths 216, 219, 224, 230, 233. *See also* path
five strengths 55
five treatises of Maitreya 32, 43, 224, 230. *See also* Asaṅga
form realm 155, 220, 226, 231, 241, 245. *See also* three realms
formless realm 155, 220, 231, 241, 245
Foundation of All Excellence, The 183
four aspects of fearlessness 3
four immeasurables 55, 139, 231
four keys 165–167. *See also* analysis
four mental activities 203
Four Noble Truths 15, 19, 22, 80, 176, 229, 231, 248
four rivers 136, 161, 165. *See also* defilements
four stages of perfection 20, 215, 224, 231

four ways of assembling 3, 11, 163, 199. *See also* bodhisattva
future lives 88–89, 92, 102, 104, 112–113, 119–122, 136, 152–153, 156, 173, 175, 229. *See also* rebirth
Gaganagañjaparipṛcchanāmamahāyānasūtra 193
Gaṇḍavyūhasūtra 186
Ganden Monastery xx, 43
Ganden Tripa Ling Rinpoche 213
garuḍa 178, 232
Gautama Buddha 24, 31, 50–54, 232. *See also* Buddha Śākyamuni; Siddhārtha
Gelug xiii, 43, 246
Gendun Drup 12, 43, 147
Gendun, Prince 45, 65–77
geshe xi, xx, 232
  degree xix, xxv
  studies xxiv
giving 9, 84–85, 89, 92, 101, 114, 120, 139, 152–153, 162–163, 177, 200, 216, 232. *See also* transcendences
golden age 39, 226, 232, 240
Gomang Monastic College xix, xxiv–xxv
Gonpapa, Geshe 101
Great Stages of the Path, The 43, 173
Guhyasamāja Tantra 210, 232
Guhyācittavyaptisūtra 191
Guide to the Bodhisattva's Way of Life 99. *See also* Śāntideva
Gyigandakmo 80
hearing, thinking, and meditating 16, 101, 111, 118, 186, 188, 192, 207, 210–211
  wisdom of 111, 113
heedfulness 115, 184, 191, 194–195
hells 37, 49, 190, 227, 229, 242
  rebirth in 23, 109, 190. *See also* six realms; lower realms
high resolve 133, 148, 161–162, 197, 199, 241. *See also* bodhi-mind
Hīnayāna 6–7, 9, 30, 42, 192, 224, 231, 233, 242–244, 248. *See also* arhat; arhatship; Theravāda
Huashang Mahāyāna 40
hungry ghost 37, 189, 227, 229, 233, 242. *See also* six realms; lower realms
  rebirth as 190
ignorance 13, 15, 17, 56, 129, 136, 161, 165, 179, 191, 193, 221, 230. *See also* defilements; fettering passions
  root of saṃsāra 124, 230, 233
Ijlin Tourgüt xxv
illusion 86, 96, 108. *See also* magician's illusion
illusory 7–8, 96, 113, 118, 206
immovable actions 193. *See also* actions; deeds; karma;non-virtuous actions; virtuous actions
impermanence 7, 113, 115, 118, 189, 192–193, 219, 228
  meditation on 95, 102–103, 114–115
imputation 118, 166, 168–169, 203, 206
  basis of 8, 203, 217
  of concepts and terms 8, 203
Indra 29, 48, 56, 61, 63, 133, 233
Indravarma, King 47, 53, 55
initiation xvi, 12, 172, 206–208, 233
intense insight 95, 169, 180, 184, 200–201, 203–206, 223, 233, 236
  benefits of 201. *See also* abiding tranquility; wisdom
isolation 87, 93–94, 97–98, 101, 117, 121
Iṣṭadevatā 249. *See also* yidam
Jambudvīpa 4, 59, 65, 147, 174, 234–235
Jangchub Öd 40–42
Jātakas 5, 234
Jentsen, Tourgüt xxi–xxii, xxiv
jñānakāya 228. *See also* trikāya
joy 47, 95, 139, 164, 179, 231. *See also* compassion; equanimity; four immeasurables; love

just-thatness 193, 201. *See also* voidness; empty of true existence
Kadam Thorbu 83
Kadampa 13, 42–43, 83, 246
kaliyuga 89–90, 93, 98, 234. *See also* degenerate age
Kalmykia xii–xiii, xv, xxi, xxiv–xxvii
 devotion to Buddhism xiv
 part of Russia xii
 refugees from, in America xxvi
kalpa 19, 230
Kalyāna Śrī 41
Kamalaśīla 40
Kanakavarṇa 66
Kangyur 45, 234
Kapila 53
Kargyu 43
karma 15, 96–97, 137, 154, 164, 169, 187, 192–193, 197, 212, 218, 234, 244. *See also* actions; deeds; non-virtuous actions; virtuous actions
 and voidness 170
 as affected by field, motivation, etc. 154
 bonds of 136, 161, 165, 191, 201
 effects of 15, 26, 45, 64–65, 81–82, 89–90, 96, 98, 118, 136, 153–154, 156, 176, 184, 188–190, 195, 218, 234
 three types of 189
Kāśyapa 63, 77
Kauśambi 53
Khampalungpa, Geshe 113
Kharawa, Geshe 114
Kimmilimālā 21
kriya tantra 243. *See also* tantra
Kṛṣṇa, Ārya 24
Kṛṣṇayamāritantra 209
Kushri Kabchu Sudhi 183, 185
Kyang Chadotsul 103
Lam-rim Chenmo 43, 173
Lamaist Buddhist Monastery xxvi, xxxi–xxxii
Lamp of the Bodhi-Path 14, 42, 173. *See also* Atīśa
Land of Snow 12, 33–38
Langdarma, King 40
Langri Tangpa, Geshe 116
leisure and opportunity 16, 111, 113, 118, 136, 152–153, 155, 172, 176, 181, 183, 187–189, 195
Lekshiwa 72–77
Lha Jangchub Öd 87
Lhasa xi, xvii, xix, xxiii–xxv, 42–43, 86, 90, 234
liberation 89, 102, 108, 118–119, 188, 192, 195, 239, 242. *See also* bodhi; buddhahood; nirvāṇa
 attainment of 83
 five paths to 51. *See also* five paths
 from saṃsāra 173
 goal of Buddha's teachings 6, 17
 obstacles to 105
 of other living beings 9, 151, 160, 243
 path to 3, 9, 100, 117, 161, 19; taking refuge on 12
 process of 173
 wish for 101, 117, 121, 135–136, 147, 151, 156, 172, 177, 179, 184, 192, 194. *See also* renunciation
Licchavis 22, 47, 53, 56
lineages, two 14, 41–42, 174, 219
 of extensive deeds 14, 32, 42–43, 142, 196, 235
 of profound view 14, 42, 142, 235
living beings
 as mother 108, 113, 116, 137, 140, 148, 157–159, 165, 184, 197–198, 207, 241
 kindness of 158–160, 197, 241
 repaying the kindness of 160, 197, 241. *See also* bodhi-mind
 sufferings of 6
Losang Chökyi Gyaltsen 45–46
Losang Drakpa 42. *See also* Tsongkhapa
Lotsomo 98
love 6, 9, 48, 55, 93, 95, 98–101, 106, 113, 139, 142, 151, 163, 209, 231,

235, 244. *See also* compassion; bodhi-mind
cultivation of 103, 106–107, 112, 160, 241
meditation of 24, 57, 95
loving-kindness 65, 88, 209
lower realms 35, 165, 187, 233
causes of 107
rebirth in 11, 68, 78, 92, 99, 102, 104, 111, 115, 120, 155, 160, 176, 189–191. *See also* rebirth
sufferings of 152, 190
three 155
Lushipatsi, King 62–63
Madhyamaka xxiv, 7–8, 30–31, 43, 123, 179, 217, 235, 239, 243, 248. *See also* tenets
founded by Nāgārjuna 25
Magadha 21–23, 50
magician's illusion 7–8, 86, 96, 105, 128, 168, 180, 204, 206. *See also* appearance; illusion; illusory
Mahākāla 27, 133, 235
Mahākāśyapa 19–21
Mahāmadhyāntikā 23
Mahāmudrātilakatantra 207
Mahāshakuli, King 61, 63
Mahāyāna 6, 30. *See also* bodhi-mind; bodhisattva
bodhi-mind in 94, 177, 198
cf. other vehicles 6, 207, 249
compassion in 114
deeds of 117
final goal of 9
four wheels of 171
gateway to 12, 195
great entrance to 14
in stages of the path 42, 173
learning 198
meeting 119
mind-practice in 9
Nāgārjuna and 30–31
path 9, 172, 180, 195, 199; entering 96, 195, 197
renunciation in 192
tenets 7, 226, 235, 248
transcendences in 163
wisdom and deeds in 96
Maheśvāra 26–27, 29, 235
Maitreya 3, 32, 41, 142, 174, 204–205, 219, 232, 235, 246
and Asaṅga 31–32
five treatises of 32, 43
maṇḍala 142, 146, 209, 235
Mañjuśrī 3, 15, 31, 40–41, 43, 123, 138, 142, 147, 151, 170, 174, 219, 235–236
mantra 7–8, 30, 38, 110, 170, 206–207, 209, 236
Mantrayāna 12, 41–42, 114, 172, 180, 206, 233, 236, 243, 247, 249
gateway to 12
vows of 114, 172
Māra 23–24, 52, 59–60, 236
Marpa 40–41, 236–237
Mathurā 23
Matimāt 216
Mātṛceta 4–5, 26, 28
conversion to Buddhism 30
debate with Āryadeva 4, 26–30
Maudgalyayāna 241
Māyādevī 60, 63
meditation 9, 11, 16, 84–86, 101–102, 104, 114, 139, 162, 177, 179, 188, 195, 200, 202, 204, 208, 216, 229, 236, 245, 249. *See also* abiding tranquility; contemplative equipoise; samādhi; three precepts; transcendences
analytical 170. *See also* analysis; four keys
definition of 86
focusing 170, 179–180
of bodhi-mind 38
of compassion 24, 95
of delusion 105

of filth and stench 105
of love 24, 57, 95
of mother or sister 104
of repulsion 104
of restoration 38
of shame and self-reproach 104
on egolessness 95
on impermanence 95
method and wisdom 6, 147, 150, 180, 199, 207
Milarepa 41, 236
mind-practice 9, 94–95, 183, 185, 187–188, 191, 196–198, 213, 223
three branch methods 95
mindfulness 84, 91, 101, 188, 229, 240
misery 68, 105, 160, 193–194, 201, 234, 239
causes of 17, 58, 89, 108–109, 119, 154, 177, 184, 192
of change 156, 161
of conditioned activities 161, 191, 218, 245
of lower realms 190
of misery 156, 161
of saṃsāra 9, 11, 78, 89, 136, 153–156, 160
three types of 136, 161, 165, 191, 218, 245
value of 109, 121
Mongolian xix
clans xiii
culture xii–xiii
history xiv
Kalmyk xi–xii
language xi–xii
monks entered Drepung xxiv
moral practice 9, 11, 16, 84–85, 89, 95, 101, 104, 109, 113–114, 117, 139, 152–153, 162–163, 178, 188, 195, 200–201, 216, 236, 245. *See also* three precepts; transcendences
three types of 184, 198–199, 236
Moscow xviii–xix, xxi
Mount Meru 144, 146, 178–179, 190, 234, 237
mudrā 141, 237
Mūlamadhyamakakārikā 123, 216
Munīndra 46, 216, 237
Nāgārjuna 3, 5, 14, 26–28, 30–31, 41–42, 111, 123, 132, 148, 174, 213, 216–217, 219, 236, 239, 243
death of 25–26
life of 24–25
nāgas 23, 25, 28, 30, 65, 69, 237
king of 63
Nakchuka xvii, xix–xx, xxii–xxiii
Nālandā 4, 25, 27–28, 30, 41, 237
Nambarpa, Geshe 118
Nāropa 41, 236–237
Neysurpa, Geshe 116
Ngag-rim Chenmo 43
nihilism 96, 124, 230, 237. *See also* extremes, two; eternalism
nine states of mind 202
nirmāṇakāya 10, 206, 238, 240–241, 246. *See also* trikāya
nirvāṇa 11, 109, 117, 137, 146–147, 160, 169, 217, 224, 230, 238–239. *See also* arhat; arhatship; liberation
non-attachment 84, 101, 110–111, 148
non-duality 86, 113
non-returning 20, 52, 58, 65, 99, 103, 231, 238
non-virtuous actions 50, 59–60, 68, 77, 82, 85, 107, 113, 115–116, 119, 154, 176, 184, 188, 190–191, 193, 195. *See also* actions; deeds; karma
Nyingma 40, 43, 238
Nyugrumpa, Geshe 112
Oṃ āḥ ra pa tza na dhi 170
Oṃ maṇi padme hūṃ 36, 38
omniscience 5, 9, 14, 49, 83, 101, 108, 114, 188–189, 226, 228, 238. *See also* bodhi; buddhahood
of Buddha 4
six kinds of 55, 242

once-returning 20, 65, 231, 238
One Hundred Thousand Verse Prajñā-pāramitā Sūtra 25, 141, 219
Padmasambhava 40, 238
Pallis, Marco xxv, xxxi
Pañcakrama 210
Panchen Lama 223, 238
first 45–46
fourth 135, 138
pandit 4–5, 27, 31, 141, 215, 238
six 19, 45–46, 48, 50–54, 56, 60, 63
pāramitās 3, 9, 85, 216, 239, 245. *See also* transcendences
Pāramitāyāna 207, 245, 249. *See also* Mahāyāna
parinirvāṇa 5, 13, 19–22, 30–31, 94, 145, 239
path 189, 211–212, 239. *See also* five paths
Mahāyāna 94, 96, 141, 171, 177, 180, 195, 199; entering 197
of accumulation 219, 225, 230, 241
of application 216, 219, 230
of cultivation 219, 230
of extensive deeds 3
of insight 216, 219, 224, 230, 233
of mantra 207–208, 210
of nirvāṇa 103
of no-more-learning 219, 224, 230
of profound view 3
stages of 14, 16, 123, 183, 185
to enlightenment 161. *See also* bodhi-path
to liberation 3, 9, 100, 160–161, 185, 192, 194
Vajrayāna 171
patience 9, 32, 84–85, 89, 91–92, 101–102, 106, 108–110, 113, 120, 139, 152, 162, 178, 200, 216, 239. *See also* transcendences
how to practice 106–107
Pawo Dorje 147
Potowa, Geshe 94, 100, 102–103
powers
five 55
four 176, 219, 231
six 202
Prajāpatī 63, 77
prajñā 248. *See also* wisdom
prajñāpāramitā xxiv, 16, 33, 217, 235, 239. *See also* sutra; wisdom
Prajñaprabha (King) 59–60
pramāṇa 86
Prāsaṅgika 7–8, 31, 123, 217, 235, 239
Prasenajit, King 47, 53–54, 77, 163, 218
pratimokṣa 220. *See also* vows
pratyekabuddha 11, 64–65, 81, 162, 194, 205, 224, 230–231, 239
Pratyekabuddhayāna 207, 249
prayogamārga 216, 230. *See also* five paths
precept xxix, 13, 42, 83–84, 87, 90, 98, 101, 104, 118, 122, 172, 174–175, 181, 210, 216
definition of xxix
Precepts Collected from Here and There 83
prophecies 30, 34, 37
by Buddha 3–5, 24, 33
Puchungwa, Geshe 94, 111–112
purification 5, 9, 11, 13, 82, 98, 109, 138–140, 142, 170, 176, 194, 205, 229, 231
of defilements 56
purposes 162
of self and others 99–101, 108, 195
two 5–6, 130, 248
Rāhula 65
Rājagṛha 20, 50, 52–53, 225
rakṣa 69, 239
Ralpachen, King 40
rebirth 23, 189, 220, 225
in higher states 5, 33, 35, 54–58, 99, 112, 114, 150, 152–153, 160–161, 187, 189, 191, 200–201, 217
in lower states 78, 99, 102, 104, 115, 120, 160, 176, 189–190
in saṃsāra 154, 160

of bodhisattvas 11
repeated 78, 136, 154, 165
various, of the Buddha 4
refuge 33, 80, 125, 129, 138
benefits of 10
foundation of all practice 12
having none 35–36
objects of 140, 142, 219, 231
prayer 12, 138
taking 4, 9, 11–13, 56, 138, 170, 176, 190
three levels of 11
remembrance 17, 92, 115, 184, 191, 194–195, 202, 205, 240
renunciation 9, 42, 80, 109, 135–137, 151–152, 156, 165, 171, 184, 192, 218
meditation of 152
of desire 93
of saṃsāra 84, 118–119, 177, 195, 198
of this life's activities 84, 92, 100, 102–103, 115, 120
of worldly existence 91, 93
right view 42, 96, 114, 135, 151–152, 169, 171, 218, 229, 240. *See also* wisdom
cultivation of 165, 169
Rinpoche Gocha, King 65–66, 68–70, 73, 75–77
rishi 22–23, 25, 64, 66, 81, 240
root lama xvi, xviii, 141–142, 149–150. *See also* disciple; spiritual teacher
root text
use of 135, 183
roots of virtue 86, 98, 105, 114, 139, 148, 191. *See also* dedication of merit
rūpadhātu 231. *See also* three realms
rūpakāya 24, 94, 96, 151, 238, 240–241. *See also* trikāya
Rushibaza, Princess 62–63, 65
Śāktiman, Prince 25–26
Sakya 43. *See also* tenets
Śākya clan 4, 48, 56, 80, 173, 240
samādhi 47, 94–95, 180, 202, 240. *See also* abiding tranquility; contemplative equipoise
three branch methods of practice 95
Samādhirājasūtra 206
Samantabhadra 143–144, 146, 240
śamatha 223
saṃbhāramārga 225, 230, 241. *See also* five paths
saṃbhogakāya 10, 206, 238, 240, 246. *See also* trikāya
Saṃdhinirmocanasūtra 204, 226
saṃsāra 6, 9, 77, 108–109, 111, 114, 117, 119, 136–137, 139, 146, 150–151, 154, 169, 177, 179, 184, 197, 236, 241, 249
beginningless 158
causes of 193. *See also* attachment; defilements; fettering passions; ignorance
faults of 89, 160
liberation from 173, 239, 243. *See also* liberation; nirvāṇa
misery of 105, 118, 155, 160–161, 176, 184, 192, 194, 196–197, 245
nature of 11
prison of 105, 113, 156, 191, 201
rebirth in 157, 160, 165
root of 137, 177, 179
Śāṇavāsika 22–23
Sangbochok 34
Saṅgha 10, 15, 21–22, 45, 95, 109, 225, 241. *See also* refuge; Three Jewels
actual 10
as attendants 10
as object of refuge 10, 13
relative 10
Śāntideva 99, 106–108, 123, 213, 218
Sarasvatī 27, 29, 48, 131, 241
Sarba, Geshe 117

Śāriputra 241
Saundarananda xviii–xix
Sautrāntika 7, 244. *See also* tenets
scriptures
  definition of xxix
self. *See also* ego; self-nature
  of person 110–111
  of phenomena 110
self-grasping 108, 111, 129, 136, 165, 169. *See also* ignorance
  innate 166–167
self-nature 30–31, 86, 96, 105, 107–108, 125–128, 204, 217, 227, 229–230, 243. *See also* ego; self
Serlingpa 41
seven acts of worship 142–145, 217–218, 235
Shabogaypa, Geshe 118–121
Shachin Lama xvi, xviii
Shingtanimi, King 59–60
Shun Tsin, King 47, 49, 53, 55, 57
siddha 41, 241
Siddhārtha 4
siddhi 84, 86, 101, 114, 185, 207–208, 211, 241–242
Śikṣāsamuccaya 218
Śiva 27, 242
six aspects of preparation 135, 138, 217
six realms 37–38, 242. *See also* lower realms; saṃsāra; three realms
six sense objects 201, 227
skandha 218. *See also* five aggregates
skillful means 14–15, 143, 174, 195
smṛti 240
Songtsen Gampo, King 39
spiritual teacher 14, 37, 105, 118, 132, 142–143, 160, 174, 185, 190, 211–212, 219, 232, 234. *See also* disciple; root lama
  as Buddha 13, 118, 149
  best is monk 207
  blessings of 118
  despising 209
  embodiment of Three Jewels 13
  enemy as 107
  false 24
  kindness of 3, 89, 132, 149–150, 181, 186, 213
  manifestation of Vajradhara 149
  precept of xxix, 13, 83, 87, 187
  qualified Vajrayāna 172, 207
  qualities of 4, 13, 16, 84, 113, 115, 117, 147, 175, 186, 207–208, 210–211
  relationship with xvi, 121, 146
  reliance on 13, 87, 101, 114, 117, 123, 147, 149–151, 153, 172, 175, 180, 183, 185–187, 190, 219, 239
śrāmaṇera 207
śrāvaka 11, 81, 114, 162, 194, 205, 224, 230–231, 242
Śrāvakayāna 207, 249
Śrāvastī 47, 53, 77
Stages of Mantra, The 43
stream-winning 20, 23, 65, 231
stūpa 22, 243
Subhūti 198, 243
sublime wisdom 197, 200, 216, 244. *See also* transcendences
Sudarśana, Ārya 24
Śuddodhana, King 63, 77
sugata 143, 196–197, 209–210, 243. *See also* Buddha; tathāgata
Sukhāvatī 34, 223, 243
Sulashen 63
Sulipala, Queen 59–60
śūnyatā 248. *See also* empty of true existence; voidness
sutra 243
  -piṭaka 15, 21, 41, 215, 234, 246
  and tantra 14, 172, 206, 211
  and Ānanda 21
  as scriptural authority 183
  followers 40
  Mahāyāna 163, 165
  prajñāpāramitā 16, 25, 235, 239

reciting 100
translation into Tibetan 39
Sūtrayāna 123, 172, 180, 206, 243, 246
Suvarṇadvīpa 41
Suvarṇavarṇa 21
svabhāvakāya 228
Svātantrika 7–8, 30, 123, 217, 235, 243
taking and giving 164
Tampa Dokar 4
tantra
and sutra 14, 172, 211
followers 40
four classes of 224, 236, 243
root and explanatory 211
three lower classes 206, 210
ḍākinīs in 227
Tantrayāna 123, 173, 246
Tārā 5, 36, 38–39, 90, 216, 243
tathāgata 5, 33, 49, 52, 133, 143, 185, 196, 200, 244. *See also* Buddha; sugata
tathāgatagarbha 195. *See also* buddha-essence; buddha-nature
Tathāgatagarbhasūtra 196
ten aspects of opportunity 187, 244. *See also* leisure and opportunity
ten non-virtuous actions 59, 119, 153–154, 190, 244. *See also* actions; deeds; karma
ten virtuous actions 58–60, 77, 119, 154, 187, 244. *See also* actions; deeds; karma
tenets xxiv, 6–8, 123, 223–224, 226, 235, 239, 243
four schools of 7
Tenpe Nyima 135
Theravāda 173, 244. *See also* Hinayāna
thirty-five buddhas of confession 144
Thomi Sambhota 39
Three Baskets 15, 104–105, 215, 223, 245. *See also* Tripiṭaka
three entanglements 102
three great purposes 146, 195, 220
Three Jewels 10–13, 33, 52, 95, 101, 118, 139, 146, 176, 190, 211–213, 241, 245. *See also* refuge
as remedies to illness 10
qualities of 10
three levels of beings 14, 42, 173, 175, 183, 188
highest level 196–198
lower level 188
middle level 191–192
three miseries 197. *See also* misery
three poisons 9, 13, 17, 56–57, 191, 212, 221, 230, 233, 245. *See also* attachment; defilements; desire; fettering passions; ignorance
three precepts 11, 16, 104, 188, 195, 245. *See also* meditation; moral practice; wisdom
how to practice 104
three principles of the path 55, 137–138, 140, 148, 150, 170–171
Three Principles of the Path, The 123, 135
three realms 84, 118, 174, 191, 227, 231, 241, 245. *See also* saṃsāra
three vows 83–84, 144, 152, 218. *See also* vows
Tibetan Buddhist Learning Center xxvi
Tigitsashiri 53
Tolungpa, Geshe 117
transcendences 198, 200, 245. *See also* individual names of each transcendence
six 3, 9, 11, 55, 85, 101, 153, 162–163, 188, 199, 228, 232, 236, 239, 242, 244, 248
ten 39, 200, 216, 244
Trijang Rinpoche 213
trikāya 10, 147, 206–207, 238, 246
Tripiṭaka 15–16, 20–21, 41, 83, 104, 215, 223, 234, 244, 246–247
Trisong Detsen, King 40

truth of suffering 176, 189. *See also* Four Noble Truths
truth of the cause of suffering 177. *See also* Four Noble Truths
Tsaidam xvii, xxii
Tseta 49, 57
Tshenama, Queen 61, 63
Tsongkhapa xiii, 3, 5, 12, 14–15, 42–43, 123, 138, 140–142, 146–147, 151, 170–173, 183, 213, 217, 246
  visualization of 141
Tsunba Jegom 83, 122
Tuṣita heaven 4, 32, 43, 224, 235, 246
two truths 147, 162, 246
  absolute 246, 248
  relative 246, 248
Udrāyaṇa, King 47, 49, 53–54, 58
Ulan Ude xvii, xix–xxi
Umapa, Lama 43
Upagupta, Ārya 23–24
Upāli 21
upāsaka 36, 99, 102, 247
upāsikā 247
Urga xvii–xxi
Utpaladok, story of 45, 77–82
Vaibhāṣika xxiv, 7, 244. *See also* tenets
Vaiśālī 19, 22, 53
vajra throne 19, 247. *See also* Bodhgayā; Buddha Śākyamuni
Vajradāka Tantra 208
Vajradhara 141–142, 146, 149, 185, 207, 210, 212, 247. *See also* spiritual teacher; tantra
Vajrapāṇi 40, 48, 56, 247
Vajrayāna 185, 198, 206–207, 247. *See also* Mantrayāna; tantra
  entering 207
  five aspects of 206, 208, 210–212
  two stages of 171–172, 185, 210, 246
Vārāṇasī 19, 53, 55, 64, 81
vessel 97, 170
  suitable 16, 185, 206, 208
  three types of 16–17
Vijñānavāda 7, 226. *See also* Cittamātra; tenets
Vikramaśīla 41, 247
vinaya 16, 21, 43, 247. *See also* pratimokṣa; Tripiṭaka; vows
  -piṭaka 15, 21, 41, 215, 234, 246
vipaśyanā 233. *See also* intense insight
virtuous actions 17, 55, 59–60, 81, 83–84, 89, 103, 109, 113, 122, 145, 153–154, 184, 188, 190–191, 193, 208, 218–219, 231, 237. *See also* actions; deeds; karma; non-virtuous actions
voidness 6, 14, 36, 83, 85–87, 89, 94, 97, 107, 116, 120, 124, 126, 128, 137, 142, 169, 179, 193, 196, 201–203, 205, 216, 219, 227, 246, 248. *See also* ego; egolessness; empty of true existence; self; self-nature
  absolute bodhi-mind 94
  and appearance 117, 170, 204
  and compassion 84, 95
  meditation on 103, 112
  realization of 6, 9, 16, 85–86, 103, 126, 137, 180, 206, 233, 240
vows xvi, xxiv, 10–11, 36, 77, 90, 101, 107, 199, 218, 236, 247. *See also* pratimokṣa; three vows; vinaya
  maintaining 91, 98, 185, 199, 206, 208–210
  of Avalokiteśvara 12, 33, 37
  of bodhisattvas 114, 184, 199, 225
  of individual liberation 22, 25, 83, 184, 194–195, 220, 247
  of tantra 84, 114, 172, 185, 206, 208–209
Vultures' Peak 19, 65
Wangyal, Geshe xi–xviii, xx–xxvii, xxix–xxx
Wensa, lineage of 139
wheel of the Dharma 19, 141, 145, 218, 226, 231, 235, 239, 248

White Lotus Sutra 33
wisdom 9, 11, 16, 46, 84–86, 96–97, 101–102, 104, 111, 114, 120, 162, 179–180, 188, 195, 200, 211, 216, 227–228, 240, 245, 248. *See also* three precepts; transcendences
definition of 86
wisdom-eye 39, 104
wisdom-horse 113
wish-fulfilling jewel 45, 69–73, 77, 91, 113, 141, 174–175, 177, 187, 207
world sovereign 59, 61, 63, 65. *See also* cakravartin
worldly concerns 12, 16–17, 78, 84, 89–91, 100, 102–103, 108–111, 115, 119–120, 122, 176, 189, 191–192. *See also* eight worldly concerns; renunciation
yakṣa 248
Yama 111, 248
Yerbay Shangtsun 101–102
Yerpadrak 90
Yeshe Barwa of Olgud 90
Yeshe Öd 40–41
Yeshe Sung 113
yidam 142, 146, 249
yoga
of contemplative equipoise like space 169
of four sessions 172, 185, 210
of illusoriness 169
of the divine mantras 205
symbolic and non-symbolic 210
treatises 41
yoga tantra 243
yogi 40–41, 118, 132, 172, 179, 209, 236–237, 249
yoginī 249

Wisdom Publications

WISDOM PUBLICATIONS is a non-profit publisher of books on Buddhism, Tibet, and related East-West themes. Our titles are published in appreciation of Buddhism as a living philosophy and with the special commitment to preserve and transmit important works from all the major Buddhist traditions.

If you would like more information, or a copy of our extensive mail order catalogue, and to keep informed about our future publications, please write or call us at: 361 Newbury Street, Boston, Massachusetts, 02115. Telephone: (617) 536-3358. Fax: (617) 536-1897

THE WISDOM TRUST

As a non-profit publisher, Wisdom is dedicated to the publication of fine Dharma books for the benefit of all sentient beings. We depend upon sponsors in order to publish books like the one you are holding in your hand.

If you would like to make a donation to the Wisdom Trust Fund to help us continue our Dharma work, or to receive information about opportunities for planned giving, please write to our Boston office.

Thank you so much.

Wisdom is a non-profit, charitable 501(c)(3) organization and a part of the Foundation for the Preservation of the Mahayana Tradition (FPMT).

Care of Dharma Books

Dharma books contain the teachings of the Buddha; they have the power to protect against lower rebirth and to point the way to liberation. Therefore, they should be treated with respect—kept off the floor and places where people sit or walk—and not stepped over. They should be covered or protected for transporting and kept in a high, clean place separate from more "mundane" materials. Other objects should not be placed on top of Dharma books and materials. Licking the fingers to turn pages is considered bad form (and negative karma). If it is necessary to dispose of Dharma materials, they should be burned rather than thrown in the trash. When burning Dharma texts, it is considered skillful to first recite a prayer or mantra, such as OM, AH, HUNG. Then, you can visualize the letters of the texts (to be burned) absorbing into the AH, and the AH absorbing into you. After that, you can burn the texts.

These considerations may also be kept in mind for Dharma artwork, as well as the written teachings and artwork of other religions.

Wisdom Publications

LIBERATION IN THE PALM OF YOUR HAND

A Concise Discourse on the Path to Enlightenment

Pabongka Rinpoche

edited by Trijang Rinpoche, translated by Michael Richards

In 1921, Pabonka Rinpoche gave an exeptionally important twenty-four day *lam-rim* teaching in Tibet to some 700 monks, nuns, and laypeople. This was masterfully edited into its present form by Trijang Rinpoche, tutor to the Dalai Lama and Pabonka's closest disciple, and published in Tibetan in 1958. *Liberation in the Palm of Your Hand* is the English translation of that famous teaching, which is a clear, step-by-step explanation of the path to enlightenment, the fruit of over one thousand years'study, practice, realization, and transmission of the *lam-rim* teachings.

"This guide has given me a friend whom I may consult and appreciate through the years...an accessible, pragmatic view of the path of liberation...a spiritual classic."—*The Reader's Review*

"...the richest and most enjoyable volume from the *lam-rim* tradition that has been published to date..."—*Golden Drum*

"...an accessible literary style, this text is a straightforward guide on how to meditate on each step of the path."—*Tricycle Buddhist Review*

980pp, $37.50

Also by Wisdom Publications

HOW TO MEDITATE
Kathleen McDonald

What is meditation? Why practice it? Which technique is best for me? How do I do it? The answers to these often asked questions are contained in this down-to-earth book written and compiled by a Western Buddhist nun. *How to Meditate* contains a wealth of practical advice on a variety of authentic and proven techniques covering the whole spectrum of Tibetan Buddhism.

"This book is as beautifully simple and direct as its title...earnestly recommended to every seeker on the path." —*Yoga Today*

227 pp. $10.95